The
Private
Heinrich Himmler

The
Private
Heinrich Himmler

Letters of a Mass Murderer

EDITED AND WITH COMMENTARY BY
Katrin Himmler and Michael Wildt

TRANSLATED BY
Thomas S. Hansen, Ph.D.
and Abby J. Hansen, Ph.D.

St. Martin's Press
New York

www.stmartins.com

Designed by Kathryn Parise

LIBRARY OF CONGRESS CATALOGING-IN-PUBLICATION DATA

Names: Himmler, Heinrich, 1900–1945. | Himmler, Katrin, 1967– editor. | Wildt, Michael, 1954– editor. | Hansen, Thomas S. (Thomas Stansfield), translator. | Hansen, Abby J., 1945– translator.
Title: The private Heinrich Himmler : letters of a mass murderer / edited and with commentary by Katrin Himmler and Michael Wildt ; translated by Thomas S. Hansen and Abby J. Hansen.
Description: First published in the United States by St. Martin's Press. | New York : St. Martin's Press, 2016. | Original German edition: Munich : Piper Verlag, 2014.
Identifiers: LCCN 2015042404| ISBN 9781250064653 (hardback) | ISBN 9781466870895 (e-book)
Subjects: LCSH: Himmler, Heinrich, 1900–1945—Correspondence. | Himmler, Margarete, 1893–1967—Correspondence. | Nazis—Correspondence. | BISAC: BIOGRAPHY & AUTOBIOGRAPHY / Historical. | HISTORY / Military / World War II. | HISTORY / Europe / Germany.
Classification: LCC DD247.H46 A413 2016 | DDC 943.086092—dc23
LC record available at http://lccn.loc.gov/2015042404

Our books may be purchased in bulk for promotional, educational, or business use. Please contact your local bookseller or the Macmillan Corporate and Premium Sales Department at 1-800-221-7945, extension 5442, or by e-mail at MacmillanSpecial Markets@macmillan.com.

Originally published in Germany as
Himmler Privat: Briefe eines Massenmörders
by Piper Verlag GmbH

First U.S. Edition: March 2016

10 9 8 7 6 5 4 3 2 1

Contents

The
Private
Heinrich Himmler

Introduction

I

In the spring of 1945, in the immediate aftermath of the war, a U.S. intelligence officer in Gmund am Tegernsee[1] encountered two American GIs who had obviously been helping themselves to "souvenirs" from Haus Lindenfycht, the private residence of Heinrich Himmler. The officer was a historian and quickly recognized what the two men were carrying. When he tried to buy their spoils, one of the two agreed. The officer was thus able to obtain a bundle of papers containing private documents of the Himmler family. Manuscripts of the *Tagebücher* [Journals] of the young Heinrich Himmler from the years 1914–22 were among these papers. The other GI moved on, unwilling to sell his trophies.

The officer sent home the diaries and other documents he had purchased, and paid no further attention to them until 1957, when a discussion with a friend of his, the German-Jewish historian Werner Tom Angress, reminded him of them. He then produced them for historical inspection. Working with a young colleague, Bradley F. Smith, Angress transcribed the manuscripts. Both men reported on the discovery in an essay in *The Journal of Modern History* (1959).[2]

-----

[1] Gmund is a town on the north shore of the Tegernsee Lake in Bavaria, not far from the Austrian border. [—Trans.]

[2] Werner Tom Angress (1920–2010) used to tell this story again and again, and in a footnote to the article coauthored with Bradley F. Smith, "Diaries of Heinrich Himmler's Early Years,"

Other versions of this story exist, but must ultimately remain unsubstantiated because neither of the GIs could ever be positively identified. Angress later presented the diaries, along with the other documents, to the Hoover Institution on War, Revolution, and Peace at Stanford University, where they were made available to the public. This "Himmler Collection," which contained the letters of Marga Himmler to her husband, has been a treasure trove for primary historical research for years. After protracted negotiations, the Bundesarchiv (Federal Archives) in Koblenz purchased the originals from the Hoover Institution in the mid-1990s. They are now catalogued as the *Nachlass Himmler* (Himmler Papers).

A further collection of private documents from Heinrich Himmler's family surfaced in Israel in the early 1980s. These apparently represent the "souvenirs" that the second GI kept for himself. This material, on microfilm rolls, comprises around two hundred letters written by Heinrich Himmler to his wife in the years 1927–45. The rolls also contain the microfilms of Marga's *Tagebücher* from 1937 to 1945, the originals of which are now in the collection of the United States Holocaust Memorial Museum in Washington, DC. In addition, the collection in Israel contains the originals of Marga Himmler's *NSDAP-Parteibuch* [*Party membership book*]; her *Jugendtagebuch* [*Childhood Diary*] from 1909 to 1916; a *Kindheitstagebuch* [*Childhood Journal*] about her daughter, Gudrun; the daughter's *Poesiealbum* [*Friendship Album*] and *Mädchentagebuch* [*Girlhood Album*] from 1941 to April 1945. The collection also contains Marga's notebooks with entries about household expenses, Christmas presents, recipes, official documents, and official Hitler Youth certificates for their foster son, Gerhard von der Ahé. In addition, there are numerous personal photographs, some of them loose, some mounted in an album.

It is unclear how these materials reached Israel. Several stories survive. In the version dating from the end of the 1960s, the man who owned them for years, a Holocaust survivor, claimed to have bought them at a flea market in Belgium. In a different version, he claimed to have purchased them in Mexico from the former secretary of Himmler's confidant Karl Wolff, and kept them in his pri-

---

The Journal of Modern History 31, no. 3 (September 1959), he briefly recounts it. For more on Angress, see his . . . *Immer etwas abseits. Jugenderinnerungen eines jüdischen Berliners, 1920–1945* (Berlin: Edition Hentrich, 2005).

vate possession for years. An Israeli filmmaker supposedly had a plan to use them in a documentary about Heinrich Himmler, but he died before his project could come to fruition. At times there seem to have been negotiations about selling the documents to the Bundesarchiv in Koblenz. To that end, in 1982–83, the Bundesarchiv undertook a comprehensive expert examination, including an inspection of the materials, in order to authenticate the documents. The result of this research was the verdict that the documents were unquestionably genuine. Although the originals of Himmler's letters are not available, a comparison of the handwriting and the references to dates and content in his [microfilmed—Trans.] letters with those of Marga Himmler confirms their authenticity beyond all doubt.[3]

In the meantime, these materials have become the property of the Israeli documentary filmmaker Vanessa Lapa. Her film *Der Anständige* [*The Decent One*, Berlinale 2014] presents these documents, which had never before been seen by the public.[4]

Taken together, these collections of source materials comprise a dense corpus of Heinrich Himmler's private documents, the like of which does not exist for any other member of the National Socialist Party (NSDAP) leadership. It is well known that Hitler left neither journals nor private records behind; and Hermann Göring, the highest-ranking National Socialist to sit in the dock in Nuremberg in 1945–46, left only what is contained in the official written documentation of the Third Reich. Joseph Goebbels wrote a megalomaniacal diary, many thousands of pages long; its function was primarily to document his political role as a National Socialist leader, and he conceived of it as the basis for later publications. But when it comes to intimate details of private life, Heinrich Himmler is the best documented among the highest-ranking NS perpetrators.

Himmler's letters to his wife, Marga—published here for the first time in

---

[3] Gutachten [Reports] des Bundesarchivs Koblenz, Gesch.-Z. III2-4211. Himmler, Archivdirektor Dr. Josef Henke, from March 12, 1984. In a later letter, from February 18, 1997, Dr. Henke again confirmed "that the authenticity of the material preserved in Tel Aviv can be considered as beyond any reasonable doubt."

[4] The original documents are in Tel Aviv. After the completion of Lapa's film, they will be given to an archive to be catalogued and made available to interested members of the public for scholarly use.

English, along with her responses—combine to constitute a comprehensive correspondence from their first encounter in 1927 to the end of the war in 1945. The early letters at first seem extremely trite; nothing suggests that the Heinrich Himmler of 1927 would later develop into a mass murderer. Two rather unpretentious people, one a party functionary of the NSDAP and the other a divorced nurse, meet at the end of the 1920s and declare their love for each other in numerous letters. They marry, establish a self-sufficient business [poultry farming—Trans.] in the country, have a children and later take in a foster child. During the following years, while the husband is mostly traveling on official business, the wife stays at home, cares for the children and the house, and looks after the business of the farm. Over time the letters become more earnest: the husband's career is prospering; the couple correspond about daily worries; they telephone each other almost every day, even after the husband has had a mistress for a long time and conceived children with her. The war appears only sketchily in these letters: she writes of nights during the bombardments of Berlin; he writes about the "lot of work" he has to do on the Eastern Front. Once it becomes clear to him that the war is lost, the correspondence ends with a farewell letter from him.

As prosaic as this description may sound, further inspection reveals how clearly this daily correspondence between Heinrich and Marga Himmler shows their perceptions, assumptions, and worldviews. The discrepancy between Himmler's almost completely concealed murderous daily routine and the private idyll evoked in the letters decreases to the same degree that violence and lack of empathy in everyday life become noticeable in the petty routines of the Himmlers.

II

Heinrich Himmler was born on October 7, 1900, in Munich, the middle son of the Gymnasium [high school—Trans.] teacher Gebhard and his wife, Anna. He grew up with his brothers, Gebhard and Ernst, in a solid middle-class environment. The sons received a comprehensive humanistic education in which secondary virtues such as obedience and duty played a large role. At the end of World War I, when Heinrich's wish to become an officer had not been fulfilled, he went on to study agriculture and subsequently became involved with the folkish[5] cause, eventually as a speaker for the National Socialist movement. From 1929 on, his title was *Reichsführer-SS* [a designation created uniquely for him—Trans.], and after 1930 he was a delegate to the Reichstag. In 1936, after the National Socialists had come to power, he was put in charge of the entire German police system, responsible for the terror, persecution, and destruction of European Jews and other victims of the regime. As *Reichskommissar für die Festigung Deutschen Volkstums* [Reich commissioner for the strengthening of the German national character], he was responsible for undertaking a huge program of resettlement and murder in both eastern and western Europe. Toward the end of the war, in 1943, he advanced further to become *Innenminister des deutschen Reiches* [Minister of the interior for the German Reich] and ultimately, in 1944, he advanced to the position of *Chef des Ersatzheeres* [Commander in Chief of the Army Reserve]. After being arrested, he took his own life on May 23, 1945.

Marga Siegroth, née Boden, was born on September 9, 1893, in the Pomeranian town of Goncerzewo (Goncarzewy), near Bromberg (Brydgoszcz), the daughter of the landowner Hans Boden and his wife, Elfriede. She grew up with two brothers and three sisters. She lost her older brother in World War I, received training as a nurse, and worked in field hospitals. In 1920 she married, and after this marriage failed, she worked from 1923 on as head nurse in a private clinic in Berlin, in which, thanks to her father, she was also a stakeholder. After marrying Himmler in 1928, she joined the NSDAP, and in 1929 gave birth to their daughter, Gudrun. After 1933 she also cared for the couple's foster son. During World War II, Marga Himmler worked as *Oberführerin* [female senior leader] of the Deutsches Rotes Kreuz (DRK) [the German Red Cross] in Berlin, in which capacity she traveled through occupied European countries. After the war, she and her daughter were interned. She later lived in Bielefeld and in Munich, with her daughter. She died there on August 25, 1967.

Heinrich Himmler and Marga Siegroth met on September 18, 1927, on a train trip between Berchtesgaden and Munich. Marga had been on vacation in Berchtesgaden, and Heinrich had stayed there for professional reasons. Her blonde hair and blue eyes represented the façade of Himmler's ideal of

---

[5] *Völkisch*: National Socialist term blending meanings of an idealized German people with an archaic notion of the people as a primitive tribe, suggesting the concept of "nation" as an ethnic unity based on blood ties. This text translates the term as "folkish." [—Trans.]

femininity. They also agreed in many areas: for example, their common rejection of democracy, their hatred for "das System Berlin";[6] their hatred of Jews, whom they labeled "Jewish rabble"; and their misanthropy ("how false and bad human beings are"). Soon they were dreaming of life in the country together—not only because they wanted to supplement Himmler's modest party salary through their own venture raising animals and vegetables, but also because this corresponded to the folkish idealization of a "return to the soil." The "beautiful, pure home" they wanted to establish was supposed to be a "secure castle," and a place to keep the "filth" of the outside world at bay.

It is striking, however, to note what is absent from these early letters. Neither Heinrich nor Marga shows a real interest in the other. Neither one asks questions about everyday life, family, the past, or the other's desires. The letters occasionally mention "very interesting" experiences or conversations, without the "interesting" nature of these ever becoming tangible. In short, on both sides lack of curiosity and empathy are the rule. Their mutual love is expressed in stereotypical formulas and endless redundancies, which are simultaneously attached to grandiose, egocentric expectations ("do not forget you belong only to me"). Receiving the daily letter from the other person is more important to each of them than its content, which varies little. But it is precisely this redundancy that serves to promote amity between them. Doubts about this rapport are seldom allowed to emerge because they have no place in this narrow world in which they exist together ("we must agree; it cannot be otherwise"). Neither one is capable of articulating the basis of his or her attraction to the other. Feelings are expressed, at most, as sentimentality ("so profusely endowed with love and kindness"). Prior to marriage, for their infrequent meetings they arm themselves against impending boredom with puzzle magazines.

The letters clearly show how consistently Himmler behaved through these years, how rigidly he lived and conducted himself according to his ideological convictions. From 1924 on, it was his goal to promote the success of the National Socialist movement through his numerous appearances as a speaker and his relentless efforts to strengthen its structures and networks throughout the entire Reich. He was by no means the insignificant secretary of a splinter party that was always in financial difficulty whose career suddenly blossomed after

---

[6] *Das System*, or *die Systemzeit*, was a pejorative National Socialist term used for the constitutional democracy of the Weimar period. [—Trans.]

1933. On the contrary, it is apparent [from these letters] how important his position in the party really was, and how great his proximity to Hitler in the early 1920s. Himmler organized Hitler's speaking engagements and often traveled with him ("am on the road with the Boss"). He himself delivered speeches for the party for years—as a man who had studied agriculture, he agitated in rural areas that were crucial to the NSDAP. At the same time, when he was on-site with his SA and SS units, he was also able to build up those organizational structures and personal contacts upon which he could rely after 1933 to create his powerful apparatus of terror: the SS, police, and Gestapo.

Himmler himself liked to romanticize his work as a struggle, and in his letters to Marga, he styled himself as a *Landsknecht*,[7] a term with which he tried to distance himself from the common office routine of a "boring working stiff." The extent to which Himmler moved in his own element throughout these years becomes clear over the long period covered by the correspondence and the early references to people who later belonged to the leading cadre in the NS regime. The letters show how important the network of these "old comrades" was in all their later careers. Himmler's cliques within the movement proved inseparable from his private life. Even before his marriage, he kept company almost exclusively with like-minded individuals. Afterward, upon his return to the countryside, he realized in the private sphere what he had been propagating in his speeches and through his membership in the folkish Bund Artam.[8]

Years before the National Socialists seized power in 1933, the married couple lived in a world peopled by those of similar convictions, with whom they shared their rejection of democracy, their anti-Semitism, their belief in the victory of national socialism through its continued struggle, and their own staunch hubris. Furthermore, Marga Himmler was by no means an apolitical wife. After her marriage she quickly joined the local unit of the NSDAP in Waldtrudering near Munich, a group that her husband had founded. She soon proudly reported to her husband that her house was the meeting place of all the National Socialists in the town.

---

[7] *Landsknecht*: originally associated with mercenary soldiers, the term connotes roughness and strength. [—Trans.]

[8] The Bund Artam [Artam League] was a radical, folkish group with an agrarian ideology in the right wing of the Jugendbewegung [youth movement], which was absorbed into the Hitler Youth in 1944. [—Trans.]

From their home, Marga followed political developments with intense interest ("How I would really like to be present at all these great events"). From 1928 on she was a regular reader of the party newspaper, the *Völkischer Beobachter* [Folkish Observer—Trans.] and even hired her housemaids through notices in this right-wing propaganda organ. She was able to persuade Heinrich to take her along on trips several times.

The more mundane letters from their first years of marriage consist largely of daily reports, which seem devoid of content and rarely go beyond listings of facts and names. Nonetheless, it becomes clear that Marga suffered under her husband's constant absence. Himmler rarely had time to devote himself to their farming enterprise. In the letters he wrote from all corners of Germany, he expresses regret that his wife—first as a pregnant woman and, later, with a small child—has to do all the difficult work at home alone. At the same time, however, his role as delegate to the Reichstag frequently required his presence in Berlin. Furthermore, thanks to government-mandated free train travel, the party involved him in an ever-increasing schedule of speaking events.

Only a few of Marga's letters from 1933 to 1940 have been preserved, and not a single one from Heinrich Himmler survives. This was the time when he was pursuing his career as the head of the German police, SS, and Gestapo; it was when the family purchased Haus Lindenfycht in Gmund (in Bavaria), and moved into his official residence, Villa Dohnenstieg, in Berlin-Dahlem in 1937. The only private information we have from these years comes from Marga's *Childhood Journal*, which she wrote about her daughter, Gudrun, and foster son, Gerhard. Further information comes from the memoirs written during the war by Marga's sister, Lydia Boden, who lived with them in Gmund after 1934 and looked after the children when both parents were in Berlin. While the *Childhood Journal* ends in 1936, Marga's own *Journal* from 1937 on records information about her new social life, which she owed to her husband's advancement and enjoyed to the utmost when she, for example, organized invitations to tea or bridge parties for the ladies of high society, or when she herself was invited to dinners by them. For the most part, we do not learn much more than the bare facts, such as which people were present at which events, or at best that the experience was "very nice." Beside all the trivia and Marga's narrow-mindedness, something else can be discerned in these journals: pride in the proximity to power ("It was nice to converse with the Führer in peace and quiet"). Then there was the conviction of justifiably belonging to this new elite ("I hold the firm view that I have earned this place in the sun for myself"), and the toleration of the ruthless persecution of those who qualified as "enemies of Germany," for example, when she expresses a wish concerning "lazy" domestic staff: "why aren't these people all put behind bars and made to work until they die?" After the pogrom of November 9, 1938, she writes impatiently, "this Jewish business, when will this rabble finally leave us so we can enjoy a happy life."

III

During World War II Himmler seldom resided in Berlin or Munich, but rather, like so many others in the NS leadership, spent most of his time in special trains. These functioned as mobile military headquarters in the vicinity of the shifting theaters of war. In the spring of 1940, during the western campaign, he was on the road in a special train for two months and in Berlin for the rest of the year. The war against the Soviet Union saw this mobile field command post become his permanent residence. A few days after the attack on the Soviet Union in June 1941, his quarters became the "Sonderzug Heinrich" [Special Train Heinrich] near Angerburg, in East Prussia, near Hitler's Wolfsschanze.[9] In the middle of 1942, when Hitler set up his headquarters in Winniza in the Ukraine, a further field command post was established near Zhytomyr (Jytomyr) under the code name Hegewald. In the following years, Himmler would frequently return to Berlin or Munich for short periods, but he was primarily stationed only in the East.

With the beginning of World War II, Marga began working as a nurse again and often spent many weeks at a time in Berlin, for, according to her principles, she thought, "If everybody helps out, the war will soon be over." By no means did she merely carry out apolitical tasks. As a high-ranking Oberführerin [female senior leader] in the DRK, she administered numerous field hospitals and, with other Red Cross functionaries, traveled through occupied European countries in order to assess the care of German soldiers and oversee the repatriation of the so-called *Volksdeutsche* [ethnic Germans from eastern Europe—Trans.], which her husband was organizing.

For the period after 1941, numerous letters between husband and wife are

---

[9] Wolf's Lair, Hitler's first headquarters on the Eastern Front. [—Trans.]

preserved. From 1942 on there are only those of Heinrich Himmler, in which he frequently mentions letters from his wife to him. Furthermore, during the war years, Himmler telephoned to speak with Püppi[10] (his daughter, Gudrun) in Gmund. He telephoned Marga almost every day when she was in Berlin.

In contrast to the assumption in much scholarly literature that Heinrich Himmler's marriage foundered early, we know that he did not restrict himself merely to contact with his daughter in Gmund. The letters and supplementary documents further show the unanimity of the Himmlers in their anti-Semitism and their racism ("The Polacks, the indescribable filth"); in their absolute faith in Hitler; and in their enthusiasm for the war ("The war proceeds magnificently. We owe everything to the Führer"). Furthermore, Himmler was concerned with Marga's health, and considered it important that she read the texts of his speeches. He sent her sweets, while she sent him home-baked cookies at his military postings in the eastern theater of war. Marga's activity with the Red Cross was a constant source of contention with her husband, who preferred to see her back in Gmund with their daughter. Yet she prevailed, stating, "Without work I could not be part of this war."

The intimacy between husband and wife did not change when, at Christmas 1938, Himmler started a clandestine love affair with his private secretary, Hedwig Potthast, twelve years his junior. During the war, they had two children. As early as 1940, Marga complained that her husband was "never at home in the evenings anymore." After 1942 his letters are often only hasty notes given to an adjutant through whom he supplied Marga with gifts. Nonetheless, he devoted considerable time and money to provide not only his daughter, but also his wife with sweets, bouquets, and useful things, such as paper of all sorts, that were difficult to procure during the war. As ever, he felt closely allied to his family, as in 1944, when he regretted that for the first time he was not able to celebrate Christmas with them, or when he arranged by telephone that all three of them, both in Berlin and in Gmund, would light their Yule lights at the same time so that they might think of one another and strengthen their mutual bonds.

The many short visits to Gmund and Berlin noted in the official schedule and in Himmler's personal pocket calendar show that during the war he saw Gudrun and Marga no less frequently than he saw Hedwig Potthast and their

---

[10] Püppi, their pet name for Gudrun, is an affectionate diminutive for *Puppe*, "doll." Himmler occasionally uses related diminutives, Püppchen or Püpperl. [—Trans.]

children, who at first lived near the SS clinic Hohenlychen, in Mecklenburg, and later in Schönau, near Berchtesgaden. As early as 1939–40 Himmler made the decision to have children with Hedwig Potthast. This was at the same time that he publicly proclaimed his *Kinderzeugungsbefehl* ["Edict to Propagate"] in support of producing extramarital children by entering into second marriages without dissolving the first ones. In cases of such a so-called *Friedelehe*,[11] the first wife retained all her rights. As far as his official duties and the war allowed, Himmler was thus living out the concept of two families with absolute conviction, just as he had promulgated it for his SS. The formulaic nature of Himmler's declarations of love, and his emotional poverty, which was clear from the first letters to Marga, reappear in a letter to Hedwig Potthast. Not only could the style and content almost be taken for that of earlier letters, but the closing words are even identical with those written sixteen years earlier to his wife: "I kiss your dear, good hands, and your sweet mouth."

In contrast to other wives in the NS elite, such as Gerda Bormann, Marga had a difficult time adjusting to her existence as a wife whose husband also had a "concubine." In her *Journal*, she alludes to her distress only obliquely: "I cannot write about whatever else is happening outside of the war." Because she was just as convinced as Heinrich of the NS ideology, and with it of the urgency of producing sons for Germany, she could hardly present solid objections to his decision. However, she doubtless found the situation humiliating, not only because she viewed the infidelity as a betrayal of the marriage they had once both idealized, but also because she herself could not bear any more children after the difficult birth of their daughter.

Himmler barely alludes to his homicidal daily routine during the war years in his letters to his wife: "the struggles, especially those of the SS, are very tough." As he had done earlier, he was fond of emphasizing his huge workload ("there is a lot of work!"), and he sent harmless photographs of his short trips along the Eastern Front: "I am enclosing a couple of little pictures of my last journey to Lublin—Lemberg—Dubno—Rowno—Luck." Only the historical context reveals the truth about the trips mentioned in his letters. He undertook journeys in his role as "commissioner of settlement," with its attendant plans to expel and resettle portions of the population ("the trip to the Baltic was very

---

[11] State-sanctioned concubinage for the SS, who met Aryanization guidelines, to promote a higher birthrate. [—Trans.]

interesting; our tasks are huge"), and also regularly traveled to review SS troops who were responsible for mass shootings of Jewish men, women, and children after the attack on the Soviet Union ("my journey now takes me to Kowno—Riga—Wilna—Mitau—Dünaburg—Minsk"). In 1941–42 only subsequent knowledge of the historical context makes it clear that his travels—"in the coming days I shall be in Lublin, Zamosch, Auschwitz, Lemberg"—were actually visits to concentration camps.

In the last year of the war, when Himmler was not only minister of the interior, but also commander in chief of the Reserve Army and head of an army himself, he complained to his wife about the ever-increasing responsibilities that weighed heavily upon him. Nonetheless, up until the last, he presented himself to Marga as a joyful, optimistic, forceful man of action who, despite his poor health (chronic gastric problems) selflessly shouldered ever-greater burdens because he understood them to be a necessary "service to the German people." His wife's pride in his growing authority is reflected in her *Journal*: "How magnificent that he is called to such great tasks and can master them."

Gudrun's *Journal* also contains references to his "tireless diligence" and the difficulty of his assignments: "the whole nation looks up to him; he always stays in the background and never steps into the limelight." Her father's "great responsibility" was apparently a topic of conversation not only between mother and daughter, but also in the telephone calls between father and daughter. Her father's continual absence made him into an ever more distant hero for Gudrun, and despite her worry about him, she was proud of him and of being the "daughter of such an important man." Presumably she knew hardly anything of his true activities.

Behind the solid middle-class façade, violence and severity are discernible, the origins of which may be traced in part to so-called *Schwarze Pädagogik*,[12] which left its mark upon Heinrich and Marga as it did upon their entire generation. A further source is the National Socialist ideology itself, which declared violence, severity, and ruthlessness to be lofty virtues in all aspects of life. Severity toward oneself justified an equally merciless attitude toward others, as well as—even especially—toward one's children.

---

[12] This poisonous pedagogy (literally, "black pedagogy") was a traditionally authoritarian and repressive technique of child-rearing that included corporal punishment and other methods to control and indoctrinate the young. [—Trans.]

Marga's *Journal* entries about their first years make this attitude toward Gudrun clear: in the strict regimen of cleanliness; in the blows from her parents when she was disobedient; in Heinrich's strict dealings with his little daughter ("she obeys Pappi much better than me"). When their foster son, Gerhard, came to them at age four, Marga predicted that he would be a good influence on her three-year-old daughter: "the boy is very obedient; let us hope Püppi also learns it quickly." The initial enthusiasm about the boy's good manners soon waned, since he regularly infuriated his foster parents, teachers, and other authority figures with his pranks. Gudrun, however, who in the early years had begged her mother never to tell Father when she had been mischievous, apparently fulfilled her parents' expectations with increasing flawlessness. On the one hand, she was often sick and got bad marks in school, but on the other, her parents were proud that Püppi helped out with canning preserves "for hours at a time" and that she produced handmade presents for soldiers at the front and read the ideologically correct tracts her father regularly included in packages to his wife and daughter. The foster parents' behavior toward Gerhard was far less loving, and as he grew older, they became ever stricter, ostensibly to prepare the boy for his future role as a soldier. In the supplementary documents, the *Tagebücher*, and the personal reminiscences of the foster son, it is clear that, for years he feared Himmler's visits in Gmund, because he was always punished with brutal blows. This did not preclude occasional peaceable fishing expeditions with the boy, who recalled, "He could also be a normal father." Marga Himmler soon had nothing good to say about the boy ("He lies beyond belief"), and she refers to the ten-year-old's "criminal nature." Himmler finally advised his wife temporarily to stop signing her letters to her foster son with "Mother," adding, "If he improves his behavior," that might be possible later. Shortly before the end of the war he sent the sixteen-year-old Gerhard for SS training with a tank division, which, finally again earned the boy Marga's respect: "he is very brave and likes being with the SS."

Thus Himmler reveals himself in his private letters as not only a sentimental husband and father, but also a severe, National Socialist parent. In this, he knew himself to be in complete agreement with his wife to the end. High expectations were placed on both children—much higher on the boy, as a future warrior, than on the daughter. Obedience was the highest commandment; misbehavior led to corporal punishments and withholding of affection—a form of violence that without doubt affects the capacity for empathy just as destructively as physical blows.

IV

In these private letters, Heinrich Himmler shows himself to be a person who acts out of deep conviction. His was never a split personality, dominated either by a figurative Dr. Jekyll or a Mr. Hyde. In no way did he separate his activity as head of the SS, responsible for carrying out the extermination policies, from his private life, as though he ever had to conceal the fact of mass murder.[13] He did not boast about this to his wife, but rather considered mass murder a necessary duty that was placed upon him from above, and which he had to carry out conscientiously.

In his letters not a glimmer of doubt or pang of conscience is communicated to his wife. Moreover, he knew that they were united in a belief in the "righteousness" and "necessity" of his activities. From the very beginning, Marga not only shared his anti-Semitism and racism, but after the National Socialists came to power, she endorsed the exclusion of Communists, Jews, and "asocial types" from the community of ethnic Germans. It is unlikely that the increasing violence of Jewish persecution (from expulsion to systematic murder) can have escaped her notice, even if her husband never discussed these things openly with her. In her letters as well as in her private notes, there is no uncertainty whatsoever about the rectitude of her actions.

No "banality of evil" surfaces in these letters. Himmler was by no means what Hanna Arendt incorrectly thought she recognized in Adolf Eichmann, namely, a small cog in a totalitarian mechanism, a person no longer capable of developing an understanding of what his actions meant. Himmler wanted to do what he did, and he wanted to do it thoroughly, dependably, and "decently."

"Most of you will know what it means to see 100 corpses laid out together, when 500, or when 1,000 lie there. To have endured this, and in doing so nonetheless remained decent, that has made us tough—with the exception of a few human weaknesses. This is a glorious page in our history, which has never been,

---

[13] *Pace* original German text, it is clear that Himmler did protect his family from the details of his role in mass murder. His letters to Marga do not contain such information, and they both agreed to shield their daughter from the most upsetting aspects of the war (see letter to Marga of August 2, 1941, regarding the death of a family friend's son). His speeches to the SS, on the other hand, are completely candid about the necessity of murder. [—Trans.]

and never will be, written." These were the core sentences in the first of Himmler's two infamous Posen (Poznan) speeches on October 4, 1943. He committed mass murder with the same self-assurance and moral certitude with which, in the early years, he took note of his brothers' and friends' behavior, raised his own children, and showed himself in his letters to be of one mind with his wife. As Raphael Gross and Werner Konitzer have emphasized, it was not emotional deformity, but rather conviction and "decency" that made mass murder possible for Himmler when he considered it necessary.

These letters allow the reader to see this distortion of normalcy: violence cloaked in innocuousness, the icy coldness that goes hand in hand with a specious solicitude. "Decency" and fulfillment of duty—even when these qualities assist in monstrous crimes—were the guidelines of Himmler's actions. He himself wanted to be a paragon, as a husband as well as head of the SS, as a paterfamilias as well as the one responsible for the Final Solution. In these letters, we see expressed the single-mindedness of a German couple who believed they were participating in "great times," a couple incapable of recognizing that these were, in fact, great crimes. Even if the letters occasionally elicit laughter, one must always remember what lies beneath this apparent middle-class normalcy.

Organization of the Edition

The correspondence between Heinrich and Marga Himmler from 1927 to 1945 forms the core of this edition. Heinrich Himmler's handwritten letters from the collection found in Israel and those of Marga Himmler from the Bundesarchiv Koblenz were transcribed in their entirety and printed in their original form for the first German edition. The rules of orthography that applied at the time were preserved, as well as all errors of grammar and spelling.[14] This edition reproduces only a selection—especially for 1928, when the couple was just getting to know each other. These are excerpted because they contain countless repetitions of formulaic phrases. On the other hand, the increasingly brief letters from the years before the National Socialists came to power and from the war years are retained with almost no deletions.

We have included further supplementary documents from the collection of the archive in Tel Aviv, especially selections from Gudrun's *Journal* and the *Childhood Journal* that Marga Himmler kept about her daughter and later about her foster son. Furthermore, we have included selections from Himmler's *Taschenkalender* [Pocket Calendar]; letters from Gudrun to her father; and documents and letters from Hedwig Potthast. Other sources were also extraordinarily useful: the exhaustive biographies of Himmler by Peter Longerich

---

[14] This translation uses modern German orthography, normalizes grammatical errors when they make the text incomprehensible, and expands their more obscure initials for the sake of clarity. [—Trans.]

(2008) and Klaus Mües-Baron (2011), and the editions of Himmler's *Dienst-und Taschenkalender* [official appointment books and pocket calendars] from 1937, 1940, and 1941–42.

The reader will find thematically organized commentaries inserted throughout the transcribed correspondence. These sections have been added to provide relevant context and background for the most important people, events, and places mentioned. An appendix at the back of the book contains more complete information about the persons in the text. Here we have consciously made a selection that includes information pertinent to these letters. We have avoided biographical sketches of people who may otherwise be found easily in handbooks, dictionaries, and other research tools about the Third Reich.

For the commentary and the biographical appendix, the following sources were consulted: the extensive holdings in "Bestand NS 19" ([Inventory NS 19] *Persönlicher Stab Reichsführer-SS* [Personal Staff of the Reichsführer-SS]), as well as countless other holdings of the Bundesarchiv in Berlin-Lichterfelde. These include *SS-Führungsakten* [Regulations of the SS], *NSDAP-Parteimitgliedsakten* [NSDAP Members' Files], as well as personal files of the *Rasse- und Siedlungshauptamts* [SS Central Office for Race and Resettlement].

To make the text more readable we have kept notes to a minimum and have not included citations to source material. An extensive apparatus of sources and scholarly literature may be found in Appendix 2. In the commentaries, we have retained the common German place names used in the letters. The translators have included a glossary of German terms that occur frequently, especially NSDAP ranks and titles that have no obvious English equivalents.

Translators' Introduction

This, the first English translation of the correspondence between Heinrich and Marga Himmler, reproduces the tone and meaning of the original documents as closely as possible, while also presenting a text that is readily comprehensible to English-language readers. Certain aspects of expression present direct challenges, and we have thus chosen various strategies to make the original transparent. For example, political terms such as government positions and especially military ranks of the SA and SS, have a variety of English equivalents. Our glossary, therefore, cites the most comprehensible English translations. When such terms first occur, English equivalents follow the original in square brackets. In subsequent occurrences, we retain the German titles.

Endearments and nicknames can seldom be rendered literally. The best example of this usage is a favorite word repeated in the early letters: *Dummerle* (literally, "stupid little thing"). In context, however, it is obviously a teasing endearment, more like "silly little thing." At times it appears to convey something interior, such as doubts or depression (see letter 39 from 2.2.28). German frequently uses adjectives as nouns to designate people. *Gut* (good), for example, then acquires a flavor different from English. For example, *Guter* or *Gute* convey "good man/husband" or "good woman/wife." The word *Frau* can be translated as either "woman" or "wife," depending on the context, just as *Mann* corresponds to "man" or "husband." How, then, to choose between "my good woman" and "my good wife"? This translation switches from "man" or "woman" (in the early letters) to "husband" or "wife" once the couple is making wedding plans. The endearments Mutti and Papi (literally "Mommy," "Daddy") have been retained, as has Püppi, Gudrun's pet name in the family, which connotes "little doll." When she is called this by another form (Püppchen, Püpperl, or Püpperlein), we retain Püppi for consistency. Nuances of intimate language are explained in the glossary and notes.

Landsknecht, as Himmler styles himself, is a different example retained here in German, because it best conveys the archaic notion of a "military follower of a king or other superior."

The writing style of any intimate correspondence necessarily contains inconsistencies, errors, repetition, redundancies, and shorthand techniques. These letters are no exception. While the German edition retains the writers' spelling and punctuation errors, this English translation, in all but a few cases, tries to avoid reproducing them as much as possible, because retaining them would make the letters opaque. When such errors or idiosyncrasies convey significant information about the letter writer, however, we have retained them. The English text does not reproduce the abbreviations that the Himmlers inconsistently used to save time and space as they wrote by hand, often in haste or under pressure. We have expanded "B." to Berlin; "M." to Munich; "R." to Ribbentrop; "H." to Herr; "a. Teg." to am Tegernsee," etc., to make reading easier.

When the letter writers use a German place name that has since changed, the modern version follows in parentheses, e.g., Kulmhof (Chelmno).

All dates in the correspondence appear as in the German original. Thus, one reads the day before the month: 13.12.30 is December 13, 1930.

Thomas and Abby Hansen
Wellesley, Massachusetts
March 2015

Correspondence with Commentary

Letters

1927–28

"All that is filthy is kept far from our
home—our castle."
HEINRICH HIMMLER, FEBRUARY 15, 1928

After a long search, Heinrich Himmler finally found employment in the illegal
National Socialist Party (NSDAP) in the summer of 1924. In May of that year
Gregor Strasser (a pharmacist from Landshut), the chief party functionary, was
elected to the Bayerischer Landtag [Bavarian parliament] on the ticket of the
Völkischer Block (a folkish splinter party), a front for the NSDAP. In December
he was even elected to the Reichstag at the national level. Because Strasser no
longer had the time to devote to party organization in Lower Bavaria, the young
Heinrich Himmler took over that administrative function within the party. In
August 1924 he described his new activity to an acquaintance: "I have an enormous amount to do. I am in charge of organization and expansion in all of
Lower Bavaria at all levels. Given all the work I have, there's never a moment to
think about finding the time to write a letter. The organizational work, which I
supervise by myself, suits me well. What would make the whole thing particularly wonderful would be knowing that one were preparing the imminent victory and fight for freedom that lie before us. But as it is, we in the folkish
movement are engaged in selfless work, which will not bear visible fruit in the
near future, always knowing that the fruit of this work will ripen later and that,
for the moment, our business is to fight what seems to be a losing battle."

But the battle was not lost. In May the Völkischer Block won 17.4 percent of
the votes in Bavaria, as many as the Social Democrats won; in these elections

the right-wing parties were also able to win an above-average number of votes for themselves. In December 1924 Adolf Hitler was released from prison,[15] and in February 1925 he reestablished the NSDAP, even though the ban on public speaking that had been imposed on him was valid for a few more months. In Bavaria the ban lasted until March 1927, and in Prussia until November 1928.

It was now Himmler's task to integrate the one thousand or so party members in Lower Bavaria (who were organized into twenty-five local groups) into the reconstituted NSDAP. Given the difficulties of issuing new party members' documents, collecting membership dues, etc., this was no easy matter.

This also meant that he was on the road a lot in Lower Bavaria visiting local groups, giving speeches, and clarifying organizational details on-site. Between 1925 and May 1926 alone, he addressed twenty-seven different meetings in Lower and Upper Bavaria and another twenty in Westphalia, Hamburg, Mecklenburg, Schleswig-Holstein, and elsewhere. In his incessant travel commitments he was no different from other party functionaries. In 1925–26, Joseph Goebbels was also tirelessly on the road, speaking all over Germany and supporting local National Socialist groups. In April 1926 Goebbels even came to Bavaria on a lecture tour. "In the afternoon, with Himmler, in Landshut," Goebbels noted in his diary on April 13, and he continued: "Himmler: a good fellow, very intelligent. I like him."

At the *Reichsparteitag* [annual party rally of the NSDAP] in Weimar in July 1926, Gregor Strasser was made *Reichspropagandaleiter* [propaganda chief] and Himmler rose in the ranks accordingly: he was named acting chief of propaganda, transferred to party headquarters in Munich, and at the same time became acting *Gauleiter* [regional leader] of Lower Bavaria. Whereas he had previously been responsible specifically for Bavaria, his sphere of activity now spread to encompass all of Germany. Since Gregor Strasser was completely occupied as a delegate to the Reichstag and a high-ranking party functionary, the daily propaganda work fell to Heinrich Himmler. He had to make sure that propaganda material was sent out. He also stayed in contact with the local groups, had to coordinate party speaking engagements throughout Germany, and most

---

[15] In February 1924, after the failed putsch attempt in Munich, Hitler was sentenced to serve five years in prison. He was, however, released early.

important, had to organize the so-called *Hitlerversammlungen*.[16] As a result, a very special role in the party apparatus fell to him, for on the one hand, it was up to him to determine which local group would enjoy the privilege of an appearance by Hitler, and on the other hand, he kept in close contact with Hitler in order to arrange his speaking engagements. Despite the fact that in retrospect a picture of Himmler as a pale party functionary has emerged, he was actually at the very heart of the power center of the NSDAP and enjoyed very good contacts with the "Boss," as Himmler refers to Hitler in his letters, and as he was generally known by those in his inner circle.

On his travels Himmler read, among other things, Hitler's *Mein Kampf*, then still in the two-volume edition. The first volume, which presented a stylized political autobiography of Hitler, had appeared in 1925; the second volume, which outlined the political program of National Socialism, appeared in 1927. Himmler bought the first volume as soon as it appeared in July 1925 and, as his handwritten marginalia show, began to read it immediately. He interrupted his reading, however, and did not finish the book until 1927, according to an entry in his *Leseliste* [reading list]. "There are amazingly many truths in it," he noted. "The first chapters about his youth contain certain weaknesses." Perhaps this was the reason he interrupted his reading.

Himmler also bought the second volume immediately upon its publication. By December 17, 1927, he had reached the end of the third chapter, and on December 19, when he had already been in Berlin with Marga for a day, he read to the end of the eighth chapter. This suggests that Marga might also have been reading *Mein Kampf* in these days.

If one follows the checkmarks and underlinings, it appears that Himmler was especially interested in Hitler's statements on *Volksgesundheit* [racial hygiene] and racism. He underlined this sentence: "The assertion that defective people must be prevented from producing other defective people is an assertion of purest rationality and, in its methodical application, signifies the most humane deed of humanity." He noted in the margin "lex Zwickau." With this Himmler refers to the initiative of Gustav Emil Boeters, the doctor from Zwickau, who in the 1920s unsuccessfully demanded a radical law requiring enforced sterilization, which was later passed by Hitler's government in July 1933. Hitler had issued a

---

[16] The first *Hitlerversammlung*—a rally at which Hitler addressed a mass audience—was held in Berlin in November 1929. [—Trans.]

vehement warning against miscegenation and against the danger for the racially pure that occurs through products of racial mixing. Himmler commented: "The potential for undoing racial mixing exists." In a note to Hitler's demand for "the recognition of blood"—meaning "racial bias in general" and also "for individuals in the population" who must be evaluated differently according to their "racial affiliation"—Himmler writes this question: "Are consequences drawn from this?"

Himmler also emphasized Hitler's program to structure all education and training to give every young German "the conviction of being absolutely superior to others. In his physical strength and agility, he must recover the belief in the invincibility of the entire "Volkstum."[17] Himmler's comment on this was "education of SS and SA."

He continued to travel a great deal, both in Bavaria and throughout Germany. In January 1927 he held speeches in Thüringen preceding an election to the regional parliament. In February he was in Westphalia; in April, in the Ruhr; in May, in Mecklenburg and Saxony; in June, North Germany; and in July, Vienna. On one of these trips, in September 1927, on the train that returned to Munich from Berchtesgaden, he made the acquaintance of Marga Siegroth.[18]

Marga Siegroth, née Boden, had spent a week's holiday at Berchtesgaden and stayed on for a further week in Munich before returning to Berlin. She had been unhappily married from about 1920 to 1923, but nothing is known of her first husband except his family name, Siegroth. Marga's father, Hans Boden, a former landowner in Goncerzewo (Goncarzewy), near Bromberg (Bydgoszcz) in Pomerania, had purchased a thousand-dollar gold savings bond as his portion of a private women's clinic in Berlin at the height of the inflation. The clinic was located in a block of flats at 49 Münchner Strasse, in the middle-class neighborhood of Schöneberg, where Marga lived and worked as head nurse.

---

[17] "Racial essence," an NS term replacing *nationality*. [—Trans.]

[18] The later letters by Heinrich and Marga indicate that they met on the train from Berchtesgaden to Munich on September 18, 1927. Himmler's letter of December 26, 1927, states, "[A]t that time, on the train, I immediately considered you to be a very energetic creature," and that of January 10, 1928, where Heinrich Himmler defends the movement against an attack by Marga because "If it had not existed," he writes, "I would never have gone to Berchtesgaden on 18 September." As for the fact that their meeting did not take place on the trip to Berchtesgaden, but rather on the return trip, it is established by the postcard sent on September 19, 1927, by Marga, which carries a Munich postmark and in which she informs him that she is staying at the Hotel Stadt Wien (in Munich).

There is absolutely no doubt that if she attracted the attention of Heinrich Himmler, it was not merely because of her blonde hair and blue eyes, but also because of her profession—all the more because during World War I she had taken a job as a Red Cross nurse, which in his eyes was an exemplary occupation for a woman. In their subsequent letters, they both write about that war and refer to it specifically, as when Marga writes, "Ever since the battlefield I have gotten used to writing without a table" (22.12.27).

As the head nurse in this private clinic, she led a very independent, rather comfortable life with a workday of only a few hours. She had her own maid, and her meals were provided by the clinic's cook. There was time in the afternoons and evenings for shopping in the city and dates with friends to attend cultural events. Nonetheless, she does not seem to have been happy with her life. Although her employment contract ran until the month of April 1929, she often considered leaving this position before the end of her tenure, or even changing clinics. One reason was clearly her bad relationship with the doctors in the establishment: "If only it were not for these impossible doctors," she complains repeatedly. It may be that she also considered her work as a desperate move after the failure of her marriage, especially since the status of a divorced woman was hardly a glorious one at the time. The clinic secured her financial independence—but she would soon voluntarily abandon her work to enter into her second marriage.

Marga Siegroth not only dreaded human company, but was almost "terrified" by anything that disturbed her routine and her daily tranquility. As she never ceased to emphasize later on, dealing with others was nearly always a source of "annoyance" or "disappointment" for her. Her misanthropy ("There are also very different sorts of individuals," letter of 4.11.27), coupled with an extremely high standard for other people, and her own rigidity and lack of warmth in dealings with others, later quickly cooled her relations with the Himmler family. Although they welcomed her cordially at first, they soon limited their contacts to infrequent formal visits.

Her skepticism about other people in general, and men in particular, is a theme that reappears chiefly in her first letters, when Heinrich Himmler hopes that she will stop mistrusting him. But this is difficult for her, for in her own words, she has "lost faith, in particular, in the honesty and sincerity of a man's respect for a woman" (26.11.27).

During the train trip of nearly three hours, both certainly had occasion to note what separated them: a Prussian mentality on one side, Bavarian on the other; a Protestant religion for one, Catholic for the other; and the fact that Marga was not only a divorced woman, but also seven years older than Heinrich. However, they not only shared the same aversion to the Weimar Republic and the Jews ("this rabble"), but also had common interests. As his journals show, when Heinrich was a student of agriculture, he had dreamed of one day owning a property with "a beloved girl." With Marga, an old dream suddenly came back to life because, although at that time she was a confirmed city dweller, she had a much better idea of actual country life than he himself did—more than most young girls of good family could ever have, because she had grown up on a large farm. Marga thus had practical experience with cultivating fruits and vegetables and raising animals. Not only could she preserve food for the winter, but she could also turn over the soil in the garden beds and even slaughter pigs. In addition to that, she was a head nurse with bookkeeping skills, and not least of all, Himmler found it appealing to think that she could care for him and his delicate health. Marga, too, was soon filled with enthusiasm at the prospect of moving to the country and building a life there together with her new husband.

They clearly got along well enough that, on the very next day, Marga wrote him a formal postcard (showing a scene of Berchtesgaden) in order to make plans to meet. She told him where she would be staying in Munich, at the Hotel Stadt Wien, right near the central railroad station. Their first disagreements became apparent during a long walk together along the Isar River ("the path where we nearly came to blows at the time," 25.12.27). Both of them later refer frequently to their early disputes. At one point Himmler writes, "you know, in the early days, *we* argued, and for as long as we live, we *never* have to do that again" (13.2.28). And she confirms this: "I believe you are right, in the early days we argued enough to last us the rest of our lives. Every sentence was an argument and a doubt" (14.2.28).

19.9.1927[19]
Herr Heinrich Himmler
Diplom-Landwirt [certified agronomist]
Munich
Barerstr. 44/II

Am staying at the Hotel Stadt Wien.
Cordially
M. Siegroth

———

Himmler's first letters have been lost, but in his correspondence folder, he notes that he first wrote to Marga Siegroth ("M.S.") on September 26, 1927. After the date of Marga's letters, he also noted, by hand, the date on which he received them—as he did with all his correspondence. The editors have indicated this convention with parentheses. All other parentheses in the letters are by Heinrich and Marga Himmler themselves. Editorial notes are in brackets and and set in italics.

———

Berlin West 30. 29.9.27 *
(Munich. 4.10.27, 9:00)

Dear Herr Himmler!
        Thank you for your lovely note. It found me in a less than good mood, for I have found more annoyances here than I ever would have believed possible. I will and must put an end to this business. But it is difficult to start from scratch; but that is why it must be done.
        How are you? Your health? How about the mustard, vinegar, and onions? Have you been back to a "good" café? If so, then please write me a card.
        Say hello to the Hofkino for me [a local movie theater—Trans.]. (Sarcasm, as usual!!) I await the promised letter. Demanding as always, don't you think?

———

[19] This postcard bears a Munich postmark, as mentioned earlier.
* 30 designates the postal code. [—Trans.]

I have read your writings with great interest. What can I send you in return? Just the red book, yes?

The weather is so beautiful. And it rained so often in Munich.

　　Very cordially yours,

　　Frau M. Siegroth

Berlin W. 30. 16.10.27

Münchener Str. 49

Dear Herr Himmler!

　　Today is the first quiet day, and I have enjoyed it to the hilt. As for the rest, just work and boredom. How are you? Much to do, surely, and your health? But whatever you can do, you want to do, and whatever you want to do, you can.

I have so often said this to myself lately, when I thought I could not go on.

The weather must still be absolutely magnificent where you are. Are you traveling a lot? When are you coming to Berlin?

　　Otherwise, I am all right.

　　Very cordially yours

　　M. Siegroth

Berlin, 2.11.27

(Munich. 4.11.27, 24:00)

Dear Herr Himmler.

　　At last the final monthly accounts are done, now I just want to thank you for your correspondence and for the newspapers. As for the latter, one can also buy them in Berlin, which I have done. So I ask you to send me some from Munich. I have also read the ones from Weimar.

As to your letter, I shall keep silent: I certainly did not laugh. "Actually, one should not be decent and nice." Incredible, the number of things you have undertaken. Your stomach is just taking revenge for what you constantly put it through. This is understandable, since it has good reason.

One works to be able to pay taxes, at least that's fun: taxes!

I read Ludendorf's [*sic*] book on the Freemasons.

The book criticizes the Jews, I find that the facts speak volumes, so why all these remarks? Life truly offers too many pleasures.

With my regards, yours

Frau M. Siegroth.

Marga had obviously read the recently published pamphlet by Erich von Ludendorff, the former imperial general and military leader of World War I, who was also a committed Folkish nationalist and anti-Semitic politician. His *Vernichtung der Freimaurerei durch Enthüllung ihrer Geheimnisse"* [Destruction of Freemansonry Through the Revelation of its Secrets] (Munich, 1927) was full of hatred toward the Jews. According to Ludendorff, the goal of the Freemasons was "the Semitification of populations and the institution of the reign of the Jews and Jehova." According to Ludendorff's own information, the text published at the author's expense rapidly found its public, even though the middle class press had barely mentioned it and the bookstores had at first boycotted it. By the end of 1927 more than one hundred thousand copies had been sold.

Berlin, 4.11.27 (Munich 9.11.27, 11:00)

Dear Herr Himmler.

Well, we seem to have written to each other on the same day again. But it should not happen again this time, that is why I am writing right now.

So you have a somewhat bad conscience after all. Things do not seem to be quite as far along "after all" with your new achievements. The fact that you do not want to be good, I can understand. Young, unattached, but decent, I cannot get over it. You just wait at least until you have been in my beloved Berlin. All at once is too much of a good thing.

You see, when the stomach is treated well, it gets better.

If you only have to deal with inwardly dishonest people, be glad. There are also very different individuals, not to say humans. I would be grateful to fate if it would show me just a few people whose life had real substance.

Through them, one comes to the realization that life, whatever it may bring, has a purpose, a goal.

I am waiting for the day when I attend a rally (I have never yet been to a political rally), what an impression it will make on me! Won't I leave with the sensation that this is all just empty slogans? Is it not romanticizing to want to help people who do not really want any help! Nonetheless, one has to do it, if only for oneself. Even though there are so many good-for-nothings, you do not have to be one yourself. Yes, the thought makes my blood boil. I cannot even open the Ludendorf [*sic*] book anymore, it infuriates everything in me. To think that there have existed, and still exist, free German men who do not even care that their outward behavior is unworthy of them.

I will be as silent as possible about my own troubles. My contract runs until April 1929, and I will honor it up until then. And I think I will be able to do that. One can do what one wants to do! I have sometimes thought it will not work, but it must. Why it "must" be, that is what I just do not know. *When all is said and done, I'm sure I'm certainly not brave enough.* Whenever one starts something new, things will be better! I doubt it.

Now I have to write the second part of the letter. In the first version of it there was too much of my own "ego." You are also careful with my letters?

So, in one month you will be here. Will the long stay in Berlin suit you? Naturally, we can be more peaceful with each other, but whether we shall be, only the future can tell. I look forward to fighting and teasing [. . .]

   Many regards,
   As always your, M. Siegroth

W.30. 13.12.27 (Bützow 17.12.27)

Dear Herr Himmler

  By now you will have safely survived both of the "Little Parises," and when you are in Berlin, I will see how well. Or not!![20]

---

[20] In mid-December Heinrich Himmler had taken a trip lasting several days through Mecklenburg-Vorpommern [Mecklenburg-Pomerania]. Clearly he had informed Marga about most of the stops along this trip, because he picked this letter up on December 17 from general delivery in Bützow (near Rostock)—just a day before he continued on to Berlin for a three-day visit with her. Like the other towns where Himmler spoke, Bützow and Stolpe (near Parchim) were located in regions where the National Socialists already had a relatively high proportion

When I read in the V.B. [*Völkischer Beobachter*] that you were speaking in Stolp[e] on Saturday (today), I also understood your telegram, which at first seemed very odd to me. Thank you very much for it, and also for the letter.

What must you have "thought," surely something very bad, since you did not write it, or have saved it for when you come? Your suggestion is absolutely correct. Please do not let me wait too long. Otherwise it will be so late even in Potsdam, but you can hardly even be there at 11:30, because you are going to be arriving at the Stettin Railroad Station. And you have forgotten the big city, it is not like Munich. Go ahead and laugh, you will soon know it as well as I do. A compliment?!

You will receive my letter on Saturday, it was too late for Parchim. I came home late last evening from my father's birthday.

Just think, so much annoyance these past few days. Christmas, so many errands, which I usually do happily, sometimes are no fun. Theater, I was pleasantly disappointed.

We will speak later about January—Munich.

Why did my Stolp[e]-Pomerania[21] please you and not my Berlin, or does your "Dickkopf"[22] not let you admit that Berlin is actually more pleasant than you thought. Please do not make a big fuss over it. Maybe you are getting to know me a little by now, and?! Rather than continue in this tone, I want to stop now!

This week I have to have guests, I think it will be very nice. Really it is a shame that you understand me so little, I would so gladly continue "teasing." But it is possible that it reads quite differently than it is meant. I will make up for everything I've been holding back.

---

of the vote. Among other towns, Güstrow, which is situated near Bützow, was called "Little Paris." Marga regularly read the *Völkischer Beobachter*, presumably to be able to follow Himmler's speaking itinerary.

[21] Stolpe is a town and surrounding area in Pomerania, Prussia, now in Poland. [—Trans.]

[22] The correspondence contains several instances of this teasing endearment. It sometimes appears in the North German dialect form *Dickkopp*. Both mean, literally, "thick head," and connote stubbornness. The variant, *Dickschädel*, or "thick skull" is also used (see letter of December 31, 1927). The German words will be left untranslated in subsequent passages. [—Trans.]

God, does Dr. Goebbels ever look "Jewish," even his comb-over; it made me think of all my sins. You left your pencil here at my place. But what on earth did you experience in "Little Paris"? Oh, curious!

Until we meet again, your,

M. Siegroth

––––––––––

Heinrich visited Marga in Berlin from December 18 to 21. As usual he had planned a full program in advance. In keeping with that, on the very day of his arrival they apparently went out to Potsdam to tour Schloss Sanssouci. The following letter of Marga's shows a noticeable change in their relationship. Not only do they now use the familiar pronoun *Du*, but suddenly the tone changes from the friendly teasing of a superficial acquaintanceship to the intimate and caring tone of lovers.

How close they actually became, whether they merely declared their mutual love or actually went to bed together, does not emerge clearly from Marga's reserved wording, or from Himmler's next letter.

For Heinrich Himmler, celibacy before marriage had always been a steadfast principle; perhaps he viewed this less strictly with a divorced woman. Certainly it is possible that his persistent idealization of Marga as a "high, pure woman" (albeit not "pure" anymore, in the old-fashioned sense, because he was not her first husband) is a clue that restraint before marriage continued to be important to him. Therefore it is quite conceivable that they declared their love for each other in Berlin and merely sealed it with a few kisses and the shared *Du* form. Whatever the case, they had already decided to see each other in Munich in January.

––––––––––

1.[23] W. 30. 21.12.27 (Munich, 23.12.27, 7:30)

Now it really has gotten late before I managed to write you, my dear Dickkopf. I sense your disappointed face, and would have gladly written earlier, but it was impossible. But tomorrow is our Christmas and then it will

––––––––––

[23] The numbering of the letters is explained in Himmler's letter of 23.12.27. He apparently numbered this letter of Marga's himself, as well as, later, the one from 22.12.27.

be peaceful. Today a nice nurse came to visit me, and I just could not get rid of her. You have now safely landed in "your" Munich, and have a lot of work. Please be good, let Christmas pamper and take care of you, so you can recover a little. Be sweet and do not forget that there is an infinite distance between recklessness and cowardice. Yesterday we were still chatting together, today we are far apart. One has no answer to one's questions. Tomorrow I will have a letter from you, you good man, and I, I will be better, that is, I want to be. And what one wants to do, one can do, and that is possible—isn't it? Was it ever cold last night, you must have frozen. Did you also pay a visit to "uncle doctor?" Go there in January!

My dear good man,

Your Marga

At the time, Heinrich Himmler was renting a room with the Prachers in the Maxvorstadt area on Gabelsbergerstr. 2. The Alte Pinakothek [art museum] and the Technische Universität [Technical University], where he had studied from 1919 to 1922, were also on this street. Ferdinand von Pracher was the stepfather of Heinrich's best friend, Falk Zipperer, whom he had known since his school days in Landshut. Despite their acquaintance, he called Falk's parents by the title "Excellencies." Although he came "home" to this place daily from his office, he obviously still thought of his real "home" as that of his parents. They lived in a rented apartment on the top floor of the Wittelsbacher-Gymnasium from 1922 to 1930, where his father was active as principal until his retirement. Heinrich sometimes stopped by briefly for lunch with his parents; on Sundays, the whole family regularly gathered there for dinner. Heinrich Himmler also spent the Christmas holidays in his parents' house with his younger brother, Ernst ("Ernstl") and his older brother, Gebhard, with his wife, Hilde, and their little daughter, "Mausi." The school lay a few streets to the west of his rented room on Marsplatz, a sprawling, inhospitable square near the railroad tracks with a view of a barracks and the tent top of the Circus Krone, where Hitler had given his first speeches at mass rallies.

Maxvorstadt, which was situated north of the city center, and Schwabing, which bordered it, were known before World War I as bohemian artists' quarters. After 1921, however, there was also an NSDAP section in Schwabing, which by 1925 had five hundred to six hundred party members, four times as many as other party sections in Munich. In the rear courtyard of 50 Schellingstrasse, Heinrich Hoffmann, Hitler's photographer, had his first photographic studio. In 1925 he vacated several rooms for the NSDAP, which used this address as its head office until the end of 1930. The business office of the party was staffed by Hitler's inner circle: Philipp Bouhler as managing director, Franz Xaver Schwarz as treasurer, and Max Amann as director of the party's publishing operation, the Eher Press.

The editorial offices and press of the *Völkischer Beobachter* were situated one intersection away, at 41 Schellingstrasse, from 1927 to 1931. Hitler's favorite restaurant, the Osteria Bavaria, was also on Schellingstrasse. The writer Oskar Maria Graf, who lived in the neighborhood from 1919 to 1931 and was a frequent patron of this bohemian tavern in the Italianate style, wrote this: "There Hitler was surrounded by his future 'Paladins,'" among whom Graf mentioned Heinrich Hoffmann, Rudolf Hess, Hermann Göring, and others. The "bull-necked, thick-headed Gregor Strasser and the bespectacled, small-eyed Himmler with his officious-looking head clerk's face came there every now and then."

After September 1927, Photohaus Hoffmann was located just a few buildings farther along the street, on the corner of 25 Amalienstrasse and Theresienstrasse. It was here that Hitler presumably first met Eva Braun in October 1929. The atelier was located right above the famous Café Stefanie, which had been the meeting place of the artists in Schwabing up until World War I but in the meantime counted leading NSDAP politicians among its clientele. Heinrich Himmler was well acquainted with this neighborhood. Up until age thirteen he had lived with his family on Amalienstrasse, and he had often stood with his brother looking through the window of Café Stefanie. Gebhard recalled them watching impoverished artists playing chess, sitting "over a glass of water and a toothpick." Six years later, in 1919, Himmler returned to this neighborhood to study after he had finished school in Landshut and spent a short interlude as an officer's candidate. Here he could reach everything on foot from his furnished room: the university, the lunch and dinner meals with his circle of friends at Frau Loritz's, and the gatherings of the student club, Apollo.

Not until January 1, 1931, did the central headquarters of the NSDAP move from the back annex of the building at 50 Schellingstrasse to the imposing and

lavishly renovated Barlowpalais at 45 Brienner Strasse (better known as the
Brown House), which had been bought in July 1930. From mid-January 1933
on, the entrance to the building was guarded day and night by SS men.

After the National Socialists seized power in 1933, Munich was declared to
be the "capital of the movement," with the primary responsibility of glorifying
the history of the party and its ascent. To this end, a new center of power was
established around Königsplatz and Karolinenplatz, where every year in memory of the failed putsch of November 9, 1923 a commemorative celebration
was held with an enormous swearing-in ceremony of SS candidates.

On Christmas Day 1927, a warm, sunny day, Himmler and his younger
brother once again walked the same path that Heinrich had walked with Marga
in September: "We walked on Maximilianstrasse, on the banks of the Isar (the
street where back then we almost came to blows), to the Friedensengel [Angel
of Peace statue], to Prinzregentenstrasse, the English Garden, the Monopterus,
Ludwigsstrasse, all streets well known to you. You can imagine how little I
thought of you" (December 25, 1927).

The following letter (from him, numbered 3; see his commentary in letter
number 4) is the earliest surviving letter by Himmler on the Israeli microfilms.
Save for scattered exceptions, he always writes the pronoun of address, *du, dein,
dir, dich*, etc., in lower case.

---

3) Special Delivery Munich, 23.12.1927, 14:00

My dear, good Marga!

Your letter came this morning by special delivery. How it delighted me,
and how happy it made me when I went out. I ran a few errands, then to the
office and now quickly home, and here I find your dear little package. What
can I say about it, you sweet spendthrift, you!

Now why don't you make some Christmas wishes for yourself. Be happy
about the holiday and do not be the slightest bit sad, and have no doubts; for
you must know that you have a man you can call yours, who is deeply grateful
to you for your love and whose every free thought that the struggle permits
him, is of you—and who loves and honors you as the sweetest, purest thing
he has.

You must believe, and should therefore be happy when we celebrate Christmas together, even if it be from a distance. I send you my two pictures, so that you can sometimes see your Dickkopp up close.[24]

And just this morning I got a book for you that I think you will like, you, the dear woman with the beautiful blonde hair and the good blue eyes. Tomorrow afternoon I shall go home and stay at home on Sunday and Monday and rest a bit there and be happy.—But what a feast it would be if my little woman were sitting by me and we were being sweet to one another—I must not even think of it.

And now, do not have any worries about me; absolutely nothing is happening until 6 January, even we are taking a break. Tomorrow morning I am off to Uncle Doctor; it simply was not possible any sooner. I amaze myself at how good I have actually been. At home I am going to have to really pull myself together, so that the whole world will not be shocked at how "docile" I am. There, you see!

I hope that everybody is nice to you, that nothing gets on your nerves, and that you do not have to wrinkle your brow. I stroke your dear forehead and kiss your dear mouth.

     Your Heini

4) Munich, in the office, 23.12.1927, 21:00

My dear dear Marga!

     Listen, I do not think I ever thanked you for your lovely present today. [. . .] And what is more, I will be sure to use the little writing case on my trips so the little woman always gets news.

I have numbered this letter, I think that is quite practical. The numbers begin at *our* 18 December.

I kiss you, my dear little woman!

     Your Heini

---

[24] On December 24, Marga replied to him, "Your pictures, they are incredibly good. [. . .] But why are you holding your hand in front of your face? Is that supposed to cover your chin? And the part in your hair!"

3. W. 30 22.12.27 (Munich, 1:00, 25.12.27)

Ella from next door just brought me your dear letter, you can imagine how I breathed a sigh of relief. Because tonight I have to celebrate Christmas, and what's more, I have to be "in good form." Oh my good Dickkopp, how I laughed at this word, because it actually means "Kopf" [head]. You were good, sweetheart, really good, and you got some sleep. You really do know how to be "good"! I shall find out in January. [. . .]

Your letter is so sweet, if only I could write everything that way, but it is not my style, and you know my thoughts and my love for you. You know what I think and how peaceful and quiet everything is with me. I have such a horror of Christmas, it is a celebration of peace, and what a horrendous year it has been. And yet on the other hand it was good, amazingly beautiful, restored my faith in humanity. I can believe again, trust. You do not know what that means. I am rich in treasures thanks to you and your love.

My dear good Dickkopp you should get nothing but joy from me, as much joy and love and kindness as I can give. You know what a weak sex we women are.

Now I have to go next door for the festivities. If only all this were in the past. I really dislike playing "head nurse." My associate, who has left already, gave me a beautiful big pillow. I really have to put up with everything. Deep breath, and now over to the merriment.

11 o'clock, as many presents as a princess, kissed like a lover, at last I have landed safely back at my place. After the official part had been taken care of, I saw only happy faces and almost everyone hugged me. My life had a purpose again. It made me downright happy. Four of my employees were also here last year. [. . .]

And now, my beloved Dickkopp, I would like to wish you a very happy holiday again. Happy and good days with much joy and peace. You especially need the last one. Are you still annoyed at Berlin? It makes me sad. But I cannot do anything about it. It does not bother me. My home is my world. [. . .]

> My dear, good beloved Dickkopp, all my very best to you
> Your Marga

7) *Munich, 26.12.27, 23:00*
In my room, Gabelsbergerstr.

My dear, dear little woman!

It is almost 11:00 and I have just gotten in after taking the streetcar from my parents' place and have arrived in my nice room, which at the moment I am calling my home. I have put on my old fur vest that I got ten years ago when I joined the German army as a green young soldier. There is no one in the apartment but me. I have just found what I need in this unfamiliar kitchen and made myself some tea, and now I am sitting here and I want to put a few thoughts on paper. A cumbersome process! How wonderful it was eight days ago when I knew that after work, I could go spend a wonderful couple of hours with my little woman, who would be sweet to me—and then knowing we could chat together and tell each other everything that we would otherwise never tell, because other people just do not understand, and because we are both too proud to bare any piece of our souls to others who might possibly laugh at us.

And that is the way it will probably always be with other people, and so both of us must resort to paper and say in words that which our souls whisper to each other across all distances, and sense through the vibrations of feeling without any physical contact.

But now I should give you a bit of a report on all I have been doing, otherwise the "angry" little woman will not believe that I have been "good." So, on Saturday morning I did not get up until 9:30, and then I chatted until around 11:00 with my friend Falk, who was driving to Schliersee with his associates. I was in the office at 11:00. There I met only a couple of the gentlemen; the employees were allowed to stay at home. Lunch at 2:00 p.m. At 2:30, to the doctor's. I have already written to you about the good results. And now I will say again that the notion that I am a "Dickkopp" (that is how they say it in North Germany)—that is certainly not true. A few more errands, then back to the office again. Here I finished some work, then quickly back home; I packed my things and got on the road. It suddenly occurred to me that I still had nothing for "Mausi," my little niece, so I found a colorful little ball for the little creature, which can be attached to the canopy of her cradle. Now I was happy that I had everything, and I took the car and rushed over to my parents', where I arrived with military punctuality (I do not hear anyone saying "for a change"). Naturally, great joy at the return of the prodigal son.

Just like every year, a beautiful celebration in front of the tall (4 m.) Christmas tree and the old illuminated crèche. Around 8 o'clock (20:00) we went over to visit my married brother who lives ten minutes from my parents' apartment and spent the evening with him and his truly lovely and good wife. At midnight my brother Ernst and I went to Mass as we do every year. It is not like me to be devout in church very often, but I am always devout at Mass, especially in the high Gothic cathedral. I do not often bother God much with my affairs and my worries, in good or bad times, but I did pray for you, my dear and good woman, and for our love.

After midnight Mass, I came back here to my room and discovered your sweet letter, which made my Christmas joyous. I then wrote you the special delivery letter, took it to the station, and went home with my loyal little brother at around 3:00 (Marsplatz, parents). (I always have to write that for you specially, otherwise you will not know what your Landsknecht means by all these mentions of "home.") I read your good letter once again and then slept wonderfully until lunch. In the afternoon, from 14:00 to 17:00, the walk with Ernst that I described to you yesterday, then my brother Gebhard and his wife came to tea and stayed until dinner. We chatted together. After dinner and into the night we and the parents played two games, harmless and happy, as though we were still children. At midnight I then wrote you a short note; it was actually lazy of me, but I knew what a good little woman you are and that you would not be angry if one letter ends up a bit shorter than another. Then I had a wonderful sleep. This morning I went into town with Ernst and wrote you a note. At noon we went to Mass, then back to my parents'. The weather was bad, so we could not go walking. From 14:00 to 16:30—you will be amazed at this—we went to the movies (not to your favorite Munich movie theater, but to a different one) and saw the Christ film "King of Kings." I liked the film a lot. Apart from a few distortions and kitschy places, it is very good. Afterward, home, where we chatted together, then Ernst and I paid a short visit to Gebhard, his wife, and little daughter. After dinner we played a bit more, and with that, our two days of peace and innocence under the parental roof were over. As beautiful as it was, I had to get out by 22:00, I wanted to be alone in order to be together with you.

How pleased I am that your people were good to you; by God you earned it, you dear good creature. Look, now a sentence has just occurred to me, one you will like, and one I have often repeated aloud to myself when I sometimes despair about people: "Even the worst of worst human beings is connected to humanity by some tiny thread." You can often see this during a holiday like this, when even the roughest types become good and grateful, if only for a moment.

You use the word "little" about yourself when you write to me. You must be joking. Oh I can just imagine you in your clinic and elsewhere, you know that back in the train I first thought you were a very energetic creature, but nonetheless, for me, you are my dear "little" woman, whom I would always like to hold in my arms and protect so that no one can hurt you. And furthermore, you sweet scamp, I hardly have to explain to you that it is never meant to demean you, but you know well enough what I mean. That is just the fate of us "sawed-off giants,"[25] so we shall stick with "dear little woman."

And then you also write about "Berlin." Nowadays Berlin is dear to me because you live there, for the same reason that the poorest little village would be dear to me if that were your home. I hate the Berlin "system,"[26] which cannot touch you, you good and pure woman—and I shall always hate it. But that is no reason for you to be sad, I do not have the tiniest thought that could make you sad. So please, for my sake, do not be sad, you dear, dear little woman.

Another thing in closing: be assured of one thing, that I shall always remain true to myself. Do me the kindness of never having another thought like those that I read on the last page of your letter!

You will *always, always* be able to sit with me and feel protected, the way you did when you sat with me eight days ago. I told you once I neither wish to nor will *ever* disappoint you. You can rely on this, just as I rely on your love. My fate is something I cannot guarantee. The worry I have is always the question of whether I have the right, because of this love, perhaps to cause a human being whom I love so infinitely, much bitter sorrow someday because of this love. I can never neglect my duty—and may someday pull you into the vortex of sorrow, pain, and fate. We Landsknechte of the fight for German freedom should really remain lonely and outcast. Dear, dear child, ponder

---

[25] Himmler uses the colloquialism "abgebrochener Riese," literally, "broken or cut off giant," derisive slang (roughly equivalent to "half pint") for a short man. Marga later refers to this image. (letter of 28.12.27) [—Trans.]

[26] See section II of the introduction for the note about the so-called "System." [—Trans.]

everything I say, for it is not written lightly, but I can already imagine many horrors in the future, and because I truly love you. In any case, *you* will never be a burden to me, never have that thought again. But the fact that I could someday cause you sorrow and pain weighs heavily upon me. I wish to talk to you about this in person.

Tomorrow I will again receive another sweet letter from you, and I will write to you in the evening. But for now it is time to close. It is 1:30 a.m. I am going to take the letter to the post office, which is just a few buildings away.

I embrace you and kiss you, my dear woman,[27]

Your Heini

———————

For the native Bavarian Heinrich Himmler, Berlin represented a dystopia, symbol of the "hated system" of Weimar democracy. Popular opinion had been divided about Berlin since the city became the capital of the German Reich in 1871 and enjoyed a rapid boom. For some, it was the place of urbane culture and the artistic avant-garde, of scientific progress, and industrial power. For others, Berlin represented the very concept of detestable modernity, a place of vice, decadence, and greedy capitalism. For the folkish Right, the metropolis was both a target par excellence and also an object onto which they could project all those characteristics of modern society that they perceived as negative. In addition, Berlin was a bastion of the workers' movement. The counterrevolution was attacking this hegemony of Social Democrats and Communists; Red Berlin was being marked for ultimate destruction.

Marga, however, lived in Berlin and was certainly not going to let a native of Munich like Heinrich spoil the city for her. "Just wait at least until you have been in my beloved Berlin" (4.11.1927), she wrote, trying to soothe him. Or she teased him: "Why did my Stolp[e]-Pomerania please you and not my Berlin, or does your "Dickkopf" not let you admit that Berlin is actually more pleasant than you thought" (13.12.27). Or she tried to enlist his sympathy: "Are you still annoyed at Berlin? It makes me sad. But I cannot do anything about it. It does not bother me. My home is my world" (22.12.27). He tries to pick up on this in the previous letter: "Nowadays Berlin is dear to me because

———————

[27] In this letter Himmler addresses Marga with the word *Frau*, which has a root meaning of "woman," but also, and especially in this context, can mean "wife, spouse." [—Trans.]

you live there, for the same reason that the poorest little village would be dear to me if that were your home. I hate the Berlin "system," which cannot touch you, you good and pure woman—and I shall always hate it. But that is no reason for you to be sad, I do not have the tiniest thought that could make you sad. So please, for my sake, do not be sad, you dear, dear little woman" (26.12.27).

Eventually, however, Marga does an about-face and adopts the resentments of her fiancé. At the beginning of the New Year, she still pokes a bit of fun at him in reference to his impending visit to Berlin: "You do not have to be afraid of the 'metropolis,' I will do my best to 'protect' you" (4.1.28), or "Just think, Berlin is a metropolis (and how, I hear you say), but people know how to drive cars, and your naughty scamp does not get in trouble here so easily. In small towns people have to learn it—how to drive, I mean. But if you are still afraid of Berlin, then write to me in time and I will pick up my Landsknecht, the fearful one, and protect him well and loving to him" (2.2.28). But once it becomes clear that she is going to leave Berlin, she turns to look at the city and writes: "A good thing that I do not have to live here in this dirt forever" (13.2.28). Or she writes, "Berlin is too polluted, all people talk about is money" (22.4.28). But one thing is certain for her: it is in Berlin that they will marry.

---

6. W. 30. 28.12.27 (Munich, 30.12.27, 10:30)

My dear Beloved, this morning your sweet letter arrived promptly as usual. At 9:00 I ordered myself tea and the mail, and Hanna appeared with the words, "Here is the letter." She had put all the others aside. I have just read it, all that love and sweetness. How good of you to have written such a long letter. My good, dear Dickkopp, that is what I am going to keep calling you, and you are satisfied with that, right, and even if you "are" so *good*. Because I know that is now what you are going to *become*. I had to laugh out loud several times at your sweet message.

Listen. About the fur vest: don't you have heating? And you've bought a little ball, I would have liked to have been there when you did, and then your brother's sweet good little wife, how incredibly well-mannered that all sounds—I laughed out loud.

Lately things have been going well for me; I have more activity again. Things to write, shopping errands, and visitors in the evenings, my parents yesterday, Helmut today, I hope nobody tomorrow. Friday evening theater, Saturday, New Year's. My parents,[28] Ella, and I are meeting, and plan to take a stroll through Berlin. I have never done that, I wonder what we shall see!

In what category of "giants" do you count yourself? I shall carry my fate proudly, you will help me, dear Dickkopp, for "sawed-off" giants cannot do it alone.

My "favorite movie theater," that would be the Hofkino—let us say what we mean.

You write that you might one day *pull me down* into a vortex of sorrow and pain. It should certainly rather be *pull me in.* It is not possible for you to pull me down any more than you can pull yourself down. Wherever we may stand, we shall always stay the same. "We *Landsknechte* should really remain lonely and outcast," surely a sentence beginning with "but" following this is missing. Otherwise I would have to assume that you regretted it, but that you can always stay lonely, outcast seems to be quite impossible. Would that then make the last page of my letter that you mention so completely unjustified!? Do not think about so much horror in the future. In this regard, leave the future alone. *May it bring us joyous and magnificent hours. And all the sorrow that love may still bring me, I shall bear, because I know that to love means to experience and to sacrifice.* If I could not do that, I would never have loved you. And then I also know that you will help me. What else do I need if only you truly love me.—

They are calling me to come and eat. Helmut is here too.

Be sweet and good, and do not worry.

How I would like to have you here.

> My Dickkopp
> Your Marga

---

[28] Shortly before, Marga's father had moved from Berlin to Röntgental, near Berlin, with his second wife, Greta.

10) Special Delivery
Munich, 30.12.27, 15:00

My dear little woman,

I have always known that you, by all "E" [?] are an infinitely sweet and good creature. Your special delivery letter, however, brought that home to me again. How I would like to kiss you for this letter.

In the meantime, you will surely have noticed that I am far from such a nasty Dickkopp. See, I was just being honest enough to write you a thought that once surfaced in the corner of my "black" soul. I certainly never acted accordingly, and with the exception of Christmas Day (December 25), I wrote to you once a day, otherwise once or twice a day. Believe me, I have to chat with my little woman every day, I do not know what else to do and I do not want you to fret unnecessarily for a single moment. Sweet, "mischievous" good woman, I hardly feel guilty at all, but I would gladly accept the punishment every day if it were only possible. At least we will each be able to get *revenge* in January.

For the last paragraph of your letter, you have my very special affection, you good person.

I am very sorry that you fretted over my letter. You dear, dear silly little thing, believe me that there is never anything in my letters or words to you that should ever make you worry. Things are sometimes poorly expressed because of brevity and haste, but there is certainly no cause for fretting. How could I ever cause you pain? Will my dear, silly little thing learn that and never again worry about such things; I think so, the little woman knows how fond I am of her.

Now just a few more words about your letter number 6. I discovered it when I came home this morning at 10:30 from Passau. A special delivery letter came at 10:45. I had to laugh about your [maid] Hanna. She is quite fresh.

About the fur vest. Of course there was heat, usually too much (steam heat). Often I just turn it off and open the windows. No, my old fur vest that I always used to wear when I was a soldier in my quarters is what you call a housecoat, and that is just a habit of an old Landsknecht. What is more, I like the softness of the fur.

Be a little careful on your walk through your exalted Berlin. Many people start the New Year with an excess of alcohol and subsequent fistfights, in which innocent bystanders can sometimes get hurt.

You write that the sentence "We Landsknechte should really remain lonely and outcast" really ought to have a next clause beginning with "but." That is true. Let me write it for you so that you understand me completely in this matter. "But I did not stay that way and now know—because to some extent I can imagine the horrors of the future—that sooner or later I shall cause the person I hold dearest on this earth worry and grief. Believe me, I know that you would gladly take upon you every worry and every sacrifice for the sake of love. But love willingly *endures* concern for the other, and the worst thought for love is to know that the other suffers and worries for the sake of love." That is the way you think and that is the way I think, and that is the way I meant it.

You are right. Because we truly love one another we shall survive any future, as far as that is within the bounds of human possibility.

By the way, what else do you miss in my letters? You must write and tell me, for I do not know.

Send me your sweet pictures soon. A good thing that the letter from the "mischievous" Landsknecht did not arrive until later. (He never changes . . .)

Now I have to tell you a few things. Yesterday morning I went from Landshut to Passau with Strasser. We had very good conversations in the train. We are longtime comrades in the struggle and friends. [. . .]

Now I am on my way to the office again. In the evening I will go to Schleissheim (12 km from Munich) and will visit the people from my first group of Storm Troopers from 1922. Back home again at night.

Now I am being telephoned again; somebody is waiting for me.

I shall keep my wish for the new year brief. Whatever one can think that is good and loving, I wish for you. You, my dear, dear woman!

I kiss you

Your Heini

12.) Special delivery, Munich, 31.12.27, 19:00

My dear, good, little woman!

Before I go out to my parents' to celebrate the New Year and stay out tonight, I must send you another special delivery letter so that you have something tomorrow. The last thing I write in this year should be something to you, just as the first thing tonight at 1:00 a.m. will be a letter to the little woman.

Today I should really scold, you *impossible* little woman. I did not receive any letter today, and would liked to have had one. I assume—because I am an old optimist and because I know my good Marga—that the post office was at fault and not the little woman.

Just a quick report before I go out. Yesterday afternoon at 4:00 (16:00) I met a very dear acquaintance in the office, went with him to his laboratory, had a lot to discuss with him, and by 20:00 arrived happily at my old friends' in Schleissheim,[29] where I was received very cordially. Back again [to Munich] at 23:00. To the office this morning. Lots of work. Meetings from 11:00 to 16:00 (3 of them), in the meantime I visited my parents for half an hour and quickly explained to my good father the necessity of street combat and then disappeared again. At 18:30 I returned home after working two hours at the office.

And now I hope that mail will arrive tomorrow. Once more! A good new year and infinite love to you, my dear, good, sweet woman.

My dear, sweet child, I kiss you!
Heini

Do not forget, little woman, that you may not wrinkle your brow anymore.

10. W. 30. 31.12.27 morning (Munich 2.1.28, 19:00)
My dear, beloved, Dickschädel,

My good, my best man—today around 11:00 your sweet letter arrived by special delivery. My dear Dickkopp got something wrong: it was only number 10. You see with me the word "only" is right up front—an ungrateful woman! You should not always be so "naughty" and make fun of my beloved Berlin. After all, it is mine, good Dickkopp.—I am afraid I cannot share your view completely, namely that the worst thought for love is that the other person suffers and worries for love's sake. For if I am going to suffer for the sake of love, it is because I want to, then it belongs to me and is part of my

---

[29] In December 1929, Himmler was supposed to take part in an SA evening in Schleissheim (*Pocket Calendar*, 13.12.28).

love. Otherwise, what is "love." I love the sentence "a moment lived in paradise is not paid too dearly with death."[30] [. . .]

[. . .] Love without sorrow and worry is something I just cannot imagine. I have the feeling that it is no *love* at all. For love is the absolute certainty that one can sacrifice anything without one or the other in the relationship feeling it as a "sacrifice." It is love itself that demands that it be requited in this way. We will certainly be talking about this in person. [. . .]

Do you have snow on the ground now? I want to go sleigh riding. You have to make that happen. What else am I supposed to do down south there, I am really just coming for the sleigh rides. I also want to go sledding. Today I am really in a mood for arguments and sarcasm. I know you are not really against that, but are really much more for peace. [. . .]

But good, dear Heini, I have always told you I cannot do anything about my wrinkled forehead because I do not know when it's wrinkled. I am sure it is certainly wrinkled today.

If you already know your plans for the coming weeks, then be sweet and write them to me.—My new maid is expecting me. I kiss you.

> Ever your Marga

In 1928 not only were Reichstag elections scheduled for May 20, but also regional parliamentary elections were to be held on the same day in the largest and most powerful state of Prussia, as well as in Anhalt, Bavaria, Oldenburg, Württemberg, Mecklenburg-Strelitz (January 29), Hamburg (February 19) , and in Schaumburg-Lippe (April 29). The "horrible year" that Heinrich Himmler feared[31] was determined, at least in the spring, by numerous election campaigns, which for Himmler, as an NSDAP functionary, meant uninterrupted travel, countless speeches, party meetings, and the founding of new groups. For example, on the evening of January 25, he wrote of his visit to Freising, near Munich: "This evening was quite good, I founded a student SA and will come back here every two weeks in order to drill the youth."

-----

[30] Marga slightly misquotes a line from Friedrich Schiller's classical drama *Don Carlos I, 5.* [—Trans.]

[31] He could not yet have known of the impending Reichstag elections because the Reichstag was not dissolved until February.

On January 2, 1928, in order to prepare for the elections, Hitler announced Gregor Strasser's appointment as *Reichsorganisationsleiter* [Organizational Leader of the Reich] in the *Völkischer Beobachter*, and added, "As of today I am taking over the provisional leadership of the propaganda section. Pg. [*Parteigenosse*, party member] Himmler has the power to sign documents in my name."

"There is a lot of work, but otherwise everything is pleasant so far. On Sunday, 8.1, I shall be in Austria, not returning until Monday. As for geography, next week you will be getting a map from me," Heinrich wrote to his future wife on January 5. The following letters always mention the places where he is staying or traveling to. He was often on the road with "the Boss," Hitler, whom he accompanied to election rallies—which caused Marga to heave sighs: "if only you did not have to travel with the Boss anymore. He costs you so much time" (3.2.28).

It was also Himmler who organized the "Hitler rallies." For this purpose he would send party groups a questionnaire that required specific information about the size of the room ("Herr Hitler will speak only in a hall [. . .]"), the social composition of the audience, the security staff, Hitler's lodgings, the nearest garage, etc. Each party group had to channel 50 percent of its profit from the rally to party headquarters in Munich. But because Hitler attracted a large audience when he spoke, an event where he appeared was also a financial bonus for the local group leader, and requests at party headquarters in Munich increased steeply. As a result, Himmler had to turn down countless party groups—he was now the one with the power to permit or refuse the coveted Hitler rallies.

———

15) Munich, 2.1.28. 21:00

My beloved, good little woman!

Your letter (9) arrived this morning and that was enough to make it a beautiful day for me. I'll bet that you did not expect your Dickkopp to write you from Landshut, did you? I can just imagine what you wanted to write. But look, he is not a Dickkopp toward you anymore. I could not have written to anyone else, and on this evening I *had* to write to you. I never want to be harsh and rough to you and will never be that way, it might sound like the style and language of a Landsknecht, hardened by ten years of struggle; but that is just the way it sounds. My heart is always dear and good to you. [. . .]

I have to scold you just a little about the wrinkled brow. When the little woman writes that she does not know anything about that and in the next sentence, "today it is certainly wrinkled," what is that supposed to mean— that your mischievous Heini is giving you headaches.—You, at least, should be "good" and remember that, and do not wrinkle your brow anymore.— When you get a letter from me, I always want it to bring you so much joy that you can make a happy face.

I wrote you something about the birthdays. I am for celebrating both of them if it is at all possible, and it has to be possible.

I have an incredible amount of work to do, but that does not mean anything.

Dear, good Marga, my wife, I kiss your dear good hands and your sweet mouth.

Your Heini

I really like your sentence about "paradise." I will mostly be able to write you in the evenings; the mail is picked up in the mornings at 3:30:30 [?], and therefore you will get this letter Wednesday morning. Listen, my dear, Friday is a holiday here, Epiphany, and so there will be no mail delivery.

I joined the German army exactly ten years ago to the day.

Based on his physical constitution, Heinrich Himmler was anything but a military man. During his childhood he was often sickly—weak and unathletic. Even as a youth he complained of stomach pains, which would stay with him all his life. Nevertheless—or perhaps because of this—he tried with all his might to be accepted as a volunteer in the army during World War I. Probably because of his father's connections, he did receive the longed-for news that he had been admitted as an officer candidate in the eleventh Infantry Regiment at the end of 1917, yet "Miles Heinrich," as he proudly called himself, never saw action. The revolution broke out before his unit was transferred to the front. In addition to his studies, after the end of the war, Heinrich involved himself with radical right paramilitary organizations, among others, the Freikorps Epp and the

Bund Oberland. These contributed to the bloody suppression of the workers'
riots and the short-lived soviet republics such as the one in Munich. In November 1923 he was out on the street under Röhm's command as a member of the
Freikorps organization, the Bund Reichskriegsflagge,[32] participating in the
attempted putsch led by Hitler and Ludendorff against the Republic. Yet one
notices in his letters that Himmler tends to use the designation *Landsknecht*
for himself, rather than "soldier." Although absolute obedience and fidelity
certainly belonged to the virtues that Himmler demanded of the SS, his self-
image was less that of a party soldier—a member of a bureaucratically organized army—and more that of a fighter who campaigns for the "freedom of his
people."

Nostalgic reminiscences of his military days certainly come up repeatedly—
for example, when he recollects his fur vest, which he received in 1918 from
his parents, because he was freezing in an unheated room in the Regensburg
barracks. Ten years later he is still wearing this (30.12.27). Or when he writes:
"[. . .] in Nuremberg I go back to my hotel and skin myself again (I shave, put
on my uniform, report at 21:00), and once again, another bit of soldiering"
(10.2.28). All his life it went without saying that the ideal of the "tough man"
should be held in high esteem. Even later in the war, he kept training to
toughen himself, and thus styled himself as a "Landsknecht hardened by
ten years of struggle" (2.1.28). Even in his relationship with Marga: "I can
never neglect my duty—and may someday pull you into the vortex of sorrow,
pain, and fate. We Landsknechte of the fight for German freedom should really
remain lonely and outcast" (26.12.27). While the SA was conceived of as a
Volksarmee [people's army], which was meant to outrank the regular army,
Himmler chose a different model for the SS: that of an ideologically sworn order or fellowship of warriors, who did not need to wait for a command to take
action.

---

[32] The Bund Reichskriegsflagge [Imperial War Flag Union] was a paramilitary organization
under Ernst Röhm's control. The group participated in the so-called Beer Hall Putsch (Munich,
1923), which led to Hitler's arrest and imprisonment and was banned thereafter. [—Trans.]

17) Munich in the office, 3.1.28. 22:00

My good, dear woman!

It is already rather late evening and I must write you a sweet note and take it to the station so that you can get it tomorrow. In the meantime you will probably also have received my Sunday letter, which was certainly not harsh and rough. Today I had enough time to think about your letter again. What awkward little people we are, love each other so terribly, and keep upsetting each other.—But really, you dear child, do not grieve anymore, the thought would be horrible to me, just as if you truly had the feeling that I could be harsh and rough to you. That would be just as terrible as when I believed you, you of all people, thought me dishonorable.—But no, I know *my* little woman knows me now and will not be sad on my account.

You can be sure of one thing, that your Landsknecht *always* feels your love and is happy because of it.

Now I want to be able to come home to you after this day of work and worry and just be peaceful with you and in your love and be able to give you the feeling that you, sweet "little" woman, are protected by your Landsknecht, for whom you are the exalted wife, dearest woman, true comrade, and sweetest child.

I kiss you, you darling,

Your Heini.

Himmler's conviction that his love for a woman must be subordinated to the "struggle" (23.12.27) for the Fatherland is clear in the letters from the very beginning: "[. . .] for I love you with every thought that belongs to me and not to the Fatherland" (1.1.28)—even though Marga, with her blonde hair and blue eyes, epitomized the ideal image of the German woman.

As early as 1921 when he was a student, he had already described his "ideal image of a woman" in his *Journals* "I am against female vanity wanting to prevail in areas where it has no competence. A woman is loved by a real man in three ways.—As a dear child, which one may have to scold or punish in its irrationality, which one protects and shields because it is just too delicate and weak, and because one loves it so much. Then as a wife and spouse and loyal, sympathetic comrade, who fights through life alongside one, is always faithfully by one's side without hindering or restraining the man's spirit. And as a goddess whose feet one must kiss, who gives one strength through her feminine wisdom and childlike pure holiness, strength not to give up in the toughest battles, and who bestows divinity in the ideal hours of the soul."

Himmler summarizes this ideal image of woman in the concept of the *Hohe Frau* [exalted woman] who obviously had to have "Aryan blood." As early as 1920 he had made notes in his *Leseliste* about the book *Der Rosendoktor,* by Ludwig Finckh, "a fitting song of songs to woman." In 1924, after reading Werner Jansen's *Das Buch Liebe. Gudrun-Roman*, he gushed, "The Song of Songs to the Nordic woman. This is the ideal image that we Germans dream of in our youth and are ready to die for as men, an image one always believes in, even if one has so often been deceived."

In the letters to Marga he also often uses the term of address "you pure, dear, exalted woman" or styles her as "good little blonde" (11.11.29). It is unclear what meaning the word *purity* has for him in this context, when he writes, "I always see you beside me in your purity and loftiness and your boundless love for me" (11.2.28). According to conservative values of the time, Marga, as a divorced woman, would by no means have counted as "pure." Thus, for him, purity seems rather to reside in the sense of childlike innocence, which he absolutely sees in Marga, even though she only marginally corresponds to this ideal image.

Heinrich Himmler's inexperience with women, which becomes clear in the first letters, and his initial insecurity about them recede rapidly because, thanks to his sex and education, he feels superior to the "little woman" (whom he sometimes teasingly calls *Dummerle* ["silly little thing"]. For her part, Marga is basically convinced of the correctness of this assignment of roles: "You know what a weak sex we women are," she writes to him on December 22, 1927. Nonetheless, accepting her new role is made difficult by the fact that she had been independent for years. In the following months, she is torn between her joy at having found a man at her age and the fear of the changes and restrictions that she must accept as a result: "Do you know, my dearest, sometimes I have a horror of everything. So much that is new! People and things, everything around me. My darling, I have nothing but you now. Last night I thought about it and got very worried" (13.3.28). She tries to banish her fears by conjuring up happiness: "We must be happy" (13.3.28), and "Marriage shall be our fulfillment, our greatest happiness" (16.2.28).

He apparently does not take her inner conflict seriously, or rather does not understand it, when he tries to comfort her: "I certainly know that when my good little woman is a little bit prickly now and then, she is not that way because of a mood she's in, but because she is worried about her naughty man" (3.3.28). Or another time: "the little woman scolded like a shrew" (7.5.28). He basically seems to have avoided conflicts in the relationship more often than not. Thus on February 13, 1928, he categorically announces to her: "Cannot help you, my dear little brat, your good man is not going to argue."

From the very first letters it became clear that Marga Siegroth and Heinrich Himmler had little interest in each other's daily life and social sphere. Moreover, they seem to serve each other as projections of the ideal of a partner.

———

15) W. 30. 4.1.28 (Munich 6.1.28. 11:00 Special Delivery)
My dear, beloved Landsknecht, my good Dickkopp,

Dickkopp keeps coming up even though I admit that you truly are not one. But you are *mine*, and I know that you like it a little bit.

Your sweet third letter arrived this evening and so I have to write again. Let me tell you again how happy and joyful I am. You, my good Dickschädel. (Dickschädel for a change.) Today I really wanted to be virtuous and do some reading in your good book, but now I would rather write. Later on, when I read your old letters (one day the old ones and the new ones will be read), as well as my newspaper, then, lazy as I am, I go to sleep. And so the book always gets neglected. Nor am I going to be able to mail this letter today, especially given the rain and my sore throat, both of which are a lot better. I am sure I caught a cold at my parents' again; there's no steam heat there and the rooms are overheated.

My dear beloved, do not forget the little pictures, otherwise we will be bored[33] and just think of the "revenge." My black soul is already contemplating the unthinkable.—

You, poor man, are running around all over the place and I, lazy woman that I am, sit here happy and cheerful in my own four walls. But in the mornings I still always have to get up at 7:30. Terrible!

———

[33] On February 21, before Heinrich visited her in Berlin, Marga wrote, "Will you collect little pictures? The last time you did not do it and we were so bored."

You, my impossible, dreadful Landsknecht, you do not write whether you will be coming to Berlin for three weeks. You do not have to be afraid of the "metropolis," I will do my best to "protect" you [. . .]

How is your stomach doing? It occurs to me, because in your sweet letter the word misbehaving comes up again. When I read your old letters you have no idea how hard it hit me when I read that you wanted to be naughty and misbehave.

I thought you had made up your mind to do it because something or other in life had disappointed you terribly. And that you were going to try to manage like this. I did not realize that it could also just refer to your stomach. I still have a lot to learn about medicine!

You still do not seem to have received my second special delivery letter. My Landsknecht is tough and hard, but to me sweet and good. May he always stay like that, that is the way I love him most, because he is genuine.

[. . .]

On Friday evening the Reifschneiders[34] want to visit me, he's never been here, that is to say, never been invited. When I was so sick, about two years ago, he often came along. He teases a lot, but I do not like it in him. 9:30 p.m. and I, lazy girl that I am, am off to bed to read.

I would rather *tell* you everything else, my dear; my dear good man, I am with you and I kiss you.

> Your little woman

21) Special delivery, Munich, at the office, 7.1.28. 21:30.

My dear little woman!

A day with quite a lot of work is once more over, and now I am sitting down in spirit beside my little woman and being sweet to her and telling her a bit about what her Landsknecht has been up to. First I will tell her that she is very dear and good because she has written me such good letters (15 and 16), the first of which I received last evening at 23:00 upon returning from Landshut, and the second one this morning.—How happy I am that my dear child is no longer sad. And you will never be sad again, for, look—we can never misunderstand each other.

---

[34] Elfriede Reifschneider was Marga's best friend. She was ten years older and also a nurse.

How are you coming along with your sore throat? I am just saying, how does one catch a thing like that in Berlin.—But I would come there anyway if time permitted. At the moment, however, it does not look that way. Child, how beautiful it would be to see your faithful eyes every day and to feel your good hands, and to kiss your dear mouth every day, and to show the little woman how much her Landsknecht loves her.

In the meantime, my little Marga, these are dreams. But we have to think of something to do in Tölz, because going for months without seeing each other is just impossible. Or does the "little scamp" think otherwise.

True, the "scamp" is a fresh little creature. I am absolutely in favor of spending our time on little pictures when we are in Tölz. But a little bit of "revenge" is bound to creep in. My little scamp, I am "afraid" the little photos will not be enough.

Dear child, the way you are able to sleep; I am happy for you, but do not do too much of a good thing, and be sure you go out for walks.—Make sure you do some calisthenics every day. I have started to do so myself. This is equally good for training the will and the body. [. . .]

You as a "foreigner," quite naturally misunderstood the word "quarrel." Where I come from it has almost the same meaning as "fight." We will never do either one.

Making up is lovely, but being good to each all the time is even better. That is exactly what you believe too, but you're just a little mischief maker. When we are in Tölz I am going to have to pull your little ears.

Dearest, as for peace and quiet on Sundays, for the most part that does not exist, I go for months without anything like that.—But I do have peace when I think of you. Dear woman, I can hardly tell you what you are to me.

Listen, touch your own forehead frequently; it should not have any wrinkles.—You will be thinking: this impudent rascal! But that is just the way it is, and with time, the dear little woman will no longer wrinkle her brow. Look, then there won't be anything left for you to do when you are really upset. [. . .]

My dear woman, I kiss your sweet mouth and your good delicate hands.

Your Heini

In the train from Simbach am Inn—Munich, 9.1.28. 5:30 a.m.

My dear good little woman!

Your writing case has made its first trip with me, and the first letter that will be written on it naturally belongs to the little woman. I have just gotten up at 4:45, after getting to bed at 1:00. This sort of "resurrection" is not exactly exhilarating, but what can one do.—Yesterday from 9:00 to 12:00 I traveled from Munich via Mühldorf to Simbach am Inn. The trip is quite beautiful, it was good weather, you could see the mountains in the distance. I thought and slept and dreamed (about whom, do you think??) and read Carlyle's "The French Revolution."[35] In Simbach ate a quick lunch in the railroad station while talking with the [SS-] *Ortsgruppenführer*. 12:40 continued the journey through Braunau (Austrian border station) to Neumarkt-Kallham. The party members there are very nice, capable people. The meeting was well attended (over 80 people), which was quite a lot for that small town. And around 10 red comrades were there for the first time, and after 2 hours finally sang along with "Deutschland über alles." After the public meeting I held a roll call of the Sturmabteilung (SA)[36] people and drilled with them for a while. Had dinner. At 9:00 (21:00) went to Braunau. There I was picked up at 23:00 by party members. We held a discussion for a good hour longer about various questions and around 1:00 I went to bed happy.

Now I shall be in my own room in Munich at around 9:00 (and here in the train I am already looking forward to a letter from my dear woman). At around 10:00 I will have changed clothes and shaved and be in the office, where a lot of work awaits me. At noon, to my parents' quickly, where I have arranged to have the tailor come meet me. In the afternoon again, much, much work. At 20:00 the roll call of my people. I hope that I will be finished there in an hour. Beforehand or afterward my dear child will receive a longer message from me.—Most likely I will have to go to Memmingen tomorrow.—If only Thursday were over, before then I have 6 rallies in 3 days;

---

[35] Himmler had borrowed Thomas Carlyle's *The French Revolution* (1837) from Gregor Strasser and read it while traveling. "An outstandingly good and instructive book" was his commentary. In 1924 he had borrowed a book about Schiller by the same author from his friend Falk and read it with enthusiasm.

[36] SA (Sturmabteilung), the Brownshirts recruited by Ernst Röhm to protect speakers at NSDAP rallies. [—Trans.]

it horrifies even me. But it is all right, especially when I think how sweet I can be to my little woman in 8 days and how sweet and tender the good little woman is going to be to *her* Landsknecht.

Listen, could you bring the *Rassebuch* [Race Book] with you, I would like to explain a few more things to you.

It does not look like there will be snow yet; it is raining today. I have ordered artificial ice for my dear "little Prussian girl."—If it is even a little bit nice out, we shall take a few really good long walks. I know the whole area around there very well.—That means bring your sturdy shoes with you, it isn't paved there. (Time for more revenge.)—a thing about our "revenge"—it is sweet. I am in favor of nothing else but "revenge," constantly.

Now I will get a little sleep again and dream of "Berlin" and naturally nothing else.

My dear Margawife I kiss you and cherish you endlessly, your Landsknecht.

The handwriting is horrible. But that is the train's fault.

———————

On January 5, 1928, Marga wrote him about the "Race Book": "I was just reading in your book about the Dinaric race when your letter arrived." This refers most probably to the well-known book by the author popularly known as Rassegünther. Missing from Himmler's *Leseliste* [Reading List] is the *Kleine Rassenkunde des deutschen Volkes* [Little Race Primer of the German People], by Hans F. K. Günther, a standard work for the folkish Right. According to his *Leseliste* in the years before he met Marga, he was always reading books on the topic of race. Military and historical books, specifically adventure novels, were definitely in the majority. These, however, were, either novels on the same theme (*Rasse*, by Erich Kühn, from 1921) or just short essays, for example, "Race and Nation" (1922), by Houston Stewart Chamberlain, whose major work, *The Foundations of the Nineteenth Century*, Himmler apparently never read.

32) Munich, 25.1.28. 18:00

My dear sweet little woman,

[. . .] I did not get up until 7:45 this morning, after I had first dreamed about the good woman for around a quarter of an hour [. . .]

In the afternoon I visited my parents. My good mother told me of an acquaintance who was visiting there and asked, among other things, whether or not Heini was going to get married someday, whereupon my mother assured her that he would not think of such a thing. I made a bad joke (but I was certainly not embarrassed, my dear scamp). What do they know.— Sweetie, we both know better.

This evening, more to come.—Dear child, I kiss your dear sweet mouth and your good hands

　　　　Your husband.

Must get to the train station.

————————

From January 15 to 21, Marga visited Munich. On this occasion, both apparently discussed marriage plans. From now on they each signed their letters more and more often with "your husband" and "your wife." Immediately following Marga's visit, Heinrich told his brother Ernst and his friend Falk about her: "He was extraordinarily happy, just as Ernstl was" (28.1.28).

————————

33) W.30. 29.1.28 (received Munich, 31.1.28. 21:00)

My dear Darling,

I am just back from the theater and feel I have to write to you. All the many doubts and scruples are overwhelming me again. My good dear sweetheart, you know how tenderly I love you, that you are the joy and happiness of my life. Your love for me, which belongs to me, and is my life. Dear sweetheart, this impossibility seems unimaginable. This is the way you will love me forever as I love you, it cannot be otherwise. There was just such momentary fear, your love belongs to me and will always belong to me. Do not be angry with me, my only beloved husband, now that I have written that to you, things are clear and bright for me again. Poor silly little thing gets so badly taken advantage of. My dear good man will be good to her, even when she does not deserve it.

Sweetheart, when you come home, tired and tense, and are happy to have a letter, then your naughty woman has written such a lot of mischief. That is all I know how to do! Shall I go to bed with these doubts and not be able to sleep. I know I can tell my beloved man everything. He knows his naughty little woman. His great generosity and love can understand everything.

Sweetheart, good husband, never be sad. Once I am with you forever, all this will end. Then all we shall have is *happiness*. Our happiness. You, my dear, rough Landsknecht, my beloved man,

I kiss you with all my heart,

Your naughty wife

In February and March 1928, they both produce mountains of similarly vapid letters, almost identical, word for word. Far more important than the contents was clearly the fact that each received a letter from the other every day, and that this letter contained a minimum number of lines. That placed Heinrich Himmler especially under pressure, given his long work days and his many trips. But Marga accepted no such "excuses" and decided to consider his short letters simply as "signs of life," which she accordingly refused to include in the numbering system with which they were in constant competition.

---

39. W.30. 2.2.28. 8:00
(Received Munich 4.4.28. 8:00)

My deeply beloved good man, if you were to see me now, so utterly happy in my room sitting and writing (accompanied now and then by a little drop of white Bordeaux) then you would surely be convinced that I am truly happy in having such a good, mischievous husband, who loves his naughty wife as much as she loves him.

Sweetheart, are your silly little thoughts behaving themselves? Nothing must be allowed to bother my good dear man too terribly. You know, we both want to outgrow these silly thoughts. Just send them away for good. We do not need anyone. We are enough for each other. [. . .]

People are bad, how happy we should be because we understand each other and belong to each other.

At first I could not believe your great pure love was possible, but now I know for certain how great your love is, and how true, and that it will always be so. You never need to have any second thoughts, our last time together put an end to the slightest doubts in each of us. I can only repeat I am joyous, happy, and satisfied—and for the first time in my life. For I have found a homeland, beside my dear, beloved rough Landsknecht. Beside my Dickkopp. Am I allowed to keep saying that even though it is not true? Both of these Dickköppe have now squabbled their way into each other's arms, right?

Just think, Berlin is a metropolis (and how, I hear you say), but people know how to drive cars and your naughty scamp does not get in trouble here so easily. In small towns people have to learn it—how to drive, I mean. But if you are still afraid of Berlin, then write to me in time and I will pick up my Landsknecht, the fearful one, and protect him well and be loving to him.

I often have to think of Tutzing. Everything so beautiful and so good. Write to me to say roughly when you are coming!

I want to go to my parents' place on Sunday, and then I always stay at home, I only go out if I have to go out in the morning. [. . .]

My dear, good, mischievous husband, thanks to you I am happy beyond words.

I kiss you, your naughty little wife

———

In January they were apparently not only together in Bad Tölz but also in Tutzing am Starnbergersee. On March 26, 1928, Himmler refers to it once more when he writes that he had "driven past our Tutzing" and he mentions a shared dream: "and if only one day we were to have a little piece of land on a lake!" Such a plan would of course have strained their financial resources, as each of them knew quite well.

❧

48) Munich–Plauen, in sleeping car,
7.2.28

My dearest, darling little wife!

I feel like a prince, here I am making my way gradually northward to my sweet little woman in the far north, am sitting in a sleeping car drinking a little bottle of port (toasting the health of my good woman) traveling comfortably through the countryside (through my *Gau* [district]) certain that nobody is going to annoy me, either by telephone or any other way. Furthermore, yesterday I even went to bed at 11:00 so I am wonderfully well rested, and afterward I am going to read, work, sleep, and think (poorly of course). What do you say, my dear scamp?

Incidentally, I am not such a good man, given all I eat and [illegible word] almost unbelievable! Everything, because that is what my good wife wants. You know, so compliant, [rest of sentence illegible].

I will have lunch here. I shall arrive in Plauen at 15:21, and have a meeting right away.[37]

Listen, do not tell anybody, especially the little scamp, but if nothing interferes, then your mischievous husband will come to his little wife tomorrow. Darling, how lovely that will be.

I kiss you and cherish you

Your Heini

44. W. 30. 6.2.28 4:00
(Munich 11.2.28. 13:00)

My very very naughty husband! from whom I got no mail yesterday. Two today already. But the number is not correct, that sign of life does not count as a letter. You are only at number 45.

You really are a bad man. Me not taking walks? I told you I do that, and you know (actually I do not need to mention it anymore) when I say I go for walks, then I go. [. . .]

---

[37] The regional headquarters of the NSDAP in Saxony was in Plauen before 1933, and was not moved to Dresden until after 1933.

Sweetheart, my good man, just two more days, then I, poor creature, will have to put up with scamp, shrew, rascal, sawed-off giant, Dummerle, imp, and sleepyhead. (I really am a smart woman, right?).

Sweetheart, my good man, how long do you think you will be able to stay. Your face, you are forgetting your face. I wonder if this letter will reach you! My good, naughty husband.

  1,000 kisses, your Marga.

                                              52) Munich, 12.2.28. 20:00

My dear good little wife!

  What a day it has been. From 9:00–14:15 uninterrupted meetings with around 40 people.[38] Then to Freising with the Boss, where there was a fine rally; it came off peacefully without a hitch. At 4:00 I was finally able to get a little bit to eat. At 18:45 we then traveled back. I am now sitting in a guest-house and looking forward to a meal.

  [. . .] Lovely little wife, I kiss your dear mouth and your good little hands
      your Heini.

                                              53) Munich, 13.2.28. 20:00

My most beloved little wife!

  [. . .] Dear scamp, when it comes to a little tussling and roughhousing (I will tell you a secret, also exercise and calisthenics), your mischievous man is happy to join in. You know there are times when your Landsknecht can suddenly be quite a merry, mischievous boy. [. . .]

      your husband.

                         ———————

They both apparently enjoyed little games like those alluded to here. Marga wrote on February 11, 1928, "The poor good scamp [. . .] wants to fight. [. . .] Roughhouse, run around the table." The next time "fun" could be denied just as teasingly: "no hair is going to be pulled, and no ears tweaked" (20.2.28). Or also "no thumbscrews" (30.3.28). But on March 1, 1928, she is happy

————————
[38] In his letter of 11.2.28, Himmler mentions that a meeting of regional leaders took place.

again: "only 5 more months and then the good woman is with her mischievous man again, and will be tweaked, rumpled, and 'scolded.'" Himmler constantly looked forward just as much to her punishments for his taunting. "If there's going to be more revenge, that will be great" (9.1.28). As for his all-too-infrequent letters, he writes, "Your bad husband deserves revenge" (27.6.28).

———————

53 W.30 15.2.28.
11:00 (Munich, 17.2.28. 8:00)

My dear little Sweetheart!
      Now I need to report to you right away. My parents visited, beaming and armed with red roses. So, no tempest, just harmony. How pleased this makes me. Let me tell you the way we all think about this. Just the way we talked it over. Also that you should come here on Easter if at all possible, and that you will then go visit him [her father—Trans.]. Then he asked when I intended to travel to Munich, and when I said not at all until I have settled in Munich forever, he got quite upset and said that would be impossible. If your parents feel the same way, I would have to go introduce myself to them first. Sweetheart, what do you say to this? Your parents would surely be opposed to me from the first if I did not know how to do the right thing. The whole matter seems clear to me. We should first wait to hear what your parents say about it, and then, in time, you will hear whether they agree. My father also believes that everything should happen more or less simultaneously, meaning little by little. Good sweetheart, write at length about this when you have enough peace and time. [. . .]
      I kiss you Marga.

60) Munich, 19.2.28. 19:00

My most beloved little wife!
      [. . .] This noon I went to eat at my parents' and after the meal with Ernst to visit Gebhard and Hilde. I told both of them this afternoon. In short: first; both are very happy and send their dear "sister-in-law" cordial greetings. One thing I now know, how the parents might behave, both will certainly be very sweet.

[. . .] Sweetie, do not be upset about your 132 pounds, for her naughty man, the little woman is just exactly right the way she is [. . .].[39]

>Sweetie, I kiss you
>
>your husband

---

60. W.30. 20.2.28 6:00
(Munich, 23.2.28. 23:00)

My dear Sweetheart!

[. . .] Today Hauschild started to say we could expand the clinic with a new apartment. There was nothing more left for me to say, I had no more interest in it, and so made a few hints as an explanation for it, he was very pleased, and will pay me my money right away. I might possibly split up amicably with him [. . .]

>You good man, my beloved, I kiss you,
>
>your little wife

There is little to be found about Dr. Bernhard Hauschild, co-owner of the private clinic. According to Berlin directories, he was a "surgeon, gynecologist, and obstetrician" who in those days lived at 45 Münchner Strasse. After 1933 he is listed only as "gynecologist" in the directory, and after 1935, not listed at all—which suggests perhaps that he had emigrated from Germany by that time. Hauschild held the option on Marga's interest in the clinic and sold it to her shortly before her wedding (see the later letters of 1928).

Marga seldom called the doctor by name, but rather primarily "my Jewish rabble" (27.2.28) or simply "the rabble" (28.2.28 and elsewhere). Heinrich certainly never referred to him by name, but rather spoke of the doctor simply as "the riffraff" (29.2.1928) or "the Jew."

---

[39] Two days earlier, on February 17, 1928, Himmler had mentioned that he also weighed just 132 pounds; thus in no way did he present the image of a tough Landsknecht and militarily steeled fighter to which he pretended.

64) Malgersdorf, 26.2.28. 10:30
And 27.2.28 19:00 [finished in pencil]

[. . .] My most beloved little wife!

Yesterday while writing a letter I was soon disturbed, had to go there (in Malgersdorf) to see some people and for 2 hours had to listen to unbelievable dirt about the life of this family from the woman of the house; I should either bring one of these delinquents back to the path of virtue—particularly her sister, who is the guiltiest—or see that the brother and sister leave the village. At the same time I really have to see that all this filth does not disturb our local group.

At 14:00 we took the truck to Reisbach; I excused myself from all this depressing dirt back to my exalted, pure, sweet wife and was so happy deep inside during the time when my thoughts belong to me. Let the others wallow in dirt, I have a pure paradise, your, our love, you my good angel. [. . .]

Dearest wife—I have such infinite love and kiss you
Your Heini

———————

It is striking to note what meaning "morality" (which played a major role in his upbringing by his father, Gebhard Himmler) still has for Heinrich Himmler. The close correlation between outer, medical hygiene and inner, moral cleanliness derives from notions that were prevalent most notably in the nineteenth century. According to them, dirt, chaos, and immorality were seen as threatening enemies to be fought.

On February 29, 1928, Himmler formulated his and Marga's common dream: "It will be so beautiful. Our paradise that we will build for ourselves in July, August, no one can destroy." And she declares: "We do not need anyone. We are enough for each other" (2.2.28). The categorical certainty of mutual future happiness and their home with one another was imagined over and over by both of them, as for example, when he writes, "[. . .] in the soul and in the arms of the rough Landsknecht, there is your safest and best home" (1.2.28), and she: "I know that my only home is with my rough Landsknecht" (2.2.28).

The focus on their "safe fortress" distanced from the "evil world," the "dirt of the big city" with the hated "Jewish moneybags attitude"—in other words, the despicable "cowardly citizens" and "philistines"—is, from the very beginning, important to them in planning their future together. On February 15, 1928,

Himmler had already written, "[. . .] everything dirty will be kept far from our home, our fortress." Marga writes in reference to Berlin, which she will soon leave, "[. . .] so good, that I will never have to live here in this filth" (13.2.28), and is already looking forward to "our beautiful pure home" (28.2.28). This juxtaposition comes up over and over in both letters like an incantation.

The notion of barricading themselves continually accompanies the assurance that their unity will surmount all difficulties and assure a clear sense of mutual ownership.

As early as in 1927 Marga writes, "We are surely of the same opinion, anything else is unthinkable" (31.12.27). Right after a few meetings, Himmler is also sure: "I know you so utterly and completely" (25.4.28 and elsewhere) and "There are absolutely no disappointments" (7.5.28).

The sense of mutual ownership is strengthened through the remark "in your life there is only the movement and me" (16.2.28), and he confirms this promptly with the phrase "the good woman belongs to me, to me alone" (17.2.28).

Only like-minded people gain entry to their idyllic home, which they build a few months later in Waldtrudering. In the next years they construct a tight network based on Himmler's contacts and also developed through many mutual acquaintances with old Nazis and their similarly inclined wives.

———

72. W. 30. 2.3.28 12:00
(Munich, 3.3.28. 14:00)

My sweet, good Darling,

[. . .] I have just pictured what you might have looked like as a boy, I mean *little* boy. Do you have any pictures? If you think of it, bring them along at Easter, and also some of your family.

Darling, you write: "Do not be sad, it is all outside us. How beautiful our paradise is." Good dear one, how shall I understand that?

Why are you going to a Hitler rally, you surely know what he's going to say? [. . .]

Good, dear darling I kiss you
Your little wife

Marga seldom had positive comments to make about Himmler's activity on behalf of the National Socialist movement, which she jealously considered as a competitor for the time they shared. Her annoyed question in the preceding letter shows how distant she was from her future husband's political activities. There are countless further unsympathetic and impertinent remarks in her letters, for example, on January 6, 1928: "I cannot stand this town Landshut, why do you constantly go there!" Just one day later she complains, "[. . .] I'm always short-changed. You see you cannot serve two masters" (7.1.28), and on February 3, 1928, she writes, "If only you did not have to go around with the Boss anymore. He takes up so much time."

On February 24, 1928, she temporarily took heart: "When the elections are over, then there will be peace at least for a few years," but as soon as March 3, 1928, she resumes her scolding: "[. . .] it would be really nice if you were not a member of a movement." She clearly wished he had a different occupation. On May 1, 1928, she writes, "Leave that old[40] party." On May 5, 1928, she writes, "Darling I cannot understand that you let yourself get so depressed about the party that you are not even able to write a letter. The other gentlemen certainly do not let themselves be exploited that way."

He either did not respond at all or tried jokingly to protect himself against her reproaches, as when he points out, "You scamp, do not criticize me about the movement. If it did not exist, I would not have gone to Berchtesgaden on 18 September" (10.1.28).

---

70) Special Delivery Munich
3.3.1928 19:00

My dear, sweet, little wife!

[. . .] I shall bring you pictures of my family and then of me as a boy, perhaps I will even send them before Easter. You should know what your naughty husband used to look like.

⁕

---

[40] Marga softens this criticism slightly with the dialect word *ulle*, meaning "old". [—Trans.]

With the sentence, "Do not be sad, it is all outside us . . ." I meant trouble and filth. In a letter you wrote you mentioned some kind of trouble, and I was referring to that.

I have to go to the Hitler rally. I organize these rallies and am partly responsible for them. Just think, recently my mother and my brother's mother-in-law were at the rally together and absolutely thrilled.—I send this letter by special delivery.

> My good, dear little wife I kiss you from my heart and love you
> Your husband

———

Both Himmler's parents increasingly sympathized with the National Socialists. In 1932 Himmler lent his father his *Mein Kampf*, and he read both volumes thoroughly and added comments as his son had done. His comments show that the focus of their interests lay in different areas—the son was primarily interested in leadership, race, and racial purity; the father, rather in the upbringing of youth, and church and religion. Nevertheless, they were unanimous in their fundamental admiration for Hitler. Thus the father noted in concluding the second volume, "Read to the end, with intense interest and sincere admiration for this man. 2 June 1932."

———

78) Special Delivery Munich
10.3.28. 21:00

Dearest good little wife!

[. . .] Dear scamp, I had to laugh, just imagine, as if I were a civil servant,[41] me spineless, always agreeing with my idiotic current boss, at thirty already a bit senile, and you, you darling, my wife, a party every week etc.— . . . No, it is just a shame about us.

———

[41] A day earlier Marga had written, "Just imagine if you were a civil servant!? And then I would get at least three letters a day."

But I would rather be in the revolution and help with the fight for freedom—that is our oxygen, my dear, sweet Landsknecht's wife [. . .]

Beloved, best little wife, I kiss you and love you from my heart

Your Heini.

83. W. 30. 11.3.28 4:00
(Munich 12.3.28 23:00)

My good Darling

Today your good long letter did not arrive until 12:30. I was already in the clinic. [. . .]

What a naughty man you are, good darling. You write so much about exercise that I am getting worried after all. But then comes the trick, and the bad, bad husband has *fallen* for it, really *fallen*.

Darling,

your *clever* wife. [. . .]

85) Special Delivery Munich
17.3.28 19:00

Beloved, most beloved little wife!

Early this morning I began the driving course. Up at 6:00. The cold is terrible; it went pretty well. Did not come home all day; rushing all over the place. The Boss is here again, meetings all day. [. . .]

Dear silly little sweetie, you know that scamp, good and naughty wife, *Landsknecht*, naughty and good man—all 6 are one and when one of them is happy then so are all the others, and when one of them is sad, then all the others are too.—[. . .]

Darling little wife I love you so much and kiss you

Your Heini

99) Munich, 1.4.28 12:00

My good, dear, Sweetie!

[. . .] now the Boss and I are taking the train to Chemnitz tomorrow
[. . .].

In haste, best greetings
Be kissed by your Heini

[110] *W.30. 10.4.28.*
(Munich. 11–12?.4.28. 15:30)

My dear Sweetheart!

Your telegram just arrived and so at least I know that you are all right.
But I'm wondering again whether everything is *completely* fine again with
your stomach?[42] I look forward to a letter tomorrow. I am fine. I go out for
walks often in this beautiful weather.

Darling, already 6 whole weeks and not a ray of hope?

I keep hoping for one.

Tomorrow I will go visit my parents.

I always have to take a deep breath when I think about your parents.[43]

Good sweetheart, our happiness and our love, how we shall nurture both
of these. You my good, sweet, naughty husband.

My wild Landsknecht, think of yourself.

I kiss you,
your Little wife

102) Munich 13.4.28 14:00

My most beloved of all, best little wife!

Listen, your very naughty husband did not manage to write last night.
He did not come home from the office until 12:00.

---

[42] Heinrich had spent Easter in Berlin with Marga as planned and had met her parents.
[43] Heinrich's parents did not yet know about Marga. That Heinrich and Marga both feared the
disapproval of his parents toward his fiancée, becomes obvious in several letters.

Now everything is just perfect again with my stomach. It really hurt me that on the last morning I could not be as sweet to you as I wanted to out of sheer pain, and that we just couldn't have a really good talk.—Good sweetheart, you should not think that you are getting a self-pitying husband. But it really did get pretty bad.—But now it is all right again; just a little overworked. [. . .]

Dearest, my happiness! I kiss you

Your husband

104) Munich, 15.4.28 21:00

My sweet, dear, good "very naughty" little wife!

Just think, only yesterday and today the "poor" husband got no letter from his good wife. Say, isn't that a "really naughty" little wife. On Friday she sent the letter so late that it did not arrive with Saturday's mail and on Sunday the good wife forgot that it had to be Special Delivery.—Or is there something wrong with the good wife; I am a little worried, hopefully tomorrow morning I will have one or even 2 letters. Sweetie, watch out for the automobiles;—you belong to your big bad Landsknecht. [. . .]

Yesterday I was in a bookstore and had a look around. I am sending you a flyer. I recommend that you buy the titles checked off in blue. The one checked in red is by far the best there is about poultry raising; I think we'll buy it together later on when we have worked our way through the other texts into the whole subject. I am also sending you the pamphlet about "raising capons." Here I would advise you to get the poultry castrating implements early enough for us to be able to practice outside at your parents' house on a *dead* cockerel (to begin with) on the Sunday after Pentecost when I am in Berlin. [. . .]

You my dear wife, how much I love you. I kiss you endlessly

Your Heini.

116. a. [addendum by Marga:] so that the same day always has the same number.
W. 30. 16.4.28 9:00 (Munich. 18.4.28.)

My dear Darling!

[. . .] Darling, tomorrow morning I will order the books checked in blue right away and I will also order the implements. We can then certainly practice on a dead chicken. Now I will read the book.[44]

Good darling, your good, kind sister-in-law: I do not deserve so much generosity. I am so bad at getting used to new people. And I cannot really *cope* with everybody at first. Give her my regards again, I send many thanks.

Darling, dear, what a "naughty" wife you're getting. What does make me happy, though, when they are all nice and good to you. I want only *you*.

It is a lot, but that's the way it is. When all is said and done, there is just *you* alone. You my beloved, how happy we are going to be. It will be all right with your parents, darling. Everybody wants to be nice to me, and all the while I am stealing you away from them. It is the height of goodness [. . .]

My dear wild Landsknecht I kiss you, your

Little wife

––––––––––

The problem of having a hard time getting used to new people was one that Marga apparently had only with Heinrich's family. Later on in Waldtrudering and in Munich she quickly formed new friendships. With her remark that she desires only him, she makes it quite obvious how limited her interest in his family is. In fact, in later years, he almost always visits his family without Marga's company, while on the other hand, he gets along well with her parents. According to Gebhard Himmler's recollection, which he described to the journalist Heinz Höhne in 1966, there never developed much warmth between Marga and the Himmlers. In the eyes of the family, she was "a cool, hard woman, exceptionally nervous and all too often complaining, who in no way exhibited an easygoing nature."

––––––––––

[44] On April 23, 1928, Marga wrote, "[. . .] Good darling, I am reading our poultry books eagerly, and I am in favor of us concentrating only on eggs, feed, and capons. Hands off the breeding. [. . .]"

108) Munich, 20.4.28. 14:00

Dearest beloved little woman!

Everything is going well. Not even my good mother is against us. Of course she is sad about the religious difference, but otherwise she is happy. And I think she will be very sweet to you, the same for my father. Darling, in any case you are coming to Munich at Pentecost. This has all gone well now, and it will all be fine with the house and everything. Hilde and Gebhard were actually touchingly sweet. I was at their place for an hour yesterday evening and *they* said that they would write you a card.

If only I had a bit more time and quiet. It is awful, it is 2:00 in the afternoon and I have just come from lunch. At 3:30 back to the office. 4:00 by car to Traunstein, by night to Berchtesgaden, tomorrow evening I am speaking in Passau; Sunday morning and afternoon in Vilsbiburg. In the evening back to Munich again. Sweetie, why not write to me for Sunday, then I will have a Saturday-Sunday letter when I get home from my travels that night. Dear wife, my good angel!

Now let me give a few answers to the letters (from 115 to 118). "Marrying in Berlin," we are going to have to talk about this at length at Pentecost—that means really discussing everything face-to-face. I have to see how my parents feel about it, and the same goes for yours? [. . .]

Listen, I think we should get married in early July, sweetie, why should we prolong this terribly long time for another two weeks. Beloved, now I have to close. You dear, dear woman I love you immeasurably and I kiss you wildly like a Landsknecht.

Your husband

———

The parents' surprisingly positive reaction to Heinrich and Marga's marriage plans contradicts the couple's earlier assumption that Heinrich's parents would have rejected Marga out of hand for reasons obvious in that period (older than he, divorced, Protestant). For a long time only one letter from Heinrich's mother to him was known (April 22, 1928), in which she writes, "You know, and also feel yourself, that in addition to joy, a deep sorrow fills my motherly heart." The later, quite distant relationship between Marga and her parents-in-law is by no means based on any a priori rejection of their daughter-in-law, but rather developed over the course of time.

120. W. 30. 21.4.28 4:00
(Munich. 22.4.29. 21:00)

My dear Sweetheart!

Your naughty wife simply did not get around to writing yesterday. Just too much to do now in the clinic. In the afternoon the clinic seamstress, many errands, my parents in the evening.

Darling, now about your dear parents. How good and sweet of them. I am so happy for you. And this morning the sweet card from your sister-in-law and your brother. Darling, I was speechless. Sweetheart, convey my many, many thanks. My good darling, it is impossible for me to write on my own. You good man, this is a problem you will have with me in our relationship, I am absolutely afraid of new people. When they are strangers who do not matter to me personally, then that is another matter. But now. Pentecost. Darling, please remember that I do not live with your parents. Therefore, thank them and send my regards for the card, my sweetheart.

Beloved, now to your sweet long letter 108.

You are traveling to Berchtesgaden. Good sweetheart. This letter will certainly arrive tomorrow by special delivery. I shall take it to the post office myself.

You write "marrying in Berlin," we are going to have to talk about this at length at Pentecost, that means really discussing everything face-to-face. I have to see how my parents feel about it, and the same goes for yours? You can imagine that I was *very* shocked when I read that. But now you tell me that you *certainly* did not mean it that way. We will have to discuss this at length at Pentecost—that is the *right thing* to do. Our respective parents have little or even nothing to say about it, that is my opinion. Good sweetheart, up to now *we* have done what we've wanted, and I certainly hope that is how we will continue. You know how independent I am. You whom I love and who belong to me, I know I will be able to ask you, but I can I ever ask anyone else!? Darling, up to now we have always known what we have wanted. Darling I could never imagine that later you would ever want anyone else to meddle in our affairs. Neither would I. Just to set the record straight. [. . .]

I kiss you your little wife

112) Munich, 25.4.28. 14:00

Sweet dearest little wife!

[. . .] Yesterday I was at my parents'. My good mother is very sad only about religion, not about you, but rather because I told her that for three or four years I have no longer been a Catholic. She cries a lot about that, poor dear Mama; but I cannot lie, I hope she will get over it and forget it. Otherwise, my parents send you greetings *from the bottom of their hearts.*

Dearest most beloved wife, soon you will be mine.

I love you and kiss you

Your husband

124. W. 30 25.4.28 4:00
(Munich. 26.4.28. 13:00)

My dear beloved Sweetheart.

Your sweet long letter and the pretty picture arrived today. Sweetheart, I was so happy and I had a really good laugh. Darling, you are quite the man: you just stick the picture into an envelope and send it! It arrived as countless pieces of broken glass, but they did not hurt the picture at all.

Sweetheart, you good thing, now you have finally heard your parents' opinion. We do not wish to hurt anyone, nor do we want to insult anyone. It is a custom of this country that the wedding always takes place where the bride lives, and in this case that is quite correct, for we do not have an apartment in Munich. [. . .]

In whichever region we live, that is for *you* to know.

Maybe we could even buy an old house.[45] [. . .] Yes, sweetheart, we will leave it at early July, let us say the third or the fourth. That is what I have discussed with Hauschild; the contract will be ready this

---

[45] Whereas Himmler at first argued for moving to a rented apartment and investing money primarily in the poultry farm (20.4.28), Marga preferred to live in their own house right from the start (19.4.28).

week.[46] Everything is still proceeding smoothly, I cannot keep on dealing with people. Only ten more weeks, my darling. Then I will go to my parents', they would like that so much.

My good, dear, beloved, my wild Landsknecht, you good sweet-heart, I kiss you

Your little wife

134. W. 30. 5.5.28 4:00
(Special Delivery, Munich 6.5.28 11:00)

My dear little darling!

Today was chaotic again thanks to the impossible people and their impertinence—such a big to-do that my head is still swimming. How I looked forward to your letter, and it was a ray of light, but it was hardly more than a sign of life. Darling, I cannot comprehend why you let the party rule your life so that you cannot even write one letter. What if that happened every day! I am sure the other men do not let themselves be exploited like that. And I am sure you are not sleeping at all anymore. And the upshot of all this is that you are getting sick and miserable. I would like to know what you would be good for after that.

You write, I am here for the next few days, is that supposed to mean that you will not be able to write.

It is my bad luck that I cannot understand that there are nothing but disappointments. Perhaps I can still learn.

Darling I cannot get over this.

Three more weeks, another fifteen days until the elections are over. I am going to have a look to see if my name is even on the list [of registered voters—Trans.].

Now all I need is for something to happen to you.

I am going to take a walk. Maybe I shall drive over to my parents'.

Oh my dear beloved, what kind of a bad woman am I, but I just have to tell you everything, if not to you, then to whom. It is all so sad.

Good dear darling, now you are sad too.

---

[46] The very next day, Marga wrote that she had agreed to 12,500 marks cash with Dr. Hauschild.

In three weeks, everything will be better.

My dear sweetheart. Won't you finally think of yourself for once. What a naughty, naughty man you are. I am feeling a little better now that I have told you all my worries.

My good, wild Landsknecht. You really naughty, naughty man, I kiss you,

Your little wife

120) Munich, 7.5.28. 13:00

My most beloved dear little wife!

This morning I received your dear letter (133). You good loving thing, and your naughty husband was not even able to write.—It goes without saying that I write you every day, even if I can only write a little bit, and after the elections, then for sure; that is always the hour in the day when I can chat with you, you dearest wife. In the evening before I fall asleep I always talk with your dear picture and look at your sweet faithful eyes and feel your beautiful dear body and know how happy we shall be.—and then you will be with me every day and how often you will be sitting beside me, and then we will tell each other things, and the little woman will tell me all her cares, and the wild Landsknecht will be very, very sweet to her.

Sweetie, you do not have to be afraid of Pentecost. I actually even think it will be very nice. Except for parents and siblings, nobody else will be there.

My good, good wife, when I got your special delivery letter on Sunday I was—naughty husband—not the least bit sad, but just imagine this: I laughed so heartily to myself (I knew that you had received my special delivery letter). You know, the little wife "scolded like a fishwife," and while I read it I saw your little face and pouting little mouth so clearly, and how I longed to kiss and cherish it.—But, you naughty sweetie, there are no disappointments.— You know right from the start what a "bad" husband you are getting, who only loves you "just a little bit."

But, my good sweetie, always just tell your naughty husband your sorrows, how sweet he will then be with you, and how happy and joyous he is that his good wife tells him everything, just as he does to her.

Beloved, how soon we will belong to one another; it is so wonderful that sometimes I just cannot believe it.

You sweet woman, I kiss you so sweetly and endlessly

Your Landsknecht

126) Munich, 18.5.28 14:00

Dearest beloved little wife!

Yesterday your naughty husband never got around to writing. He slept until 10:00 a.m. and then received your sweet special delivery letter. Sweetie, you good good wife!—Then to the office. At noon, to my parents'. It was Father's birthday. Everyone was there and everyone sends the most cordial greetings to you.—Home, put on uniform, 16:00 to Augsburg, home again at night by 2:00.

Slept this morning until 9:30, then office. Now, at 16:00 I am off in the car to Pfaffenberg (Lower Bavaria), am speaking there this evening and will drive back home at night. [. . .]

On Sunday naturally I went along on the trip and got soaked to the skin. From 8:00–17:00. What my people do, I do with them.[47]—Listen sweetie, go and vote (List 10)[48] and try to drag as many people as possible with you who will vote for us. [. . .]

You sweet, most beloved wife, how I love you. I kiss you

Your husband

––––––––––––

Marga never answered directly the repeated messages and cards from her future parents-in-law, but instead responded brusquely on June 17, 1928, "Sweetheart, greet your family members once and for all from me." A week before the wedding, she wrote, "Darling please make sure that in our first fourteen days we do not have to go and visit your family" (23.6.28).

––––––––––––

[47] On May 12, Himmler participated in a "propaganda drive" through Munich with one thousand SS men to accompany the election campaign (letter of 13.5.28).

[48] List 10: In the election of 1928 the ballot designated the NSDAP ticket as "Liste 10". [—Trans.]

146) W. 30. 17.5.28. 3:00
(Munich, 19.5.28. 3:00)

My good, dear sweetheart!

No letter has arrived yet, perhaps it will get here by this evening. After all I got one yesterday, when will I stop being so demanding? Probably never. You naughty darling, the revenge just keeps growing. A week from today I am probably not going to write anymore.

A week from tomorrow evening I will be in Munich at 10:50. The train leaves at 12:00. Darling, good, beloved darling!

My good wild Landsknecht, I just hope all is well with you.

Now I am off to my parents'.

22 letters in 4 days, that is impossible. So much for this huge mountain, and all the rest of the "revenges" get heaped on top of it. Hand in hand. For 3 months.

Sweetheart, write me again about your father's place of birth.

Just think, I never received a death certificate for my former father-in-law, who was already dead in 1920. I do not even know where he died. Have written to two more places. After Pentecost we have to get our papers together. Can you be here on 6 June? Sweetie, you bad boy, 22 letters.

My dear, beloved, good wild Landsknecht.

    I kiss you my sweetheart,

    Your little wife

This letter is the only source of the information that Marga married her first husband in 1920. By the end of 1923 she had already signed a contract with the clinic. It is thus assumed that the marriage lasted only until 1922, or the beginning of 1923.

---

148. W. 30. 19.5.28 4:00
(Received Special Delivery, Munich 21.5.28. 1:00)

[. . .] Darling, everybody here is voting German-National. Sachse[49] says it would be a mistake to vote for you, none of you will get through here, and

---

[49] Sachse was apparently another doctor at the clinic (letter from Himmler of 24.6.28).

you would take the votes away from the Right. I understand so little about politics. I am voting 10[50] [. . .]

The Reichstag elections on May 20, 1928, proved a disappointment for the NSDAP. The party received 810,000 votes, or 2.6 percent. The Social Democrats (SPD), with just short of 30 percent of the votes, became the strongest party—its best election result since 1919. The Communist Party (KPD) received a good 10 percent. On the other hand, the German National People's Party (DNVP) lost almost a third of its voters, but with 14 percent, it remained the second-strongest faction in the Reichstag and the dominant force on the right. The NSDAP was able to send twelve deputies to the Reichstag, among them Joseph Goebbels.

In the simultaneous regional parliamentary elections in the state of Anhalt, the National Socialists received 2.1 percent of the vote, and in Württemberg, 1.7 percent. But the vote count in Bavaria was significantly higher, with 6.1 percent, and in the agrarian North German state of Oldenburg, the NSDAP received 7.5 percent. Whereas they found less support in cities, the National Socialists did notably better in the countryside.

At the end of 1928 the *C.V.-Zeitung* (the weekly newspaper of the *Central Verein* [Central Committee] of Jewish Citizens) devoted several pages to a description of violence against Jews in the German Reich under the title "National Socialist Terror! Countryside and Small Towns Are Particular Targets." The article emphasized, in addition to Bavaria, the Rhineland, Lower Saxony, East Frisia, and East Prussia. In fact, because of this electoral success, the NSDAP began to exhibit a greater presence in rural areas and in small and midsize towns, where they organized rallies and demonstrated their strength. For this purpose, SA units were often brought in from the whole region to march through villages in close formation.

[50] Liste 10 (List 10), See note 48.

127) Munich, in the office. 21.5.28. 19:00

Dear sweet little wife!

Your naughty man cannot write you very much today. Today I slept until 14:00. During the night I was on duty for 34 hours straight with my loyal people. I am feeling great and am so happy. Sweetie, just a few more days, and then you will be here.—I found your sweet special delivery letter last night when I returned.

I will find more time to write tomorrow. Dearest, dearest wife do not be angry. How fond of you I am, you good creature.

I kiss you

Your Heini.

150. W. 30 21.5.28 4:00
(Munich, 22.5.28. 17:00)

My dearest Sweetheart!

Has something happened to you, or have you forgotten me? Yesterday I had no letter and only the telegram today. Friday was the last time you wrote. Sweetheart, write to me about what is happening, I would like to have clarity. Now the elections are over—and what poor results.

This Hauschild! Once a Jew always a Jew! And the others are no better. Oh my dear sweetheart, write to me again. Naughty naughty man. Revenge, revenge!

My dear beloved, I kiss you

Your little wife

152. W. 30. 23.5.28 3:30
(Munich, 24.5.28 13:30 [?])

My Darling!

So far still no letter from you! Maybe by 5 o' clock, and I wanted to have another one from you tomorrow as well. I thought you were always writing, and after the elections you were going to have more time. What is the reason now? [. . .]

Darling, you did not write at all about whether you have *time* for me. I will not stay very long in Munich if *you* have no time. [. . .]

The day after tomorrow at this time I shall almost be there [. . .]

Woe if I do not have any letter tomorrow. Revenge.

    Your little wife, who is so very fond of the old scoundrel

132) Marktredwitz, 1.6.28 17:00

My dear sweet little wife!

    Just think, your naughty husband slept a long time today and you, my good little wife, surely had a lot of rushing around and work, but I hope, no annoyance. I stayed in bed until 9:30 and spent my time thinking—focused on good thoughts.—Afterward I wrote a letter to Schiedermeyer in which I listed 14 points according to which the cost estimate should be structured, and I also told him that I had to have the preliminary estimate in my hand by next Friday, 8 June.—I put everything together that I need to get and take care of in June on a large sheet of paper, and on a further sheet I have written everything we still have to discuss.—At noon I went to Nuremberg; then to Marktredwitz, and here I have an hour's stopover, then I am traveling on to Wiesau. There I have a big night of speeches this evening. Tomorrow, we are off to Chemnitz.

    You should get this letter when you are still lying in your little bed. You dear sweet wife, how happy we shall be. It will be so unimaginably beautiful to be able to live together every day and to read everything in each other's eyes, and to be able to give each other the highest joy of love, and only love.

    You dearest, dearest wife, just a couple of days and then I have you again, and then three and a half more short weeks, that will be filled with work, and then you will be with me and nothing bad will ever come near you again, you dear, dear, noble creature.

    My most beloved little wife, I kiss you.

    Your Heini

———————

Two days earlier, when Marga was visiting in Munich, they had bought a small house with a large garden in Waldtrudering, east of Munich. Schiedermeyer was the architect whom they hired to do the renovations. In the following weeks before their wedding date at the beginning of July, Himmler sped up the renovations. They both recorded the detailed expenses in countless letters. One of the largest expenses was the planned purchase of a car. In total, Marga's money was barely enough for all their purchases. Himmler himself apparently had no savings.

After Marga had been introduced to her future parents-in-law at Pentecost, a week later Himmler traveled to Berlin for two days to arrange for the publishing of the banns.

———

133) Munich, 8.6.28. 19:00

My dear, most beloved little wife!

Another day has already passed, passed by quickly. I spent all last night sleeping sitting up in the train, wrapped in your good blanket, and I dreamed and "thought," but I thought good things, namely only about the little wife, just as the naughty Landsknecht has been doing since 11 December.—Arrived here (10:00) unpacked, had a cold shower to freshen up the whole lad, shaved very carefully, and then to the office at noon; work until now; now I am going to the train station and will post *the* letter to my parents, then to Kaulbachstrasse until 20:45, where I still have to speak in front of people.—I telephoned Schiedermeyer. We are driving out tomorrow afternoon; we have a date with the plumber (for heating, bathroom, and lavatory), also a painter, carpenter, and mason—all three of them are from Trudering. Tomorrow I shall get the price estimate and on Monday a few jobs can actually begin. Tomorrow evening I will send you the estimate by special delivery.—I have also spoken with the assistant head of the postal service (an acquaintance),—he will speed up our telephone installation. Tomorrow there is an incredible amount to do; tomorrow I will also send you the money.

And you, my good, good wife, stop getting annoyed with your Jews[51] and other people; just tell yourself, soon you will be with your "naughty man," who is so infinitely fond of you.

———

[51] On 8.6.28 Marga wrote, "I do not yet have the money from H. [Hauschild], I am supposed to have it tomorrow morning. The rabble!"

My stomach is not yet completely well, but better.—Listen, tomorrow, my good sweetie will get a really long report; but it is entirely possible that it will not arrive until Sunday night (9:30).

> I kiss you, my dearest beloved wife
>
> Your husband

137) Special delivery Munich, 11.6.28. 23:00

My most beloved of all!

[. . .] Dearest best sweetie, how happily we shall bear all sorrow together, and nothing can ever be so bad that we could not bear it together for one another's sake, with our great love, but just do one loving favor for me, I beg you, write to me and always tell me what bothers you.—Is the Jew making problems because of the money—or, sweetie, is it just my silly thing tormenting herself. [. . .]

I paid a visit to Hanomag-Auto. The whole thing would cost 2300, whereas a Dixi, which is significantly better, costs 2500.[52] I am of the opinion that we need a mortgage worth not 1,000 M[arks], but rather 2,000 M more. Please write to me and tell me what you think about that.

I ordered the telephone today. [. . .]

This evening I was at Frau Dr. von Scheubner-Richter's place at 8:00; she was very happy when I told her that I was getting married in July.

Sweetie, you beloved, lovely little woman, how fond of you I am, and how happy I will be when I can read everything in your beloved eyes.

> I kiss you, you dear woman,
>
> Your husband

Mathilde von Scheubner-Richter was the widow of the diplomat Max Scheubner-Richter, one of the most important of Hitler's supporters in Munich. Hitler dedicated the first section of *Mein Kampf* to Scheubner-Richter, one of the men killed in the putsch attempt of 1923.

---

[52] On June15, he wrote to her right after his purchase of a Dixi: "I did not by the Hanomag, it is daylight robbery and a Jewish firm."

Frau von Scheubner-Richter and Himmler knew each other well, which is clear from the introduction to the inventory of the main archive of the NSDAP: "In 1926, in cooperation with Heinrich Himmler, Mathilde von Scheubner-Richter was instructed by Hitler to establish a collection that would document the National Socialist press as well as the press of the opponents of the National Socialist movement. In addition, material was supposed to be collected about persons who were inimical to the movement. The involvement of the provisional Reich's propaganda leader, Himmler, suggests that from the beginning, this collection was meant to serve both a documentary and a propagandistic purpose. In 1928 the collection was taken from Mathilde von Scheubner-Richter by the *Reichspropagandaleitung* [RPL, the Reich Propaganda Directorate], which continued it.

This made it possible for Himmler to collect substantial materials about the "enemies of the Movement," in these early years, and later to have recourse to them in his role as Reichsführer SS. From the beginning, his perfectionism with regard to this data collection completely overwhelmed the abilities of the party members of the region, but paved the way for a system of surveillance of opponents that was used with great efficiency several years later by Himmler's Gestapo.

----

145) Munich, 21.6.28. 21:30

You dear sweet little wife!

[. . .] Sweetie, neither Ernst nor Gebhard can come. Ernst's test has been postponed eight days and this is just the time when Gebhard also has to take examinations. I have spoken with him and otherwise he would have really wanted to come.[53] [. . .]

Heartfelt, loving kisses from your husband.

----

[53] The youngest brother, Ernst, was busy finishing his studies in electrical engineering, while the oldest brother, Gebhard, taught trade skills in an engineering school.

147) Munich, 23.6.28 18:40

Beloved dearest little wife!

Today I bought an Alsatian dog, female, 2 years old, good pedigree, trained, for 100 M. I bought her from the policeman in Strasstrudering. I think it will be good, because on the one hand we will have a dog, and second, the policeman will be our friend, whereas the people on the local council are morons. [. . .]

Sweetie, your "naughty" husband has to close now. Kisses to his dearest wife from your wild, bad Landsknecht, who is so infinitely fond of you.

150) Munich, 27.6.28. 22:00

Best beloved sweet little wife!

Your naughty husband did not write yesterday and deserves revenge, but for all that he took his driver's test today and despite his "fabulous" knowledge, passed it. Tomorrow I will get my driver's license, and then we can take rides in our car. Sweetie, knock on wood, all will be well. [. . .]

I kiss you my dear woman, your "naughty" husband

170) Röntgental, 27.6.28 (Munich, 29.6.28. 8:00)

My dear good sweetheart,

Just as I came back from the pastor, your sweet letter was there.

Your papers have not yet arrived at the parish office in Zepernick.[54] Do not forget this.

Darling, write whether or not the wallpaper is included (340 M). Furthermore, you do not mention anything about the mortgage, isn't there one? So the fence costs an extra 150 M. You do not write anything about it, so I know that everything has gone wrong. I no longer know which end is up, or how we are going to pay for all this.

I had asked you not to buy *anything* more [continuation missing].

---

[54] Zepernick was part of Röntgental, the place where Marga's parents lived—the appropriate parish office of the church where Heinrich and Marga wanted to marry on July 3.

152) Munich, 29.6.28. 22:00

You dearest beloved little wife!

Today I received your sweet letter. How I would like to hold you and kiss you for this letter, my good wife.—You thought I had not done things correctly and you do not write a single angry word, but instead you are always endlessly sweet, you sweetheart. The naughty man knows, however, quite well what a dear little wife he is getting. [. . .]

Tomorrow there will be an incredible amount of work again. How I am looking forward to sitting in the train the day after tomorrow thinking of you, my beloved, and traveling to my best beloved little wife.

Sweetie, how I adore you, your dear, pure, high soul, and your dear beautiful, magnificent body.—Sweetie, I kiss you

     Your husband

Please give my regards to your family.

I am leaving here on Sunday, 7:35, and will be in Berlin at 18:14 (6:14 p.m.)

———

[Printed correspondence card][55]

Heinrich Himmler
Licensed Agronomist
Marga Himmler
née Boden
married
Munich—Berlin, 3 July 1928

The civil ceremony took place in the registry office of Berlin-Schöneberg, with Marga's father, Hans Boden, and her brother, Helmut, as witnesses. The subsequent church ceremony took place in Röntgental-Zepernick near Berlin, the town where her parents lived. No members of Heinrich's family attended the wedding. His brothers were unable to come, and no one expected his parents

---

[55] In N 1126/14 in the Bundesarchiv, Koblenz.

to undertake the long journey, since the married couple was about to move to Munich right after the wedding anyway.

Himmler received countless letters of congratulation from relatives, friends, and party members. Wilhelm Frick, then chief of the NSDAP faction in the Reichstag, sent him best wishes on July 10, 1928: "on the occasion of your wedding," and added, "I hope you will continue to be active in the Movement."

Wilhelm Kube, then a member of the local Prussian parliament, also congratulated him, as did Karl Vielweib and his wife, from Landshut, "with the German salute." The family of his friend Falk was apparently completely surprised by the wedding, which is evident from a letter from Frau von Pracher to Anna Himmler. Falk himself wrote Heinrich on July 29, "Dearest friend! No—I have not forgotten you. Even if my first salutation comes a bit later, you hardly need to be reassured that nonetheless it is all the more heartfelt. I was thinking of you the whole time, but you had disappeared and were as silent as the grave. This little wedding gift shall be an advance for us. In three years, when I have reached the highest salary level, then you have my word that you, as my first, oldest, and best friend, will receive a more generous present for your household, which will then still be young—a present that shall come nearer to the incomparable values of our eternal bond. [. . .] How I am looking forward to meeting your dear wife!"

Letters

1928–33

"The rally was very good,
afterward I set up an SS unit,
then off to the café."
—HEINRICH HIMMLER, APRIL 4, 1930

POCKET CALENDAR[56]

Shortly after his wedding, Himmler had to depart again to attend, among other things, the NSDAP Reichsparteitag in Nuremberg from August 1–4, 1928. Oddly, his pocket calendar contains the entry "1–4.8, Bayreuth," which is when the Wagner Festival always takes place.

In August and early September he had meetings in Bavaria. He took his vacation from September 9–12, for Marga's birthday. On September 15–16 he traveled to Bruck an der Mur in Austria. He had barely returned from Austria when he set out again on a longer trip, during which Marga wrote him the following letter:

❧

---

[56] Wherever there were long periods without any correspondence, the most important events have been reconstructed from entries in Himmler's pocket calendars.

Waldtrudering 19.9.28.

Dear Sweetheart!

It is already late afternoon, and I have to hurry.

Your sweet letter arrived today along with the puzzle magazine. On the telephone I had forgotten to ask Ernsti [*sic*] to bring me one. He will arrive tomorrow. Just think, not a word from Miens and Frida.[57] That's the way it goes.

How do you know that Grete[58] wants to leave on 1.10? You guessed it. I am very glad. Shall write to others now.

This time I will take a very young one. No mail worth mentioning. The sergeant is picking up Hitler's *Mein Kampf* today. You supposedly promised it to him. You could send me the address from Ulm, but it will probably be too late.[59]

Sweetheart, beloved—yesterday! I sleep as much as I can. Want to take a walk in the garden now.

Be well, my good beloved, and dream, and *think*. My good husband. Your little wife

POCKET CALENDAR

On October 2, 1928, the Munich beer hall Platzl appears in Himmler's pocket calendar. This was presumably a visit he made with Marga to see the singer and cabaret artist Weiss Ferdl. They had been there for the first time in January 1928 (see letter 25.1.28 from him and 18.2.28 from her).

On October 9 Himmler organized the first evening of speeches in Waldtrudering, where he had just founded a new local group for the NSDAP and, as its leader, issued a new party identification card for Marga immediately after their wedding. It may be assumed that she was also present at these evenings of speeches, which took place at regular intervals (depending on Himmler's travels) approximately every two weeks.

On November 9, 1928, a service took place in Munich to commemorate the anniversary of the Hitler putsch. In November there followed many dates in Munich and the surrounding area; on November 27, Himmler went to

---

[57] Miens and Frida Menke: Miens was a friend of Marga's (see the letters of 21.9.29ff.).
[58] Grete: a housemaid.
[59] According to his pocket calendar, Himmler was in Frankfurt September 18–20. On September 21 he was in Pirmasens, and on September 22–23 in Ulm.

Saxony and Berlin for a ten-day visit, during which he wrote Marga the following letters:

———

Lehnitz, 1.12.28

Dear good sweet little wife!

Arrived in Berlin early this morning. Unfortunately I could not write to you yesterday. Yesterday noon I arrived in Halle from Dresden in good shape. On the evening before, I was with Kapitän Leutnant [lieutenant commander] von Killinger until 2:00 a.m. He is a charming fellow.[60] From 2–4 meeting with the Gauleiter,[61] then visit with the brother of Herr Hallermann, who is an agricultural adviser in Halle. His wife is also called Marga and was a nurse at the front. They are very nice people. From 5:00 to 6:00 meeting with the Artamans.[62] Then took the train to Sandersleben. Then by car to Hettstedt. Spoke there to quite a good rally and at the end, gave a Freemason a fearsome telling-off [illegible]. At 12:00 by car to G[?]den. 1:30, to bed. Up at 4:30. 5 [?] by car to [illegible], where I arrived at 8:30. I slept those three hours, [illegible] railroad station. How I thought of you, my darling, [illegible], to the publisher of *Mein Kampf.* Meetings there about everything under the sun. Ate lunch. With Frau Reifschneider [two illegible words], she had [corner missing] and sends her warmest greetings to you. Tomorrow noon [corner missing, presumably: I will be at the Reif] schneiders'.[63] 6:00 we drove in, ate dinner at Aschinger's, and are now meeting with a politician.—Tomorrow and the day after I shall be here, then it's off to Thüringen for me.

Darling, how I am looking forward to being home when I will have you again.

You, my good angelic woman, I am so fond of you and I kiss you
Your Heini

———

[60] Manfred von Killinger (1886–1944): a former naval officer who joined the NSDAP in 1927 and was the head of the SA in Dresden until 1933.

[61] The Gauleiter of the Halle-Merseburg region from 1927 to 1930 was Paul Hinkler.

[62] For information on the Artamans, see commentary accompanying the letter of 18.11.29.

[63] Whenever he had official business in Berlin (here, according to his pocket calendar, December 1–3), he stayed primarily with Elfriede Reifschneider and her husband.

Darling, do not worry yourself so much, sleep well, eat, dream well, do not be annoyed.—Beloved, just be a good wife.

POCKET CALENDAR

On July 20, 1929 Himmler left for a longer trip: he traveled to East Prussia via Weimar and Berlin. January 22–28 he stayed in Königsberg, Allenstein, Osterode, Tilsit, and Neidenburg. The recently appointed Gauleiter of East Prussia, Erich Koch (1896–1986), who had been friends with Himmler since 1925, booked him for speaking engagements about the agricultural situation in Königsberg and the surrounding region. His letters concerning this speech have not survived.

———

Waltrudering 21.1 (Tilsit) [1929]

My dear Darling!

In East Prussia the fight is raging and you are there, I cannot wait until I have you healthy, here beside me again. I am quite well, am sleeping, taking it easy, and eating well.

Miss Ida[64] continues to be tidy. Just think, by 15 Feb[ruary] I shall have an apprentice. On Thursday I am driving in [to Munich] to the employment office for a meeting.

Do not worry about me. Think only of yourself, so that nothing happens to you. The money, 30 M, arrived today. Everything is fine. Very cold outside hens not laying. Dog "stinks" all day. Pig eating.

My good sweetheart I kiss you

Your "little rascal"

———

It was previously assumed that Heinrich Himmler only managed an unsuccessful poultry farm in Waltrudering, which was primarily run by his wife. In reality, their idea for this business venture was more thought out and complex. In addition to his salary from the party, the chickens were by no means Himmler's

———

[64] Presumably a housemaid. There was frequent turnover in the household staff, and sometimes these young women are simply referred to as "the maids" or "the girls."

only source of income. The couple also had turkeys, geese, rabbits, and a pig; they also cultivated fruit and vegetables, and raised mushrooms. Despite the worsening economic situation, they could still afford craftsmen, household staff, and a car.

In the meantime, Hitler had appointed Himmler to the rank of *Reichs-führer-SS.*

The SS was founded in 1925. The first leader of this "Schutzstaffel"[65] was Julius Schreck. As he put it, this was a "small band of men upon which our Movement and our Führer can rely." It was not their task to undertake the protection of local "meetings [of the NSDAP] from troublemakers" or to protect the movement against "professional provocateurs," but rather, their function was "to reinforce Hitler's personal escort." In April 1926, Hitler's longtime follower, Joseph Berchtold, took over the leadership of the SS, but only under the command of the *Oberster SA-Führer* (*OSAF*) [supreme commander of the SA].

Heinrich Himmler joined the SS in early May 1926, and received membership number 168. He is mentioned in the *Völkischer Beobachter* as early as April 1926, as "leader of the Lower Bavarian SS." In May 1926 Heinrich Himmler—the regional secretary of the Lower Bavarian *Gauleitung* [district administration] took over not only the leadership of the SA and SS of Landshut, but of all Lower Bavaria. Himmler rose quickly in the SS and in 1927 became the deputy to the new SS chief, Erhard Heiden; on January 6, 1929, Hitler appointed Himmler Reichsführer -SS.

The actual strength of the SS at the time Himmler undertook his new position is difficult to ascertain. It was probably no more than a scant one thousand men. From the very beginning Himmler placed great emphasis on the strictest discipline. In one of his first orders as Reichsführer-SS, he demanded of his SS men "absolute devotion to service and the greatest manly sense of honor," and the "most meticulous and precise execution of every order."

During the course of 1928, he had already built up countless SS sections in the small towns he had been visiting regularly. He was pleased with the "nice and unspoiled lads" who "become faithful and devoted" [15.2.28]. Despite his young age, he saw himself as a kind of fatherly officer who cultivated a

---

[65] The SS, or Schutzstaffel,—"protective rank, or echelon"—began as an elite guard for Hitler and later expanded to include military combat units and concentration camp officers. [—Trans.]

comradely relationship with his subordinates, but at the same time he expected absolute obedience combined with admiration. Thus, on the one hand, the relationship to his SS men consisted of making them submissive through military drill ("I have honed the brothers a bit," letter of 15.2.28); "Marched with the SS up a mountain and drilled them" (30.5.30), "Individual conferences (discipline)" (30.5.30); and otherwise to indoctrinate them with his ideological speeches.

POCKET CALENDAR

At the beginning of February 1929, he was near Heidelberg and after February 15, in Halle for several days for a conference on the Artam journal, *Bundschuh*,[66] and in Berlin. In March and April he had appointments only in Munich and Bavaria. On April 9 he finally had time again for his friend Falk. On May 1 he left for Saxony on a ten-day election trip, from which the following correspondence comes:

———

1.5.1929, 6 o'clock

My dear Sweetheart!

When you left I actually did lie down and slept until 8 o'clock. I woke up because of the noise outside, Petermann was repairing the fence (three new posts) and was ranting about you. And one more pleasant thing, the mail arrived and brought me a 43 M tax rebate, but not from the taxes that Hauschild has to pay. We were not able to work much in the garden today because it rained constantly. Half of the wood was easily split, the other half I have left for tomorrow. We cannot bring in the manure because it is wet. Now about money. I immediately paid for 1.) the potatoes 2.) my health insurance 3.) the fire insurance. Now I do not need any money, but in case you've already sent it, I will take it for Orion and Koch. Herr Koch woke me up today out of a sleep, so that tonight I shall be going to bed at 9 o'clock at the latest. I was in Haar.[67] Frau Kraut spoke to me, because I

———

[66] Concerning the Artam group, see the commentary on the letter of 18.11.29.
[67] Haar is a town about twelve kilometers east of Munich. [—Trans.]

am really showing,[68] but she was so nice that I was actually pleased. I am well. I am just very tired. I have bought carrots and Swiss chard and planted them.

My good darling, how are you then? Good naughty man, you eat well and write to your little scamp every day, even if it is just a greeting, so that I know that you are well. Otherwise nothing new. Have heard nothing from Sepp [Dietrich—Trans.]. Ten more days. There is mail for you here from Artam, do you want to have it? It is only a card saying that they have sent us a maid. I am enclosing a card from the *Donaubote*.[69] More tomorrow.

2.5. My Beloved, this letter should go out today.

Leaning over is hard for me, so I cannot do very much, although there is so much to be done.

A card from Dr. Höfle[70] [*sic*] came in today's mail, on Sunday you are supposed to be at the Opel garage at 10 o'clock, I shall telephone and say that you are traveling. The good doctor seems to forget that you are married. Otherwise a man from the tax office came by. You absolutely have to pay 3.45 M. fees from an earlier fine. I put him off until the 15th. He also came about my church tax for Berlin, but that has been paid. The Schönbohms[71] were here for a moment. Coming for coffee on Saturday. If only there were not the nights; only slept from 9:00 to 2:00 and then again around morning, when the maids woke me up because a Zeppelin went overhead. Bad luck.

My good dear fellow, be very careful. Write soon. Have you given any thought to the health insurance for the maids?

1000 greetings and kisses,

From your Marga

---

[68] At this time Marga was six months pregnant.

[69] The *Donaubote* [Danube Messenger] was a National Socialist daily newspaper founded in 1927 by Ludwig Liebl. It was very much in the style of the *Völkischer Beobachter*. [—Trans.]

[70] Hugo Höfl (b. 1886–1957), a doctor who practiced in Apfeldorf near Weilheim and Frida Höfl (b. 1886) were distantly related to Himmler. Both joined the NSDAP in 1930.

[71] Heinrich Schönbohm (1869–1941), retired book dealer, a member of the NSDAP from 1925 on, and his wife, Margarete.

Zittau, 3.5.1929

Dearest, most beloved, good little wife!

It is now 5:00 in the afternoon, and after arriving here in Zittau I am just getting around to writing to you. This morning I slept wonderfully until 9:30, and when I woke up, right away I thought about my beloved little scamp, what she could be doing and how she is.

Then I washed and gave myself a good shave, packed, had breakfast, and then bought myself a cigar and went to the Restaurant Belvedere on the Brühl Terrace, where I met with Reinhardt Herrsching. Dearest, how I thought of you; it was lovely weather; the trees are already turning green; down below, the Elbe steamers passed by, then, magnificent Dresden—except my good sweetie was not there.

Reinhardt and I discussed the whole problem of training speakers and the publication of speakers' materials. The first of these will begin on 10.6., the second will begin on 1 July. To do this, we worked through the instructions and memos that I had already prepared.

At 12:30 I ate quickly, my train was leaving at 1:45; I still had to return to the hotel, car, station, and 1 minute before the departure I was sitting in the train. There I slept for 2 hours, and then I read again and—you good little scamp—thought.—Yesterday all day it was just the same. At 11:20 I arrived, to the hotel, then to the office, ate, back to the hotel, telephoned different people, and wrote a couple of cards to local groups telling them of the change in my arrival time, then Reinhardt and Hengler came to visit me. To Klotzsche at 4:00, there meeting from 500:–to 6:00 with Max Mielsch,[72] *Bundesführer* [league leader] of the Artam Bund. Then back to Dresden. 8:00 rally, with low turnout; but nonetheless the success was excellent. Ate afterward.

And now, my good little scamp, do not work too hard. Sleep, do not worry yourself, eat slowly, take calcium.—Such a bad-tempered husband!—Sweetie, do not forget to darken the cellar for the mushrooms.

You, my good, beloved little wife, I kiss you
Your husband

---

[72] For commentary on the Bund Artam and Max Mielsch, see notes to the letter of 18.11.29.

Because of the approaching regional election in Saxony on May 12, 1929, there were many events there, beginning in March, including speeches by Hitler, Strasser, Goebbels, and others. Himmler, the trained agronomist, frequently handled meetings with farmers in the small villages. On May 1, in Gaussig, near Bautzen, he spoke about "expropriation" and "freedom and bread"; on this evening he was also supposed to speak in the tiny village of Hainwalde near Zittau on "the plight of German farmers."

In truth, Himmler was still doing most of the work in the office of Reichspropaganda. In addition, his new duties as Reichsführer-SS demanded more and more from him, while at the same time Joseph Goebbels was himself angling to become Reichspropagandaleiter.

In November 1929 it was determined that Goebbels should take over propaganda operations. "Munich, with Himmler," Goebbels noted in his diary after a meeting. "I am determining the basis of our future collaboration in the area of propaganda with him. He is a good little man. Good-natured, but probably also mercurial. A product of Strasser. But he will toe the line."

In April 1930 Goebbels was officially appointed as head of the Reichspropagandaleitung. Himmler stayed on as his deputy, and Fritz Reinhardt, the Gauleiter of Upper Bavaria who had established the extremely successful Parteirednerschule [School for Party Speakers] in Herrsching am Ammersee (Bavaria), became *Abteilungsleiter* [department chief]. In the years up to 1933, this Speakers' School trained around six thousand party members in public speaking skills in order to deploy speakers as widely as possible in rural areas.

Munich Region. 5.5.1929

My sweet Darling!

Sweetheart, your little wife was industrious today after having celebrated yesterday. The Schönboms [*sic*] were here in the afternoon. Never heard anything from the Prachers. Well, I certainly forgot to enclose the card, and a letter has arrived from Otto Strasser.[73] On Saturday the money from you, and today a sweet letter and the card from Reinhardt. You good man! My beautiful

---

[73] Otto Strasser (1897–1974), National Socialist politician, brother of Gregor Strasser.

Dresden. How I would have enjoyed sitting there with you. Now let me tell you what I have done today. Last night I read until 1 o'clock. Finished *Rulaman*,[74] then slept until 8:00. Thank God, only seven more nights. This is the worst. After being cold yesterday, the most magnificent sunshine today. Split wood first thing this morning. Then I had someone get the mail. Read it. Then I wanted to go out to check the trees to find out why not all of them are green yet [half line illegible because obscured]. 11 trees gone, completely dead. 8 pear and 3 apple. Almost every one of them could be easily pulled out by hand, their roots had died. Let us plant currants instead, we will certainly get more out of that. Then ate lunch, slept, and from 3:30 to 5:30 I took care of the mushrooms, then I watered, but the hose is much too short, and I suggest that we decide to buy circa 15 meters. Now it is quiet and I'm writing. 7 o'clock. On Saturday I wrote to a young girl who had advertised in the V.B. [*Völkischer Beobachter*].

[. . .] The package with the newspapers from Dresden has arrived. Now it is time for supper, I did my sewing and read for as long as I could. Better than not sleeping. Now then, be well dearest sweetie.

> Kisses from your little wife

Dresden, 7.5.29

My good darling little scamp of a wife!

You are getting another letter from beautiful Dresden.

This morning I rose at 9:00, shaved, had breakfast. Meeting in the hotel with a party member from Dresden.

10:00 at Kapitän Leutnant von Killinger's. What a fine, honest, and likeable gentleman. Official meeting about the SS. 11:30 in Dresden-Neustadt, meeting with a party member about financial opportunities. Then to the post office, made a deposit, enclosed find the two receipts. Went to eat at the "Italienisches Dörfchen" [Italian Village] (near the

---

[74] *Rulaman*: young adult fiction by David Friedrich Weinland set in the Stone Age. Since its publication in 1878, it continues to be read and has become a classic. In the 1930s, Himmler often gave the book as a present.

Zwinger).[75] 2–3:00 went to the picture gallery in the Zwinger. God, is that all magnificent. My little scamp, you really should have been there with me; across the Brühl Terrace to the hotel. Wrote, put together a little package for you with old laundry.

Yesterday evening at 9:00 I went to a movie theater, 10:30 in bed, slept. So you see your naughty husband is doing very, very well, eating, sleeping, reading—and always thinking of his sweet little wife, who will be the little mother of our dear little rascal. My little scamp, you dearest child, take good care of yourself, sunshine, splitting wood, do not bend over too much. Calcium, sleep, eat slowly, just do not worry!—

I hope that the Schönbohms and the Prachers have visited you.—Why not go visit Sepp again.—I will write to you again on Friday; you must have had to send someone to the post office on Thursday afternoon. Then maybe the Friday letter is already there.—Sweetie, my good woman, I kiss you so many, many times, and love you.

Your husband

Freiberg im Sachsen [Saxony], 8.5.29

My good, good little scamp!

Last night I traveled from Colmnitz to Freiberg and spent the night here in the hotel called Roter Hirsch [Red Stag]. In Colmnitz there was a lot of official mail waiting for me. This morning I telephoned Munich.—It is really hard to work with Osaf.[76] On Sunday Morning I am having a talk with the Boss in Nuremberg and will not be coming back to Munich until Sunday evening.—Poor, poor sweetheart, do not be too sad and do not be angry at your naughty husband; there is nothing he can do about it. [. . .]

---

[75] The Italienisches Dörfchen, a fine restaurant on the Elbe, not far from the Rococo palace and park area called the Zwinger. All these buildings have been rebuilt since the war. [—Trans.]

[76] OSAF (Oberster SA-Führer; supreme commander of the SA): The abbreviation refers to the titular position of supreme commander of the SS. At this time the office was held by Franz Pfeffer von Salomon (1888–1968). Heinrich Himmler was his secretary in the Munich headquarters of the NSDAP.

Sweetie, so how are you? Is our little rascal restless, knocking at the little mother's door? Be sure you do not overexert yourself!

Now I am driving to Langenau, but back here again by car in the evening. You sweet, sweet wife, how fond of you I am and am always thinking of you.

I kiss you sweetly and gently and wildly, you, my dear wife,

    Your husband

————————

The Social Democrats emerged victorious from the elections in Saxony on May 12, 1929. They received 34.2 percent of the votes; the Communists received 12.8 percent. The NSDAP was able to increase its voting tally significantly. In the regional election of 1926 they had a 1.6 percent margin. Now they received just under 5 percent of the votes and sent five delegates to the Landtag.

POCKET CALENDAR

In the following months, Heinrich Himmler again had meetings primarily in Munich, or rather, Bavaria, except for a trip to Wels, in Linz, in Austria at the end of June 1929.

Shortly before their daughter, Gudrun's, delivery date he had to go to Nuremberg from July 31 to August 5 to attend the Reichsparteitag. For quite a while the task of organizing this annual party event had fallen to Himmler, and he was very concerned that his SS should make an exemplary impression there. Two days after his return, Marga went to the clinic; a day later, on August 8, Gudrun was born by caesarean section. Marga stayed in the clinic with the baby for three weeks. During this time, according to his pocket calendar, Himmler went to the Obersalzberg[77] only once. After August 29, when Marga and Gudrun came home, he was given a two-week leave.

Beginning on September 20, he took a ten-day trip to Silesia. The following correspondence comes from this period.

∘❦∘

————————

[77] Hitler's mountain retreat near Berchtesgaden, in Bavaria, near the Austrian border. [—Trans.]

Obersiegersdorf, 21.9.29

My beloved good little wife!

Arrived yesterday at 7:00 in Sagan and still went to the river in the dark. Then ate dinner. At 9:00 to Freystadt by train, where I arrived at 10:00 and took a very pretty room in the hotel Den Kronen. Went right to bed and slept beautifully until 8 a.m. Shaved, had breakfast, then into town; to the barber for a haircut, then washed up in my room, put on clean underwear, I felt like a prince.

Wrote a couple of official letters, went looking for the Ortsgruppenführer, then to the post office.—Then I went to Schröder's leather factory. At the entrance I met Miss Elisabeth Schröder, who told me the way to the Menkes';[78] they were already expecting me and were waiting to pick me up at the station. My reception was extraordinarily cordial, ate with them at noon, saw the magnificent garden, brickyard, etc.—Now I am off to the city because I shall be staying here tonight.—In the evening, to the meeting in Niedersiegersdorf.

And now, how are you, you sweetest scamp? Sweetie, I cannot tell you how happy I am when I think of you and of being with you again in 8 days. Sweetie, life is good for us, and God has good things in store for us.

The little rascal should only cry now and then so that Mother notices that she is not alone and that she is being touched by a little piece of Daddy.

You big and little scamps, I kiss both of you, but especially the big one.

The naughty "Pappi" (as the rascal says)

My dear Marga,

That was a very nice surprise today when your husband suddenly turned up on our doorstep. I am very pleased to have him here under our roof. I have finally been able to hear about you in great detail. You have had to go through so much. I had no idea about it, let us hope that things will all go beautifully for you again soon, what a pity that you cannot be here too. I am so looking forward to your little girl.

Mieze and I send you and your little girl our most affectionate greetings,

Your Miens[79]

---

[78] See letter of 19.9.28.

[79] For the identity of Mieze and Miens, see footnote to letter of 19.9.28. [—Trans.]

Sagan, 22.9.1929

Scamp, my beloved little scamp!

On the way Freystadt to Sagan—Breslau—Strehlen. I am speaking there this evening. The reception I got from Mins [*sic*] and her sister was most touching; I had to stay and eat with them; I was just so pleasantly surprised. The meeting was in Niedersiegersdorf, the hall was packed, I think the evening was a great success.

This morning slept until 11:30, had breakfast. Despite the rain, Mins accompanied me to my car in town. I have flower seeds with me.—Sweetie, *Hollunderwein* [elderberry wine—Trans.] is not wine at all, but rather a so-called elderberry *Sekt,* [sparkling wine—Trans.] made from the blossoms. Sweetie, prepare the blossoms as a mash to be canned; you darling, do not forget the Cornelian cherries. [. . .]

Listen, darling, do not let any silly little thoughts get to you, and if they start to, then just look into the little blue eyes of our sweet child, from which Pappi also looks out, and says to Mutti that he loves her so infinitely and will be back in a couple of days; I am already looking forward to Schweidnitz. I shall be there the day after tomorrow, and there awaits me a very sweet letter from my very, very dear beloved little wife.—Say a great big hello to our little scamp and give her a kiss from me.

Beloved, I kiss you endlessly, and love you,
Your husband

Greetings to Berta.
Many, many greetings from Mins and her sister.

Waltrudering 24.9.29
Last letter

My good, dear Sweetie!

I had the first letter from the naughty husband on Monday. The big package with the newspapers was open, so everyone could read your letter. And on Monday your letter about being with Miens as well. Today your sweet letter from Sagan arrived. I am happy that you were so well taken care of at Miens's. I am going to reduce the elderberries down to pulp. And pick the Cornelian cherries too. What's next is, the plums arrived today, also have to be cooked.—Huber is working on the windows now.—Your father telephoned and asked how we are doing.—A card arrived from a Pastor Langenfass. He heard that you have a child and wants let Pastor Högner know about it. Your father mentioned it to him. Is Högner our Protestant pastor? Your parents know that the child will be christened Protestant, don't they?[80]

[. . .] Today you will find 2 letters from me in Schweidnitz. Oh, I am so curious to know everything you will tell me. Sometimes I am sad that I always have to sit at home. Today I decided how we shall celebrate your birthday. We had better discuss it again on Sunday.

Sweetie, will we ever go together to some exhibition or other? We've never done that. Some morning, and then we can have breakfast there [in town]. We will be home by noon, then we can sleep and drink tea, go for a walk, and sleep some more. What does the naughty husband say to that? [. . .]

I am terribly tired again. It is barely 8:30. Yesterday I wrote to Elfriede, today I shall write to Else. What should I say to you, good, dear beloved, you know how I am always waiting until my naughty husband comes. Write in time for me to be able to pick you up in Munich. We will have to discuss Sunday in Diessen. Today a letter came from the Ortsgruppenführer of Diessen. You are supposed to confirm that you can do it [reference unclear—Trans.]. And me too, so that I do not sit at home with the Barons.[81] Even though it is nice here, you first said—long before there was any talk about the Barons—that I should come along. I just do not understand that at all. More about this face-to-face.

You good, dear, naughty sweetie, I greet and kiss you.

Your wife

---

[80] Gudrun Margarete Elfriede Emma Anna was christened on December 28, 1929. The godmother was Elfriede Reifschneider. For this occasion, the Schönbohms presented Gudrun with a *Childhood Journal* in which Elfriede wrote her godchild the following quotation as "a guide through life": "Be faithful unto death, and I will give you the crown of life!" (Revelation 2:10)

[81] Presumably Baron Friedemann von Reitzenstein and his wife; see letter of 28.9.29.

Schweidnitz, 27.9.1929

Little wife, most beloved above all!

Today again I received nothing from my little scamp. I only got a card from my parents, in which my father wrote that he had telephoned you on Monday, and he said that you still had not gotten any news from your naughty husband. You poor sweetie, in fact he was, and is, your good husband who writes to his beloved little wife every day.

Yesterday's meeting in Freiburg was very good; arrived in Schweidnitz 1:00, discussed things with 2 speakers until 3:00. To bed. Got up at 9:00, shaved, had breakfast, then long discussion with the district SA leader, Silesia.[82] Ate lunch. Then visit to the Schönbohm's daughter, was not at home. I then, almost unbelievably, ran into her with her baby carriage on one of the streets in town. Drank tea together in a café. Her husband joined us. I am bringing along a letter for the Schönbohms. Now at 5:30 I am traveling [corner missing, by] train to Liegnitz-Neumarkt, there is [another meet]ing today, this is unbelievably strenuous, then I have two more.

My good sweetie, how are you, and what is the little scamp up to? Darling, for my sake, do not let the silly thoughts get to you, always look right into the little scamp's eyes.

I hope you are very healthy.

Sweetie, my beloved beautiful wife, I kiss you and love you
Your husband

A kiss from Pappi for the little scamp.
Greetings to the Schönbohms. Greetings to Berta.

Breslau, 28.9.1929

My dear, dear little scamp!

What a joy it was for me to get your letter. Thank God you are doing well.

Well, good sweetie, your naughty husband is arriving on Tuesday at 9:44 in the morning (Munich, main railroad station), and you, you good

---

[82] Franz-Werner Jaenke (1905–1943) had been the SA leader for Silesia and Mecklenburg since 1928.

thing, want to pick me up, but sweetie, be careful that you do not go and get run over.—It might be possible for me to arrive in Munich at 7:00 a.m., then you may not pick me up, or else you would have to get up at 5:00 a.m. If this happens, I will come out there quickly, wake up my little scamp, and then we'll sleep a little more. If I should arrive 7:00 I shall telephone you about it from Dresden.

On Monday (7.10) let us plan on this; if the weather is nice, we could, if you want, we could go to Hellabrunn, either to the zoo or to the Botanical [Garden].

And on Sunday, you good sweet silly little scamp, we shall drive *together* to Diessen [corner missing; and the little] wife will stay with her naughty husband the whole time.—Going [to the Barons'] von Reitzenstein,[83] seemed to be a good idea out of deference to you, so that you would not have to sit in a smoky room for 3–4 hours.—But, my little scamp, now all those silly little thoughts that you have had and the sad faces have to disappear. As you know, otherwise we will come to blows.

I am fine. I am speaking tonight and tomorrow evening. Then that is all.

And, sweetie, very soon I will be with you and our sweet little child.

I kiss you, my dearest, and the little scamp, and I kiss both of you from the bottom of my heart.

Your husband

POCKET CALENDAR

After returning from Silesia, Himmler had several meetings in Bavaria before he left for the next several days' trip to Baden[84] on October 11. The following correspondence is from this period. On October 27, 1929, a new regional parliament was elected in Baden. The NSDAP won 7 percent of the votes.

[83] Friedemann von Reitzenstein (b. 1888), sergeant, ret., and his wife, Elizabeth (b. 1889), were both early members of the NSDAP.
[84] Baden: a state in southwest Germany. [—Trans.]

Munich, 13.10.1929

My dear Beloved!

Today Herr Schönbohm brought me your sweet card. We are well. The little scamp is not spitting up much. Sleeps a lot. Today it was not so cold, and tomorrow we are getting the stove. Today I sat outdoors in the sun and stripped the beans. The Schönbohms were here and it was very nice. I am going there on Wednesday. I wrote to Martchen Kolbe. Today I still want to write to Else. Write me when you are arriving on Friday.— Huber was not here, I'll bet he wanted to have money first. The Rhodeländer[85] rooster was beautiful and big. They also have young hens that are already laying. When will Gertrud send the money? If she does not send it soon I intend to become more explicit.—The hens are just laying too poorly. I heated again today, so I am really incredibly good. We are eating well. Live like princes. I slept today until 9 o'clock, the little brat was so generous. This evening I am going to be reading *Die Kommenden*.[86] Berta will take the letter to school tomorrow. Now, good beloved, I intend to write to Else and Father. Tomorrow evening I am organizing your papers. I greet you and kiss you.

My dear husband, we have just spoken on the telephone, I was in the middle of supper. You did not write, that is naughty. The money will not be here by tomorrow morning, which means Berta cannot bring your shoes with her, but on Friday we will go get them together, all right?

Huber was here and fixed the door, intends to do the rest tomorrow. Schmidt has not been here. I shall telephone him tomorrow morning. It was nice and warm today, but who knows about tomorrow. Now I am going to bed and have a bath. I had a wonderful nap this afternoon and I always sleep well in the mornings until the little one begins to scream. I do not dare to rock her, I am too cold. She spits up very little. We worked hard in the garden today, but you cannot really tell.

Good, naughty one, now write.

I shall be at the station at 1:06 on Friday. Be well, I greet and kiss you

Your wife

---

[85] The Himmlers had obviously invested in a species of poultry, the Rhode Island Red. [—Trans.]

[86] *Die Kommenden* was a publication of the Bündische Jugend, an early phase of the German youth movement, which had close ties to the Bund Artam. [—Trans.]

For the most part the baby was left on her own, as was the norm for the time. People believed that newborns perceived almost nothing of their environment. A "good mother," was thus doing everything right when she took care of her child's physical needs; when it slept a lot and was protected from too much physical contact with other "harmful" environmental stimuli; when it gained weight as quickly as possible, was meticulously clean, and got enough fresh air—even if the child's hands sometimes turned "quite blue" from the cold while this happened (letter of 11.10.29). At this time it had not yet been recognized that infants need a lot of attention and that they should be talked to.

Marga documented Gudrun's special traits in the *Childhood Journal*—her language development, and especially her funny expressions. She was frequently torn between the wish that her child might be as well behaved as possible and her joy at her daughter's animated, contagious happiness. It is apparent that both parents loved their daughter and were proud of every step in her developmental progress.

Nonetheless, when it came to raising little children in the 1920s and '30s, the emphasis lay in teaching children obedience and "good behavior" as early as possible. It was the prevalent view that children's poor manners reflected badly on their parents. From the beginning, therefore, offspring were raised according to the values of order, cleanliness, and absolute obedience to adults. Only then [when their behavior reflected these goals—Trans.] were they allowed to eat at the same table as their parents and accompany them out into society.

Obedience and "being polite" were central to Püppi's upbringing, as many entries in the *Childhood Journal* show. There Marga noted that, when she was almost age three, her daughter often answered with "don't want to," when she was supposed to do something—"so that she often needed a couple of slaps," in other words, her mother boxed her ears (entry of 10.7.32). Earlier she had noted, "she obeys Pappi much better than me" (8.8.31). At that point Gudrun was only two years old.

When she was alone with Gudrun, Marga was by no means especially strict, thus she was particularly proud of the fact that her child of five months ate "without spattering food all over herself," and at six months, she placed her daughter on the potty for hours "until there was success." She describes, however, not without a touch of secret admiration, how in unobserved moments, Gudrun ran away from the potty "as fast as a monkey" or climbed out of her playpen and messed up the whole house. Of course Marga complained about the misbehavior of the little child, but on the other hand, she enjoyed her wild side and her high spirits. "She laughs so that you have to laugh along with her. Puts her hands on her belly, which she sticks out, and chatters away, too funny." When the weather was good, both spent hours in the garden, and Gudrun enthusiastically helped feed the animals. When the weather was rainy, they romped together in the house.

It is noteworthy that both Marga and Heinrich prayed with their daughter before she went to sleep (entry of 7.8.30)—despite the fact that, according to his own statement, he had not been a practicing Christian[87] since before their marriage.

———

Karlsruhe, 16.10.29

My dear, beloved scamp!

So the naughty, naughty husband is arriving on Friday at 13:10—sweetie, you good little thing, you will pick him up! How happy I will be when I see your dear, sweet little face.

Last night I was again able to sleep only from 3:30 to 8:30; I met the *Gau SA-Führer* [district SA leader] of the Ruhr area and had much important business to discuss with him.[88] Then to the office. Drove two hours to Karlsruhe. Here, conference with my SS unit. We are now driving to Liedolsheim for a speech to the farmers, back to Karlsruhe 11:00, SS review.

This trip is damned strenuous, but I can really accomplish quite a lot. Now I have to drive. I am a naughty husband, don't you think, because I have written so little. I did not get your good letter, because I did not get to Weinheim. How happy I am that I spoke with you on the telephone.

You rascal, my dearest one, how fond of you I am. I kiss you and the dear little scamp.

Your husband

———

[87] In his letter to Marga of April 25, 1928 Himmler mentions that he has not been a practicing Catholic for some years—to his mother's great disappointment. The letters cited here do not mention a rejection of Christianity per se. [—Trans.]

[88] Here he probably refers to Josef Terboven (1898–1945), who after the division of the greater area [*Grossgau*] of the Ruhr in 1928, became the Gauleiter of Essen and, simultaneously, local SA leader.

POCKET CALENDAR

According to his calendar, Himmler was still on the French border in Kehl-Freistett on October 17. On Sunday, October 20, his parents paid a visit to Waldtrudering.

October 24, 1929, was "Black Friday" on the New York Stock Exchange, which precipitated a worldwide economic crisis, affecting Germany more than any other nation.

On November 10, Himmler left again for another ten-day trip, to Pomerania, East Prussia, and Berlin. The next letters are from this period.

_____

Landsberg an der Warthe 13.11.1929

My most beloved little rascal!

I see your sweet good blue eyes and your dear little face over and over. How are you. You are probably all alone with our little daughter; I am truly worried about you, but do not overdo it, not so much that you give yourself a backache.

In Danzig I was received with infinite cordiality. On the second evening I had to spend the night there with them.[89] Yesterday afternoon we drove together to Zoppot (Sopot) on the coast. In the morning I toured Danzig with party members. I was completely overwhelmed at the sight of this magnificent culture. What these people have achieved! Sweetie, I was always thinking about you and your good mother and your ancestors, who lived here. If only you had been here.

The Polish Corridor[90] is ghastly—hideous, depressing. Now here I sit in Landsberg an der Warthe in a restaurant. The meeting begins in a half hour, and at 1:18 a.m. I shall be traveling on the local express train, 2nd class, to Königsberg, tomorrow morning to Allenstein—Passenheim.— A week from today I shall be with you again, with both my beloved little rascals.

_____

[89] In Danzig he was probably staying with Marga's relatives.

[90] Polish Corridor: the Treaty of Versailles transferred a strip of land from Germany to Poland, which separated the province of East Prussia from the German Reich in the west and granted Poland access to the Baltic. [—Trans.]

And now to finish. You sweet beloved, I kiss you and cherish you endlessly.

Your husband

Please save the enclosures.—Please file the speakers' materials.—A special kiss from Pappi for the little scamp.

Many affectionate greetings from all your relatives.

Waltrudering 14.11. [29]

My dear good man, you naughty husband!

I had no letter from you today. Yesterday, just the short one from the railroad station. The little cutie is doing very well. I fed her yesterday and today. She swallows as if she were choking but does not spit up. She drinks her bottle anyway. The mail brought a communication from the district attorney. Because you are a blameless man, you have been sentenced to a fine of 200 M.[91] What now? Do something about it. Striessberger writes that you ought to be paying even more. Bannaker writes that he is already taking care of other people, but he will take on more [clients]. in the spring.

Berta is disrespectful and lazy. The employment agency is looking into the matter, and on Saturday or Sunday they are sending a new [domestic servant] to meet me so that I do not need to go without help. Berta has to get out of here as fast as possible, because she is becoming too insolent. Still nothing from Father.

I am looking for a money order for the 80 M. But I do not find any. You have all of them in Munich.

I worked hard in the garden. Berta had to help out too. We turned over all the garden soil except for the bed where the potatoes were. Then we carted away manure and moved the pile. We worked like dogs, because I had to pick out all the stones. There are stones absolutely everywhere!

It is so cold, I am going to bed and having a bath. Will carry on tomorrow, I am taking the letter with me to Haar.

Today Herr Widhopf just left the things we had ordered in the garden because nobody opened the door for him, and the dog did not bark.

---

[91] It is unclear why he was fined.

But I have forgotten my main point. My house is the meeting place of all Waldtrudering's National Socialists. Herr Buchmann. Herr Schönbohm. Frau Drinkel. All because of the elections. The Drinkels are saying that nobody will elect you if we put Keller on the ballot. Herr Buchmann does not want his name on the ballot. Poor Schönbohm is chasing around the area, and dropped in on me today. Because the ballots do not have to be delivered until 8 o'clock in the evening on the 21st, I advised him to wait for you. It is a lot of fun for me to hear all the points of view. Be careful of Frau Drinkel. But we will have to talk about that in person.

Good night, good beloved.

Just very quickly. Both of us are well. Berta is supposed to leave today. I am going to Haar. 1000 greetings to Elfriede and her husband. Discuss everything. Now, about my parents. I wrote them my wishes, but I forgot to say thank you for the horse blankets and the blanket that we are supposed to get for the little one. You do that. 3 pieces of mail have just arrived for you. How glad I am that you were so pleased with everything. Do not be worried. On Monday I can have a new girl.

A 1000 hugs and kisses

Your Marga

It was not by chance that their house was the focal point for all the National Socialists in the town; Himmler's own ambition was responsible for this. He had made contact with the mayor (letter of 8.6.28) and the local policeman (letter of 23.6.28) before he and Marga moved to Waldtrudering and founded a local NSDAP group immediately thereafter. Within a short time the few members of this local group comprised the Himmlers' circle of friends. Marga, incidentally, writes "my house" as a matter of principle, as she will also do later about the house in Gmund.

Not only during her pregnancy, but also now, just a few months after giving birth, Marga was doing the hardest jobs such as tilling the soil, carting off manure, and dragging stones away—mostly by herself. On the other hand, these tasks seem to have given her pleasure because it was her own land she was working, and the work reminded her of her childhood on the farm. For example, once when she climbed up an apple tree to harvest some fruit, she wrote enthusiastically to her husband, "[. . .] It was too lovely. In the old days there was no tree too high for me" (11.10.29).

———————

On the train Königsberg–Berlin, 17.11.1929 20:00

You most beloved little wife!

I am sitting in the dining car, I shall be in Berlin in two hours; we will go directly to the Reifschneiders' and there I will find a letter waiting for me from my beloved little scamp. And on Wednesday evening I shall be at home again with my good wife. Darling, what longing I have for you, you good, beloved, exalted creature.

For the past two days I have had a very bad sore throat, but it is getting better now; just still a bit of a cold.

I shall visit the parents on Tuesday.

Darling scamp, I wonder how you and the child are; give her a kiss from me.

I will stop writing now; it is too difficult. I embrace you in my arms, love you and kiss you, beloved sweet wife.

Your husband

Berlin, 18.11.29

Most beloved good little wife!

Your naughty husband did not write yesterday; I just did not get to it.—In the morning I dictated a general administrative order for Artam, then went to Holfelder's grave site; memorial service for Holfelder in the great hall of the museum, which Dr. Hahne[92] held; it was moving—beautiful and solemn.—Afterward, *Reichsthing*.[93] Everything went well there too; from

---

[92] Professor Dr. Hans Hahne (1875–1935), doctor and specialist in prehistory, who researched, among other things, bodies from bog burials, which particularly interested Himmler. Hahne was also a speaker for the Artam League leadership courses [*Führerschulungen*].

[93] The *Reichsthing* was a "parliament," or meeting, of the Artam League. Himmler later cut ties with this group. For more information, see Peter Longerich, *Heinrich Himmler: A Life*, pp. 102ff. [—Trans.]

1:00 to 2:30 I met with Professor Hahne. While eating, from 3:00 to 4:15, discussion with the representative of a camera factory. The result was again very satisfactory. 4:43 traveled to Berlin. Arrived there 7:30, telephoned, and then on to the Reifschneiders', who once again were very kind and cordial. His mother and sister were there. We chatted until 1:30 in the morning. My good little scamp, what a pity that you were not there. First thing today at the Friedrichstrasse railroad station, but missed Strasser at the Reichstag. Worked for a bit in the office of our parliamentary group, made some telephone calls, and confirmed the day's agenda. At noon I shall meet Gregor and Otto Strasser, in the afternoon I am going to the Preussischer Landtag [Prussian state parliament]. In the evening, I am thinking of driving to the parents'.

So, my good darling, now you know a bit about your husband, what he is up to.—I hope you are doing well, beloved little wife. Do not get upset and do not be afraid. Thank God, the cold wave is over. And now I must stop. You beloved creature, I kiss you

Your Heini

The first Artam League chapter was founded in Halle in 1924. Its goal was to send its members, "young German lads and maids" above the age of seventeen, to farms in the east as agricultural workers, so that they might "toughen body, mind, and soul, and strengthen character," but also to "displace the foreign, especially Polish, migrant workers, from German soil." They also fought against "all un-German, 'modern' immorality and for *artecht* [racially authentic] values and peasant culture."

The Artam League was a heterogeneous collection of folkish and nationalist movements. The leadership of this league consisted of the Bundesführer, Max Mielsch in Dresden, and a *Bundeskanzler* [chancellor], who was also the general manager of the league's circa two thousand members. Hans Holfelder held this position from 1927 until his death on January 1, 1929; Mielsch succeeded him.

Holfelder was born in Vienna in 1900 and had been a member of the NSDAP since July 1925. In the Bund Artam he was the liaison with the NSDAP. In 1928 Heinrich Himmler was Holfelder's most important confidant in the party leadership for all business relating to the Bund Artam. The two men had known each other since their student days in Munich. On January 22, 1922, Himmler recorded in his *Journal* that he had cooked with Käthe Loritz, a friend of his in Pension Loritz (where he ate every day as a student), "for H. Holfelder and his pals." In November 1928 Himmler had visited his "league brother Holfelder" in the hospital in Halle, where the latter was being treated for a compound leg fracture after a motorcycle accident (29.11.28). Shortly thereafter, Holfelder succumbed to his fatal injuries.

Heinrich Himmler supported the Bund Artam from its early days. After Holfelder's death he became the leader of the Gauamt Bayern [regional office for Bavaria] for the Bund Artam, but he developed his main activity in the league in 1929. Numerous references to meetings with Artam members during his journeys to different cities exist. Thus, according to his pocket calendar, he was in Halle again for a few days in the middle of February 1929, where the issue of the Bundschuh came to the fore. The Bundschuh-Treuorden had also been founded in 1927 in close collaboration with the Bund Artam. Its central focus was "Blood and Soil" ["Blut und Boden"[94]]. On December 21, 1929, in Freyburg an der Unstrut, Himmler took part in the *Reichsthing*, as the Artam league called its meetings, recalling ancient Germanic tradition.

Der Donaubote, the journal of the Bund Artam, appeared in Ingolstadt (see Marga's letter of 1.5.29). The editorial staff of this journal was also responsible for *Der Bundschuh*, a "militant journal for the awakening German *Bauerntum* [peasantry]." It first appeared in January 1928 under the editorship of Gauleiter Hinrich Lohse. The name *Bundschuh* derives from the symbol of the Landsknechte during the Peasants' Revolt.[95] Himmler later took over the editorship of the journal, in which Strasser also published from its inception. In 1931, Marga Himmler was still using stationery with the Bundschuh letterhead (letter of 11.10.31). During World War II, Himmler named a division of the Waffen-SS[96] after Florian Geyer, a heroic Landsknecht of the Peasants' Revolt.

---

[94] The phrase *Blut und Boden* was meant to express a primitive relationship between the German peasant and the earth. NSDAP propaganda stressed this as part of the party's antiurban, anticapitalist, pro-agrarian animus. [—Trans.]

[95] Bundschuh: late medieval peasant footwear that gave its name to the Bundschuh Movement (1493–1517), a series of peasant uprisings in southwest Germany and precursor to the later Peasants' Revolt (1524–25). The peasants displayed an image of this laced shoe on their flag. [—Trans.]

[96] The Waffen-SS (armed SS) was the military branch of the SS, an army that numbered forty divisions at its height. [—Trans.]

Richard Walther Darré also belonged to the Artam Bund. Darré later became the chief of the Rasse- und Siedlungshauptamt [Central Office for Race and Resettlement] of the SS and *Reichsternährungsminister* [Reich minister of nutrition]. He exerted a strong influence on Himmler in the early 1930s with his concept of a "New Aristocracy of Blood and Soil." Other leading Nazis such as Alfred Rosenberg, Rudolf Höss, and Wolfram Sievers were also members. Darré—who gained a reputation through his books *Das Bauerntum als Lebensquell der nordischen Rasse* [The Peasantry as the Life Source of the Nordic Race (1928)] and *Neuadel aus Blut und Boden* (1930) [New Aristocracy from Blood and Soil]—was introduced to Hitler in 1930. Hitler charged him with the political restructuring of the agrarian apparatus of the NSDAP. From 1932 on, Darré led the section of the SS Central Office for Race and Resettlement. His influence, however, diminished, and he had to relinquish his leadership position in 1938. For all practical purposes, the state secretary, Herbert Backe, took over the leadership of the Reich's Ministry of Nutrition.

POCKET CALENDAR

Himmler was on the road a good deal through the end of the year, although these were mostly short trips in Bavaria. According to his pocket calendar, he did not participate in the successful election in Thuringia, in which the NSDAP received more than 11 percent of the votes in the regional parliamentary elections of December 8, 1929. As a result, the party participated in a local government for the first time, with Wilhelm Frick as minister of the interior. On the other hand, Himmler did go to the *Reichsthing* of the Bund Artam on December 20–21, in Freyburg (Saxony-Anhalt).

No pocket calendar survives from the following year, 1930.

———

Waldtrudering, 20.3. [30]

My good beloved!

Today the sweet card you wrote while you were traveling arrived here. In the meantime, you will have arrived at Elfriede's in Berlin. I am not doing very well. Today it is already the 20th and still nothing. Who knows what the future holds?[97] One cannot stop thinking about it. I am off to Haar now and will take the letter there so that you have it tomorrow. Call me on Friday evening or Saturday morning. The little scamp is doing very well. She laughs and shrieks with joy. [. . .]

One feels so very anxious. Telephone me. A thousand greetings.

With many affectionate greetings and kisses, from the bottom of my heart,

Your Marga

My precious, ask Elfriede everything possible about the clinic. I do not know what to ask. I have run out of thoughts.

Berlin, 21.3.1930

Good, beloved little scamp!

If only I could be with you to reassure you, poor dear little soul.—I spoke with Frau Reifschneider, she said that you should not take it badly. Every evening, hot baths, and red mulled wine with a lot of cinnamon. My darling, pay attention to your little heart, so you come to no harm in the bath. Elfriede suggests that above all you should do nothing now, because nothing is certain yet. In the third month it is still possible that everything will be very easy and safe.

I still believe that your periods have stopped due to autosuggestion, and from your inner anxiety. Do not be dejected, and do not despair; I am always thinking of you and I send you all my love and strength.

Sweetie, you good creature, do not forget your little pills and sleep after meals. [. . .]

I kiss you, you dearest woman:

With love and concern,

Your husband

A special kiss for our dear little Püppi

---

[97] This letter was previously understood as evidence of Marga's depressive mood. It becomes apparent from her husband's letter of March 21, 1930, in answer to this one, and from other references, that she fears she might be pregnant. After her difficulty giving birth to their daughter, the doctors had advised her not to have any more children.

Vienna, 4.4.1930

Beloved, best beloved!

I have just arrived in Vienna and am staying in a very beautiful room at the Hotel Erzherzog Rainer [Hotel Archduke Rainer]. This morning I slept until 9:30, which did me a lot of good. I did not actually see anything of Graz. At noon on Thursday I traveled via Bruck an der Mur from Klagenfurt to Graz, where I arrived around 9:00 in the evening. The rally was very good, afterward I set up an SS unit, then off to the café.—In bed at 2:30.—Good sweetie, how often my thoughts seek you when I am on the train, how often I see your good, dear little face, with your beloved blue eyes.—I just had an official telephone call with Munich and told Aumeier to telephone you.[98]

I had various meetings this morning. At 1:00 I traveled to Vienna, the trip over the Semmering Pass was very interesting. Sweetie, if only you had been there. Austria is very instructive for me, and the common people are still good. The upper class is generally not worth much.

My little rascal, but how are you now, are you taking your pills? Are you sleeping after meals? Are you not overexerting yourself? And what is our sweet little kiddy up to, the good little Püppi. Give her an extra kiss from her "Travel-Papa."

What do you think of those Deutsch-Nazionale [*sic*]?[99] They really are pigs.—

Sweetie, will you pick me up again in Munich. I will telephone you from Salzburg.

Now I am going to dinner. Then to the meeting. Dear, sweet beloved wife, I am so fond of you, and I embrace you and kiss you.

Your husband

———

In March 1930 the cabinet, led by the Social-Democrats, broke apart as a result of internal political conflict. The cabinet had been able to rely upon a

---

[98] Georg Aumeier (b. 1895) joined the NSDAP in 1922. In August 1929 he became the adjutant of the Munich SS-Standarte [a regimental command within the general SS—Trans.]. A few months after this letter he became adjutant to the Reichsführer-SS [commander of the SS] and *Reichsgeschäftsführer* of the SS. [general secretary of the SS—Trans.]

[99] The reference is to the DNVP, or Deutschnationale Volkspartei, the German National People's Party, a party on the far right of the political spectrum that competed for a similar demographic of voters as the NSDAP. [—Trans.]

majority in the Reichstag made up of the Social Democratic Party (SPD), the liberal German Democratic Party (DDP), the liberal right-wing German People's Party (DVP), and the Catholic Center Party. In the words of Reich president Paul von Hindenburg, the subsequent government under Heinrich Brüning of the Center Party no longer needed to worry about parliamentary majorities, but could rule with the authority of the emergency decrees as stated in Article 48. According to the constitution, these could be applied only in cases of danger to public security and order. Brüning formed a coalition with, among others, the Deutschnationale Volkspartei (DNVP), but could rely only on their moderate wing, not on the radical wing led by Alfred Hugenberg. As a result, Brüning did not have a majority. On April 3, 1930, the SPD and Communists (KPD) in the Reichstag submitted a vote of no confidence against the new government. A total of 252 members supported the motion while 187 voted against it. The support of the DNVP for the government was a surprise result of this vote, which is presumably why Himmler calls them "pigs" here. In July, when a majority of the Reichstag invoked its constitutional right and rejected the first emergency decrees concerning tax issues, Brüning, with Hindenburg's authority, dissolved the Reichstag and set new elections for September 14, 1930.

Himmler had begun assembling a network of contacts with Austria as early as 1928. In January 1928 he had written to Marga of a trip to Braunau and Neumarkt (Upper Austria); according to his pocket calendar, he was in Carinthia and Bruck an der Mur (Styria) in September 1928 and in the region of the Innviertel (Upper Austria) in June 1929.

The end of 1929 saw the first efforts in Vienna to constitute an SS unit—a suggestion that Himmler welcomed. On January 1, 1930, he had given Walter Turza the task of organizing the SS in Vienna, and had ordered the establishment of further SS units in "Linz, Vienna, Klagenfurt, and possibly Graz," and he announced that he would visit Austria himself in April 1930. Before now there has been no reliable evidence that he ever actually took this trip. It was considered merely probable, for on April 4, 1930, he ordered, among other things, the establishment of a twelve-man SS troop in Klagenfurt. During the train trips to Austria, he read *Judentum und Weltumsturz* [Judaism and World Conquest] (1929), by Léon de Poncins, which he considered "good and interesting."

The Austrian National Socialists, among them especially the Kärntner

Erneurer [Carinithian Modernizers]—the three Gauleiters Hubert Klausner, Friedrich Rainer, and Odilo Globocnik—stood for a "realistic annexation policy," in other words, a separation between illegal party activity and legal nationalist activity. The strictly organized NSDAP, which was outlawed after 1933, was supposed to be internally strengthened through education and propaganda, while the connections to the German Reich were to be secured. The Austrian National Socialists nurtured cooperation with Hitler, Göring, and Himmler, and they had particularly close contacts with the SS. At the same time, they attempted to gain positions in the state by means of individual "Ideenträger" [ideologues] (for example, with the appointment of the lawyer Arthur Seyss-Inquart to the Staatsrat [Council of State]). He maintained close contact with the so-called "modernizers," and after the Anschluss, would become the Reichsstatthalter [reich governor] of Austria.

One of these "modernizers," the Carinthian lawyer Friedrich Rainer (1903–47), lived in Graz, the capital of Styria, at the time of Himmler's journey to the city in April 1930. In May 1938, Hitler named Rainer the Gauleiter of Salzburg and later Reichsstatthalter of Salzburg and Carinthia and of Krain (Slovenia). Heinrich and Marga Himmler took a vacation in Salzburg at the end of 1938; in 1941, Rainer continued to invite them to the Salzburg Festival.

Rainer's friend Odilo Globocnik (1904–45) would become a willing minion of Himmler, first in Austria and then in the occupied territories in Poland. Up until 1934, Globocnik was employed as the construction foreman in Klagenfurt and, in addition, was active in the Kärntner Heimatschutz [Carinthian Home Guard]; until 1933 he was chief of propaganda for the NS-Betriebszellenorganization (NSBO) [National Socialist Factory Cell Organization]. He joined the SS in 1934, and, in the following years, established an illegal news service for the SS in Carinthia. He failed completely as Gauleiter of Vienna, 1938–39, and following that was put on probation in the Waffen-SS. Himmler later installed "Globus" as SS and police chief in Lublin, where he was responsible for the mass murder of Polish Jews.

The lawyer Ernst Kaltenbrunner (1903–46), who was born in Ried in the Innviertel was about the same age as Rainer and Globocnik and also lived in Graz at about the same time. Not only did he know Adolf Eichmann (1906–62) from their schooldays in Linz, but he undoubtedly also knew Rainer from their university studies, because both received their law degrees in Graz in 1926.

Kaltenbrunner later became Eichmann's superior in the SD.[100] For years Kaltenbrunner had fought for an Anschluss with the German Reich as a member of
the paramilitary group Österreichischer Heimatschutz [Austrian Home Guard].
In 1930 (possibly after visiting the party meeting just mentioned) he moved to
the NSDAP, and quickly made a name for himself as a defender of imprisoned
party members. He joined the SS in 1931; from 1935 onward he was a clandestine leader of the SS-Abschnitt [SS group] Linz, and after 1938, leader of the
SS-Abschnitt Donau [SS unit Danube] and *Höherer SS und Polizei Führer*
[senior SS and police chief] (HSSPF), Danube. He was also a member of the
Reichstag. In 1943 he was supposed to take over the leadership of the Reichssicherheitshauptamt [Reich Security Head Office] and the SD as Heydrich's
successor.

With the annexation of Austria on March 12, 1938, Himmler was one of the
first NS functionaries to arrive at the airport in Vienna. There he was received
by Kaltenbrunner, Rainer, and Globocnik, among others (see also the commentary accompanying Marga's *Journal* 1938).

Hotel Sanssouci
Linkstr. 37, am Potsdamer Bahnhof[101]
Berlin W 9, 2.5.1930

You most beloved sweet little wife!

How sad I was yesterday when I realized that you were crying. Poor,
poor little scamp! How I wish I were at home with you. On Monday I shall be
there for sure.

There is much to discuss here, but we are losing a lot of time. Tomorrow
we are traveling to Potsdam and Werder and on to Leipzig, Altenburg,
where we will spend the night. On Sunday noon we are in Bayreuth for a
troop review. Monday finally home. Sweetie, how I long for you; but, little
scamp, do not be sad anymore; keep thinking of how fond I am of you.—I met

---

[100] SD: Sicherheitsdienst, intelligence service of the SS, sister organization of the Gestapo.
[101] Printed stationery from hotels, from the Reichstag (Reichstagsabgeordneter), or from Der
Bundschuh are set in italics to emphasize that this letterhead is not manuscript text.

Father[102] alone; he was overjoyed at my visit and more or less poured his heart out to me. In summer he will probably visit us alone.

Sweetie, my good one, give our little Püppi a kiss from her Pappi.

And, my sweet beloved wife, I embrace you, cherish you, your pure soul and your beautiful sweet body.

Your husband

Hotel Deutsches Haus—Coburg
Coburg, 30.5.1930

Most beloved good little wife!

It is now 5:00 in the afternoon. Arrived from Pressig at 3:00—I really must make sure I tell you about it.

Arrived in Kronach Wednesday night. Fell asleep right away. Up at 7:00. 8–9:30 unpleasant meeting (squabble). 9:30 to 12:00 marched up a mountain with the SS and drilled.—Then I quickly took a look at the magnificent Kronach Castle. Ate in 5 minutes, then parade through the little town. 4:30–5:00 conference with the Führer. 4:30–6:30 individual conferences (discipline). 6:30 by car to Coburg. Very difficult negotiations there until 9:00. All very annoying. 9:00, by car back to Kronach. From Kronach to Pressig. Frieda[103] opened the door and I just had to stay there. She was overjoyed. Slept wonderfully. The children were indescribably happy. Frieda and the two little ones will come for 8 days after Pentecost, Franz maybe for 2 days.

I am enclosing an offer for butter. Frieda gets hers at 1 pound 1.49–1.60 M. They send 4, 5, 6 pound packets. Sounds really good.

In the middle of the day I drove back to Coburg.

Tonight I am speaking here.

And you, my good sweetie, so how are you? You will get this letter on Monday, so you will have something from your naughty husband in the morning.

To you and the beloved little Püppi many, many sweet greetings and kisses from the Travel-Papa, who loves his two little ones infinitely.

Your husband

---

[102] He refers to Marga's father.

[103] Frieda Hofmann was a relative, probably Marga's cousin.

The Northern Bavarian town of Coburg had been a bastion of National Socialism since the "Deutscher Tag" [German Day] in October 1922. On that day Hitler arrived in a special train with his entourage. His SA marched through the city assaulting people, and registered an enormous propaganda victory. In Coburg, after June 1929, the NSDAP had its first majority in any German city.

On the one hand, in 1930 the NSDAP was beset by internal political conflicts. At the end of May it came to a violent disagreement between Hitler and Otto Strasser. Strasser left the party in the beginning of July under the slogan, "The Socialists are leaving the NSDAP."

On the other hand, the party was in the middle of an election campaign. With the help of the Rednerschule [Speakers' School], the number of NSDAP speakers approached one thousand. A memorandum of the Prussian Ministry of the Interior from May 1920 stated that hardly a day passed without several National Socialist rallies, even in the most far-flung districts. The memo noted that the speakers were well trained, knew how to affect their listeners with their subject matter, and according to the observations of the police, almost always attracted overflow crowds and audience approval.

In Saxony, in addition to the Reichstag elections, there was a vote for a new regional parliament. As the letters show, Himmler was constantly traveling on a campaign tour during these weeks. The first sign of the future success of the NSDAP became evident in the elections to the Saxon regional parliament on July 22, 1930. Although the SPD remained the strongest party, with 33.4 percent, and the Communists made small gains, the winners of the election were the National Socialists. They were able to raise their vote tally from just under 5.0 to 14.4 percent, at the expense of the middle-class parties.

Meissen 19.6.1930

Darling, sweet, most beloved little wife!

I keep seeing your dear, good, sweet little face and attractive, good eyes. Sweetie, how I wished again today that you could be with me. I do not always wish it, for this trip is gruesome. Tuesday noon I went from Plauen to

Chemnitz, where I quickly wrote you a card. Then onward in 4 hours from Chemnitz to Neuhausen, Erzgebirge region, always by slow train in the heat and with hay fever. On Tuesday evening I spoke in Deutsch Neudorf at a small but good meeting. The village is located in the Erzgebirge Mountains, 1 minute from the border.

Yesterday noon from Neuhausen to Dresden, where I arrived at 13:00, ate lunch then viewed the Hygiene Exhibition for 3 hours, interesting although heavy Jewish influence. After that there was no time to write, from Dresden again with the slow train to Gaussi near Bautzen. A small meeting of farmers. This morning went to the station, the heat is terrible, the hay fever is improving.

Arrived in Meissen around noon. Shaved, changed, ate. Then toured the magnificent cathedral and Albrechtsburg, wonderful.—In the evening I spoke nearby in a farming village. Tomorrow morning I want to look at the [porcelain—Trans.] factory. Around midday I shall travel to Leipzig, where tomorrow I will speak nearby. Tomorrow morning I shall go to the post office again. Today there was nothing there yet from my naughty beloved wife. I have sent off a package of old laundry and magazines.

And now, you poor sweetie, how are you getting on? Does your good little head still hurt, have a good rest in this heat, and by all means, do not overexert yourself (in these days especially, get a lot of rest).

What is our sweet little kiddie up to, is she well behaved, or is she making a mess in her little bed, oh how I am looking forward to having both my beloved ones with me again.

I cannot imagine how the garden looks—the drought is awful. Dear little scamp, do not forget to have the scythe sharpened, and do not forget your little pills!

So, my dear little angel, I have to stop now.—Supper, and then to the meeting. I hope Trude[104] is enjoying herself at our place, give her a special hello from me; I am so sorry that I am not there during her visit.

I kiss you, my good beloved, and the little kiddy,

Your husband

---

[104] The identity of this visitor is unclear.

Bad Salzungen 19.7.30

Good beloved little wife!

We departed punctually in the morning via Augsburg—Donauwörth—Nördlingen. In Nördlingen we inspected the magnificent gothic cathedral, then onward to Schillingsfürst, where we were very well received. There we heard on the radio that the dissolution of the Reichstag has succeeded after all. A couple of vacation days in August will certainly come up, and afterward all [illegible].[105] Sweetie, do not be sad.

On from Schillingsfürst via Würzburg, Kissingen, Meiningen, to Bad Salzungen, here we had good overnight accommodation. Slept wonderfully. The weather is bad again today. Now it is time to move on.

Good, dear, beloved, my little scamp,

I kiss you and am so fond of you,

     Your husband

Greetings to little Püppi from me

Lehsan,[106] 21.7.30

Darling, most beloved little wife!

Yesterday I did not get around to writing, a trip like this by car is damned strenuous.

First things first, scamp, how are the two of you, I keep seeing your two sweet little faces and think of you and wish you could be with me during the pleasant hours.

On Saturday morning we drove from Bad Salzungen via Eisenach, the Thüringer Forest, and Göttingen, to Hannover. Had a quick lunch in Einbeck. Arrival in Hannover 14:30, then conversations with the Führer until late at night and SS review. Sunday morning at 8:00 from Hannover via Uelzen, Lüneburg, Hamburg, to Itzehoe—Lockstedt Camp. Once again, this

---

[105] Presumably "September." (See Marga's letter of 27.3.30.)

[106] The correct name is Lensahn. The castle and village of the same name are located in Holstein, near Oldenburg. Nearby Eutin was an early bastion of National Socialists. Hitler paid his first visit there as early as 1926.

trip was through magnificent landscapes, but cold and rainy. My God, Germany is beautiful.

At the Lockstedt Camp, conference with Hitler and SS review.

There is wonderful human material in the SS.

At 18:00 with Waldeck[107] by car to Neumünster, from there by train to Eutin, where we were again picked up by car.

A lot of activity in the castle and village of Lehsan [sic] because of an enormous horse show that was being held. Received most graciously. Got up at 9:00 today, bathed, then breakfast. 4 of the duke's children and 2 of the Schaumburgers (whom you know) are here, and you can imagine what kind of a commotion they make.[108]

We talked a lot of politics.—On Wednesday I am meeting with OSAF in Münster in Westphalia. I shall write again tomorrow. It is almost certain that I shall be home a bit earlier. Well, my good little thing, I am so happy that my good wife must already be writing me a letter that I will get in Heidelberg.

You dear, beloved sweetie, I kiss you and little Püppi,

Your husband

Greetings to the Schönbohms

———————

The parade ground "Lockstedt Camp," north of Hamburg, was a rallying point for right-wing extremists during the Weimar Republic, and was considered the cradle of the Schleswig-Holstein SA. Numerous functionaries of the Schleswig-Holstein NSDAP completed their paramilitary training courses in the Lockstedt Camp.

---

[107] Waldeck: Josias, hereditary prince of Waldeck and Pyrmont (1896–1967), farmer, and SS leader, became Himmler's adjutant shortly thereafter.

[108] Grand Duke Nikolaus von Oldenburg (1897–1970) was the brother of Waldeck's wife and was also married to one of Waldeck's sisters. Himmler's reference to "the Schaumburgers" means Stephan, Prince zu Schaumburg-Lippe (1891–1965) and his wife, Frau Ingeborg Alix (1901–66), a sister of Nikolaus. Beginning in 1928 the couple, together with Waldeck, attended NSDAP meetings in Munich.

Waldtrudering 23.7.[30]

Good beloved!

No word from you. Today I waited for a letter, but in vain. The only letter that arrived is the one from Salzungen. I was in Munich and read about the dissolution [of the Reichstag in the newspaper]. I am happy for the NS Movement. Gauleiter Loeper[109] has already inquired when and where you wish to speak. I have saved his letter here.

Otherwise bills are the only things that have come.

When are you arriving? I hope it is on Friday. If only you weren't going along to the Hallermanns'. You are needed here, and have to leave again right away.

We are working hard on the road. Nothing new here.

But September will be magnificent.

No one has gotten in touch.

I greet and kiss you 1000 x

Your Marga

Hamburg 23.7.30, 4:00 afternoon

My best, most beloved little wife!

Yesterday your naughty husband and Papa did not write. He was out hunting until 9:00 in the evening, and shot a heron and missed a roebuck. The day before yesterday I swam in the lake, yesterday slept late until 10:00. Every night, talking politics until 2:00 at night with all the various leaders of the Stahlhelm and Landvolk,[110] etc., I think it was very successful. Today at noon I left Eutin and will arrive in Münster in Westphalia at 8:00 this evening (via Lübeck, Hamburg, Minden). I shall be meeting OSAF in Münster.

---

[109] Wilhelm Loeper (1883–1935), career officer, became the NSDAP Gauleiter of Magdeburg-Anhalt in 1928. In addition he became the head of the *Personalamt* [personnel department] of the NSDAP in 1930.

[110] The Stahlelm was a militant right-wing nationalist association for ex-servicemen founded after the defeat of 1918, eventually absorbed into the SA. The Landvolk (Christlich-Nationale Bauern-und Landvolkpartei, CNBL) was a conservative splinter party during the Weimar Republic. [—Trans.]

My dear good creature, do not be despondent and sad, your naughty husband is arriving soon. How I look forward to you and little Püppi.

We are just passing Hamburg harbor, right near whole neighborhoods of new housing blocks—real Jew barracks.

My good sweetie, in August I will probably not be able to take a longer vacation, but I shall always be able to take a day here and there so that we can finish the work in our garden. So do not be sad.

Kiss and pat our little scamp for me.

I see you before me and I embrace and kiss you,

Your husband

Leipzig Hauptbahnhof [central railroad station] *20.8.30, 9:00*

Sweet, dear, beloved little wife!

I have just come from Weimar on my way to Berlin, I have an hour between trains and have just eaten a couple of slices of pâté. My dear dear little rascal, if only you were sitting here beside me!—How are you then, I hope you are well. Do not overexert yourself and always sleep after meals.— And my little scamp, take your little pills regularly. What is our little Püppi up to, the sweet little cutie, how I love both my little ones!

Now I have to tell you a little bit about myself. I arrived in Dresden on Tuesday 20:20, right to Hotel Angermann, where I had a good stay as usual. In the evening conferences until 12:00, which were quite satisfactory.

Wednesday morning to the regional parliament as well, 10:30 traveled to Weimar, worked, read. Arrived Weimar 14:29. Schirach picked me up and we drove to his place, I was received extremely cordially.[111] Meetings from 16–19:00, which were also satisfactory. Dinner with the Schirachs. 22:00— met with [?] and the delegates at the [White] Swan (Goethe's regular pub). Home at 1:00 a.m.

---

[111] Baldur von Schirach (1907–74) became the leader of the National Socialist Student League in 1928, and in 1931, *Reichsjugendführer* [Reich Youth leader] of the NSDAP. In 1925, Hitler had been an earlier guest in the Schirach household in Weimar, where Himmler was now being received so cordially.

Unfortunately had to get up at 6 a.m. today. 7:20 my train left for Leipzig-Berlin, the connection here is terrible.

I will arrive in Berlin at 1:30 a.m. and will be picked up. The burial is at 4:00 p.m., I will change my clothes at our office and will not go to the Reifschneiders' until afterward.

You good thing, how I worry about you, everything will be all right, but if not, do not despair! You good, good little scamp!

Sunday, Monday, I am going out for prey.[112] I shall write you again from Berlin, and there I am sure to get something from my good wife.

Dear, beloved, I kiss you and the little scamp,

Your husband

For the most part, both the foreign and domestic press reacted with shock to the results of the Reichstag elections on September 14, 1930. *Paris Midi* wrote, "Germany is politically poisoned." Although the SPD lost votes in September 1930, it still remained the strongest faction in the Reichstag, with 24.5 percent. The KPD was able to raise its representation to 13.1 percent, whereas the middle-class camp suffered dramatic losses. By contrast, the success of the NSDAP exceeded even their own expectations. Their vote tally rose from circa 800,000 to over 6.4 million, which put their participation in the Reichstag at 18.3 percent. Suddenly the NSDAP had become the second-strongest party, and entered the Reichstag with 107 delegates—a political landslide of a dimension that had never before been seen in the history of parliamentary elections in Germany.

One of the new Reichstag delegates was Heinrich Himmler. In the Reichstag handbook for 1930 he is listed as "licensed agronomist" and "owner of a small poultry farm." Like all National Socialists, Himmler had nothing but contempt for democracy and its institutions, especially for the "Blabber Chamber,"[113] the Parliament. As a delegate, he therefore never got involved more than was absolutely necessary. The hours during which he was obliged to be present in the Reichstag were for him categorically an arid "waste of

---

[112] *Beutefahrt:* literally, a search for prey or booty—presumably, a hunting trip. [—Trans.]

[113] The derogatory term *Schwatzbude* (roughly, Blabber Chamber), in reference to the parliament, is attributed to Kaiser Wilhelm II.

time that one regrets" (15.10.30). On the other hand, he profited unscrupulously from the advantages that the life of a delegate brought with it: a good salary, diplomatic immunity, and a travel pass, which meant he no longer had to draw upon NS party coffers for his numerous trips. Shortly after entering parliament, Himmler published a tract with the programmatic title *Der Reichstag, 1930: Das sterbende System und der Nationalsozialismus* [The *Reichstag* 1930: The Dying System and National Socialism] (Munich: Eher Verlag, 1931), 84 pp.

———

Reichstag Abgeordneter[114]
Berlin NW, 14.10.1930

My beloved little Angel!

Your naughty husband was not able to send you anything yesterday.
I write this card during a meeting of our parliamentary group; that took an awfully long time. At the Reifschneiders' in the evening; I cannot keep living with them. He is afraid for the Jews. Nonetheless, they are endlessly kind and good. [. . .]

You dearest, good one, now I am off to the post office.

I kiss you, you dear little wife, and Püppi.

Your husband

Stegmann sends his respects.[115]

Waldtrudering 14.10. [30]

Dear good husband!

The Schönbohms were here yesterday and told me that the Reichstag was not meeting today, [but] that you probably would not be coming home so soon. That is what I am thinking. Listen and be amazed

———

[114] This letter, like many that follow, is written on official Reichstag stationery, with the heading "Reichstag Delegate". [—Trans.]
[115] Wilhelm Stegmann (1899–1944) and Himmler had known each other since their student days. Stegmann was the Gauleiter of Franconia and a party speaker. In 1930 he, like Himmler, became a delegate to the Reichstag.

today. In the forenoon we worked hard in the garden, because the weather is so nice. I was lying down at 3 o'clock and was just about to go to sleep. Then the doorbell rang, which I answered, and what do you know, it was Frau Schwarz and Hitler's niece.[116] I was speechless. We had coffee together, which was very pleasant, and then Frau Bäumel arrived, and when we were out looking at the animals, the Schönbohms arrived and reported that there had been riots in Berlin. Nothing happened to you, did it? The thought just occurs to me that that was why Frau Schönbohm showed up, but she did not let on. Such foolishness. It was really very nice. Evening is coming on now. I want to read a lot and go to bed early. Tomorrow we are getting Föhn weather,[117] which means I am going get that pressure in my head again.

In the garden we are busy digging up the raspberries. It is terrible work. Indescribable weeds.

Write again soon. And I must have mail from you tomorrow. Were you at my parents'? And did you get any pears? Did you visit Lydia and Berta?[118] Did you deliver the pillow? I shall be writing to Frida[119] later today. Do not forget the two little boards and the hoe. Kassler[?]?

Now I want some supper. Püppi is feisty, lively, and cheerful.

Say hello most cordially to Frida from me.

If you are not coming home this week, I will go to Munich with the Schönbohms on Friday. I think they drive there every week. Frau Schönbohm and I want to stroll through town. Otherwise there is always hard work to be done in the garden. Maybe an outing to the woods tomorrow afternoon.

---

[116] Frau Schwarz was the wife of Franz Xaver Schwarz (1875–1947), the *Reichsschatzmeister* [treasurer] of the NSDAP, who was responsible for funding the party organizations, including the SS. Schwarz became a member of the SS himself in 1931 and was thus one of the most important party functionaries. Angelika (Geli) Raubal (1908–1931) was the niece of Adolf Hitler, who was also her guardian.

[117] The Föhn is a dry, hot wind that descends leeside of mountain ranges (here, the Bavarian Alps) and is associated with various ailments, such as headaches resulting from the pressure changes. [—Trans.]

[118] Lydia Boden and Berta were two sisters of Marga. Berta was married; Lydia was a seamstress and unmarried.

[119] Frieda Hoffmann, presumably Marga's cousin.

So be well, you good man. Let me hear from you.

When are you coming?

Greetings, kiss—

Your Marga

Berlin NW 7, 15.10.1930

Dear heart, my good little wife!

Today at 9:30 I arrived again in Berlin from Frankfurt an der Oder, went right to the post office and deposited the money; it was just was not possible yesterday, then got a haircut, then to the Reifschneiders'. Shaved, washed, changed, then had breakfast with Frau Reifschneider until 11:30. Then off to the Reichstag, various meetings there—by the way, just think, there is a Communist delegate Frau Himmler (Chemnitz).[120] Took my seat in the Reichstag, the session began at 3:00 and had not yet finished by 7:00. Election of the Presidium [Executive Committee]. It is totally disorganized. Such a waste of time. At 7:00 I hurried away and raced to the Lehrt Railroad Station by car. Just ate in the train. Will arrive at 20:35 in Stendal, where I have to go right to a meeting. Unfortunately, the Reichstag will be meeting through Saturday. It is too soon for anyone to say what will happen after that. Dear little scamp, how I look forward to being with you again. Sweetie, how nice it will be to be together and love each other so tenderly. Greet and kiss little Püppi for me, the sweet little cutie. And you, have a good rest so that the pretty little head does not hurt and so you will be all refreshed.

When I am back, we will finish the fence right away; how I am looking forward to our own land again.

Dearest, sweet wife, I kiss you and am so fond of you.

Your husband

---

[120] Johanna Himmler (1894–1972) served as a delegate of the KPD in the Reichstag from 1930 to 1933.

Reichstag Abgeordneter
Berlin NW7, 17.10.1930

My good little wife!

It is exactly 12:00 at night, and I am just leaving my parents' house—they send you their best.

How happy I was when I found a letter there from you, and how much greater was my disappointment.

Sweetie, sweetie, one does not write such letters. When I left, dear child, you made the comment about spending money, which hurt me so much, and today this letter.—Sweetie, I do not understand you, what is this letter supposed to mean? Do you regret today that we got married, and is the miserable state of affairs that you see today [?] really so bad that it overshadows and destroys our great happiness, which I believe, and have believed, we possess.—Or have you lost your belief in me and my love and care?

Perhaps the Reichstag [session] tomorrow night will be postponed, so that I can come home Sunday evening or Sunday night.

A kiss for Püppi. Little wife, I love you so and am very very sad.

Your husband

———————

The letter from Marga to which this refers has not been preserved. Since the electoral success and the beginning of Heinrich Himmler's parliamentary responsibilities, their financial worries had diminished, but Marga was now alone more frequently than before. In the missing letter she had presumably expressed her displeasure about this situation.

———————

Reichstag Abgeordneter
Berlin NW7, 22.1.1931

My sweet, beloved, good wife!

This letter will surely arrive at the same time that your naughty husband does, but now between 10:00 and 11:00 in the evening I have an hour to myself, and now I just have to chat a little with my sweetie.—The Boss's rating was excellent and so was the effect on the leaders of the

Landbundführung [farmers' association][121]—We did not finish up until today, the Boss arrived earlier and the meeting lasted until 1:00.

Sweetie, I shall be with you again tomorrow, you good good thing, and then we will have a lovely Sunday ahead of us.

My dear wife I kiss you and am so fond of you.

Your husband

An extra kiss for little Püppi

POCKET CALENDAR

It becomes clear from the entries in January 1931 that Heinrich and Marga Himmler undertook many activities together during this month. At the beginning of the New Year they went to a concert and were visited by friends; on January 4 they were at a rabbit show, and following that, guests of the Brugers in Munich-Harlaching. In 1925 Himmler had invited the folkish writer Ferdinand Bruger to speak for the first time at a meeting in Lower Bavaria. On January 6, "Hereditary Prince Waldeck and his family" visited them, as did "Frau Dr. von Scheubner and Fräulein Wolf" on January 10. In 1929 Johanna Wolf became secretary for the district of Niederbayern-Oberpfalz [Lower Bavaria–Upper Palatinate]. She worked for Gregor Strasser and Rudolf Hess. After 1933 she worked in the party chancery in Berlin and later on Hitler's adjutant staff.

On January 15 Heinrich and Marga went to a lecture by the National Socialist agriculture expert Richard Walther Darré; on January 19 they went to lunch at the home of Himmler's parents to celebrate Anna Himmler's sixty-fifth birthday. Following this, Himmler had to go to Berlin for a few days, but on Sunday, January 25, they did something together again: Gerda Schreiner, from Plattling, and Irmgard Höfl from Apfeldorf came to visit for the day; in the evening, the Himmlers were invited to the home of Dr. Ebner and his wife in Kirchseeon. Gregor Ebner, a general practitioner, who was Himmler's private doctor for a long time, became the *Ortsgruppenleiter* [district group leader] in

---

[121] The Reichslandbund, RLB [farmers' association], was the most important farmers' interest group in the Weimar Republic. In 1929 it supported the popular petition against the Young Plan, which had been initiated by the DNVP and the NSDAP. The Young Plan attempted to restructure German reparation payments. Afterward, the influence of the National Socialists grew even greater in the RLB.

Kirchseeon in 1930, and in the Ebersberg district he occasionally lectured about the declining birthrate. In 1936 he became the medical director of the first SS-Lebensborn-Heim [Source of Life Home][122] in Steinhöring, near Kirchseeon.

On January 30, shortly before Heinrich Himmler had to return to Berlin for a longer period, he and Marga attended another lecture by the NS architect Paul Schultze-Naumburg at the Technical University in Munich.

Reichstag Abgeordneter
Berlin [crossed out]
Waltrudering, 12.2.1931

My sweet beloved little wife!

It is now 11:00 in the evening and I have just come from a conference with Wagner about the plebiscite[123] and am now sitting alone in our living room.[124] Oh sweetheart, how big a little house is when one is so alone and there is no beloved little wife there with a sweet little daughter. My little scamp, how your rough husband longs for you.

I cannot go along on the hunt tomorrow. Just think, this is awful: Dr. Schreiner-Plattling, Beppi's father, died suddenly the day before yesterday and is going to be buried in the Waldfriedhof [Forest Cemetery] on Saturday, and I certainly want to go to the funeral. The poor family![125]

----

[122] Lebensborn-Heim: This name was given to the system of maternity homes and support provided to the women who bore illegitimate children fathered by SS members.

[123] Adolf Wagner (1890–1944) became the Gauleiter of Munich–Upper Bavaria at the end of 1930 and, as the most powerful of all the Gauleiters (the "Despot of Munich"), had ready access to Hitler. It is unclear which plebiscite is referred to here, for the plebiscite about the Young Plan initiated by the right wing in Bavaria at the end of 1929 had already failed in March 1930. A month earlier, on January 11, Himmler had written, "Volksbegehren Trudering" [popular petition, Trudering], in his pocket calendar.

[124] Marga and Gudrun visited Marga's parents in Berlin. According to his pocket calendar, Heinrich himself was in Berlin February 2–11. On February 10 he had picked his wife and daughter up at the railroad station and brought them to his in-laws, in the Röntgental.

[125] From 1926 on Himmler had participated in countless party events with Dr. Schreiner, Ortsgruppenleiter [district group leader] of Plattling in Lower Bavaria and leader of the SS there.

Maybe I will go along on the hunt on Saturday evening.

Everything is in fine shape in the house. The hens are laying very well, since 3.2. they have laid 31 eggs. Our Rexchen still has not had her pups.

The painter will be finished on Monday; so far he has done his work very beautifully.

It snowed heavily today, I have already visited Strasser, he is doing *very* well.

Being the very very good husband that I am, I have sent you Die Sterne[126] as printed matter. The desk is now tidy again.

So, goodnight my beloved little darling. I shall be with you a week from today—how I look forward to it. Please give my best to your parents and Elfriede.

      I kiss you, my good wife, and little Püppi,

      Your Pappi

Reichstag Abgeordneter
Berlin [crossed out]
Waltrudering, 15.2.1931

My most beloved dearest little wife!

      Your naughty husband has just spent two terrible days. On Friday evening at 9:00 I climbed into bed with a chill. I stayed there all day Saturday and got up again today. An intestinal problem with all the trimmings, just like at our wedding, but things are fine again now, thank God. Unfortunately, I could not go to Dr. Schreiner's burial either.

Pay attention, my good sweetie, it is not impossible that on the 22nd the Reichsbanner [see commentary below] will actually lash out and I would really prefer to have my two beloved ones here. I have sketched out the following campaign plan, on Wednesday and Thursday I am speaking in Saxony. I travel to Berlin on Thursday night, arriving there at 7:35, we shall meet at the Stettin railroad station, where our train departs at 8:35. In the afternoon, we will be back from Stargard. In the evening we shall go to the

---

[126] "*Die Sterne* [The Stars] was a magazine about astrology.

"Vaterland"[127] as planned. Then we can sleep late on Saturday morning and travel to Munich in the evening where we shall arrive on Sunday morning. Reply now by special delivery or telephone me on Tuesday at 8:00 in the evening when I will be home.

The painter is finished. Did his job very nicely—sweetie, do not forget the liver medicine and buy a rubber hot water bottle, dearest sweetheart, how your husband is looking forward to having you with him again.

Say hello to everyone, an extra kiss for Püppi.

I am so fond of you and kiss you endlessly,

Your husband

———————

The Reichsbanner[128] was a nonpartisan umbrella organization that was social democratic in tone. Its mission was that of a militant group dedicated to the defense of the Republic and to opposing the enemies of democracy on both the right and the left. After the electoral success of the NSDAP in September 1930, this organization tried to increase its opposition to the street violence of the SA. February 22, 1931, the day Himmler feared that the Reichsbanner could "lash out," was the seventh anniversary of its foundation and the first time that the paramilitary defense units held a parade.

———————

Berlin, 27.3.1931, 19:00

My most beloved, good wife!

I am dead tired; at 20:00 the last "conference" will begin. Gotha was a brilliant success. Schulze-Naumburg[129] was wonderful. You should come

———————

[127] The Haus-Vaterland-Betrieb Kempinski [operated by the Kempinski Hotel—Trans.] on Potsdamer Platz in Berlin, had been expanded in 1927–28 to include a large restaurant-cabaret. It was especially famed for its theme restaurants, such as the Rhine terraces with spectacular artificial weather, the Turkish café, a Japanese tea room, Wild West bar, and many more.

[128] Literally, "Imperial Banner," the black, red, and gold flag of the Weimar Republic. [—Trans.]

[129] Paul Schultze-Naumburg (1869–1949) was an architect, painter, and politician who joined the NSDAP in 1930. Himmler apparently refers to a lecture by Schultze-Naumburg that he attended.

along next time. Tonight, off to Danzig, how I am looking forward to sleeping.

How I look forward to being with you again, how often I see you and little Püppi before me. I delivered the package to the girls. Now I must stop.

Many many infinitely dear greetings and kisses to you my most beloved, and to the little child,

Your Pappi

Hamburg, 6.5.1931

My dear beloved little scamp!

We arrived here safely. I was able to have a fine talk with the Boss. On the other hand, the night was short. The car was already here when we arrived.—Ate, went for a haircut, bathed, shaved, a few long-distance calls, official correspondence, and now a short note to you, my good wife, just enough time to have tea, and then off to Eutin to the rally. Tomorrow I am driving on my own to Hannover, tomorrow night to Berlin.

Many many sweet kisses to you, my good sweetie, and our "little" daughter,

Your husband

Reichstag Abgeordneter
Delmenhorst 9.5.1931

Good dear sweet little wife!

All went well yesterday. It lasted all day, was very tiring, but thank goodness nothing happened.

On Thursday the 7th I went by car from from Eutin to Hamburg in the morning, then by train to Hannover. There in the evening, rally and SS inspection. At 3:10 a.m. I went to Berlin, where I arrived at 7:00 in the morning. My night in the first-class compartment was a bit short. I was picked up in Berlin. Immediately inspected the security guards then at 8:30, to the elegant Hotel Kaiserhof on Wilhelmsplatz, where there were a lot of people. Bathed, breakfasted, waited, waited for the trial. At 20:00, finally dinner with Röhm and Aug.[ust] Melh.[?]. This morning at 8:40 drove here to Delmenhorst near Bremen. The Boss will arrive this evening by car. Everything well organized. Change. Dinner. Then off to the rally. I shall write again tomorrow.

> You dear good thing, I kiss you and am so terribly fond of you.
> Your husband

———

Himmler came to Berlin for one day to attend the opening of the so-called Weltbühne Trial on May 8, 1931. The trial ultimately condemned Carl von Ossietzky, the editor of the publication *Die Weltbühne*, to eighteen months in prison for espionage because he had published an article that had called attention to the clandestine rearmament of the German army. The security guards Himmler inspected were obviously SS men whom he had stationed in the vicinity of the courtroom in order to be prepared for possible provocateurs. Ossietzky was arrested again in 1933 and so badly mistreated in various concentration camps that he ultimately died of the consequences in 1938.

The Hotel Kaiserhof in Berlin, whose management had sympathized with the National Socialists since the 1920s, was located opposite the Reich Chancellery on Wilhelmplatz. Beginning in the 1920s Hitler usually stayed there when he was in Berlin. From 1932 on the entire upper floor was converted into the NSDAP central headquarters.

———

Oldenburg 12.5.1931

My sweetie, my dear sweet little wife!

You are going to say you have a naughty husband because he has not written [?][130] for 3 days, but it is not a naughty husband, only a good, harassed one who thinks so often about his beloved staying at home and never stops wishing that his sweetie could always come along everywhere

———

[130] The letter is written in pencil and is illegible in places.

with him.—But how are you, if only I knew, stupid husband that I am.
I received your fine letter in the [2 lines illegible].

Of course, I am [g?] doing fine.

The Hitler rally in Delmenhorst was on Saturday evening; it came off
very well. That night we drove to Oldenburg, where we found lodgings.

On Sunday there was a great SA demonstration in Oldenburg (Rott
[*Rottenführer?*]).[131] Sweetie, your heart could leap out of your chest when you
see what a magnificent Nordic people this is. This is a source of blood for
germany [*sic*]. In the evening I was with my SS-Standartenführer [SS colonel]
Bruns [?]. Yesterday, Monday, I slept it off. At 11:30 I took the train to
Wilhelmshaven with Dr. Frank,[132] where we waited for Hitler's car until
15:00. Then we inspected the battleship "Hannover," it was very interesting.
By car to Oldenburg at 7:00, quickly on to Wildeshausen, where, with
General Litzmann, I spoke yesterday at an excellent rally. Back at night by
car, slept until 9:00 today. Wrote a letter to my sweetheart first thing, your
naughty husband has been under too much pressure. Yesterday I sent off the old
laundry.—Today I am off to Jever, Hitler rally. Tonight back here. Tomorrow,
here during the day. In the evening I am speaking in Lohne. Thursday midday
there is a Hitler rally in Cloppenburg. In the afternoon, 16:00, will leave by
car and hope to be in Munich Friday evening. Sweetie, my good thing,
would you telephone the SS so that they can make sure my car is parked at
the Brown House[133] and ready to drive on Friday evening. You dear little
scamp, you, my [?] beautiful wife, how happy I shall be when I have you
[H?] again, and see you and the [?] again.

To you and our little Püppi many thousands of kisses,
Your husband

---

[131] *SS-Rottenführer:* corporal of the Waffen-SS. [—Trans.]

[132] Hans Frank (1900–1946), a jurist, responsible for the Nazification of Germany's legal system. He became *Reichsleiter des Reichsrechtsamtes der NSDAP* (president of the Reich's Academy of German Law). Like Himmler, he had become a member of parliament in 1930. Both men knew each other presumably from their time in the Freikorps Epp division.

[133] Das Braune Haus: the "Brown House," NSDAP headquarters in Munich. [—Trans.]

POCKET CALENDAR

Himmler's return to Munich lasted only a few days, for he had already noted a Hitler rally in Berlin for May 19 in his pocket calendar. For the rest of the month of May he was on the road in Saxony, Thuringia, Franconia, Hessia, and in the Ruhr. There are no letters from those places. An entry in his *Leseliste* indicates that he was in Vienna once again at the beginning of June. In June and July he was back in Berlin.

On August 5–6 he traveled via Berlin to Hamburg-Altona and Kiel. Elections to the regional parliament were being held in Hamburg on September 20, 1931. From Hamburg, Himmler returned briefly to Berlin and shortly thereafter, on August 8–9, he traveled to Düsseldorf again for a meeting with the Führer. He was thus traveling on his daughter's second birthday. On the other hand, he was at home for practically all of September and the first week in October before departing again for a longer trip to North Germany. The following correspondence comes from this period.

———

Schwerin, 10.10.1931

My beloved, good good wife!

We arrived here in Schwerin at 9:00 in the evening after a long but entertaining journey. Captain von Loeper traveled with us as far as Halle, and we had a very good conversation with him.

We were picked up in Schwerin by car. Then had dinner, the Grand Duchess[134] is a highly educated, delightful old lady.—To bed at 11:00 and slept wonderfully until 8:30. In the morning, walked a bit along Lake Schwerin. The country house has a wonderful location. Now off to eat. At 2:00 we shall drive to Rostock. In the evening, I shall then drive to Harzburg.

A thousand kisses now to you and our little daughter.

With love, your Pappi

---

[134] Grand Duchess Elisabeth von Oldenburg, *née* zu Mecklenburg-Schwerin.

At the initiative of the conservative right-wing DNVP, "the national opposition," a mass rally was held in Bad Harzburg on November 11, 1931. The goal was to demonstrate unity in their opposition to the Weimar Republic. Additional participants included: the NSDAP, the Stahlhelm, the Alldeutscher Verband, the Reichslandbund, and individual right-ring personalities. For his part, Hitler demonstrated his distance from the other participants publicly. He showed little willingness to cooperate, and emphasized his absolute claim to leadership of the political right wing with arrogant contempt. A week later, in Braunschweig, he exhibited the independence of the National Socialist movement at their largest rally to date, which 104,000 SA and SS men attended.

"Der Bundschuh"
Militant journal for the awakening of German farmers
Editor: Heinrich Himmler
Waltrudering, Munich-Region VIII
Published and printed: "Der Donaubote," Ingolstadt.
Waldtrudering, 11.10.31

My dear, good husband!

We are both healthy and cheerful. Püppi is sassy and sweet. Out of doors a lot in this splendid weather.—

Telephoned Klussmann yesterday afternoon and found out from him that a new cabinet has been formed. If one is not a Reichstag delegate, a letter is just returned.—[. . .]

I am slaughtering my geese on Thursday, I do not have any more feed.—I wonder how things went in Harzburg!? And what else is going to happen? How pleasant for me that Klussmann wanted to talk to you, now at least I know something. I really hope that you are going to write soon. [I] am doing a lot of sewing because I have to finish by Thursday. Think of the money.— How I would like to be present at all of the great events. I keep hoping that it will soon be possible. The radio announced that Hitler visited Hindenburg accompanied by [?]ng. I wonder what for.—

I was working on a sweater and did it all wrong, so I had to unravel it.—Think of yourself and your health. You are going to need it. And be cautious in Braunschweig. Everybody knows you will *all* be gathering there.

My good beloved, write to me and I greet you most affectionately and kiss you.

From both your
"Big girls"

Reichstag Abgeordneter
Berlin, 13.10.1931

My dear, dear sweetheart!

I just arrived here at the Reichstag at 1:00 from Schwerin. Have already eaten on the train. I just got your good letter. How happy I am that both my "little ones" are so well.—Poor Sweetie, you had to unravel the sweater. So much work! Tonight I shall probably travel to Braunschweig for tomorrow and the day after. The decisive ballots are on Friday. Hitler's visit to Hindenburg was a great success; I am enclosing the payment invoice—so that my good wife will not be upset.

I am also sending money today.—I am also sending you a pile of pamphlets that I have been reading. The author of the yellow one is the Grand Duchess. Why not read it.

I just heard that we are supposed to stay here tomorrow and the day after. That would be disastrous because of Braunschweig.

Many sweet greetings and kisses to you and our "even littler" daughter,

Your husband

Reichstag Abgeordneter
Berlin, 15.10.1931

My sweet, beloved, little wife!

How I long for you.—Here it is just the same horrible old Berlin. It is getting more and more repulsive. Yesterday morning I telephoned Edit. She wants to come next week. I was at Elfriede's in the morning; she was very happy, she wants to visit one day, but her sister-in-law has not returned yet. The clinic is struggling. But at least it's surviving. There is a

Reichstag meeting later. We are not in the assembly hall, but we have to be in the building. I had loads of meetings. In the evening I ate at Ernstl's, Paula was there too and it was very nice.[135] In the evening back to my lodgings at Hotel Minerva near the Anhalt railroad station. This morning Berta called me. Before noon I went visiting, then to the girls.[136] Father telephoned too. We ate together. The girls always have work, but prices are low. They can just about make it, but they get along. Then to the Reichstag with Father and Berta. Then we sat together over coffee. Now I am in my room. [. . .]

Reichstag session here since 12:00, boring as hell. I want to get back to the Kaiserhof at 18:00. I do not yet know what is happening this evening. Perhaps I will get together with Ernstl and Paula.

And now give our little cutie an extra kiss from Pappi.

And greetings and kisses to you, my dearest, I am so fond of you.

Your husband

Reichstag Abgeordneter
Mariensee, (5) *6.11.1931*

My dear good little wife!

I am very very well. I left Munich Tuesday evening. At 7:00 we were awakened in the sleeping car because there was a fire. It was not dangerous, but everyone had to leave the car. Arrived in Berlin a bit behind schedule, was picked up by car, and drove directly to Tilsit. Lorenz got in at Marienburg and Captain Litzmann[137] picked us up in Insterburg. After our tour, by car to Didlaken, where we arrived at 3:00 and stayed at his place. Very nice. Thursday morning hunting with Litzmann and Lorenz; I shot a pheasant, in the afternoon by car to Königsberg. Sightseeing; continued by train to Marienburg, and more

---

[135] Paula Melters (1905–1985), a milliner, had been Ernst Himmler's fiancée for about a year. Heinrich Himmler was a witness at their wedding on July 8, 1933.

[136] The "girls" were probably Marga's unmarried sisters, Lydia and Martha.

[137] Karl-Siegmund Litzmann (1893–1945), career officer and farmer, son of General Litzmann. He became SA-Führer Ostland. [Germany established the Reichskommissariat Ostland (RKO), the government of occupation in the Baltic States, in 1941—Trans.]

sightseeing there.[138] Afterward, by car from Lorenz's to Mariensee, where we arrived at 4:15.[139] Slept until 12:30 today, it was lovely. Took a ride around by car. In the afternoon Count Graving arrived with his wife. Had a very good conversation with him. Soon after dinner we will have a review of the SS Mariensee. Tomorrow I shall get a good night's sleep again. This evening I am going to telephone you again so that you will get some news from your naughty husband. Tomorrow afternoon we are driving to Danzig. I am speaking in the evening.

Now good-bye for today, you good thing, I send you so many loving greetings and kisses,

Your husband

Many greetings to Aunt Elfriede, an extra kiss for Püppi from Pappi

Lauenburg, 9.11.1931

My beloved good little wife!

Your naughty husband is finally getting around to writing again. I am very well. On Friday evening I inspected the SS Mariensee; during the whole trip I was very satisfied. On Saturday we drove to Danzig and stayed in the magnificent house of Frau Lorenz's mother. In the evening I spoke at a farmers' meeting. On Sunday morning there was a large review of SS and SA, 1,500 men, Captain Litzmann was there too. We get along wonderfully. The standard that was presented in Braunschweig was handed over to the SA. Then a magnificent march thanks to the City SAF [SA leader], Martin Loetz [?]

Now much much love, I kiss you and Püppi.

Greetings to Elfriede

In 1931, Himmler was further expanding the SS. One of the basic directives was the so-called Heiratsbefehl [marriage order] of December 31, 1931. This

---

[138] Concerning Marienburg, see commentary on the letter of 7.7.39.
[139] Himmler was a guest of the farmer and SS-Führer Werner Lorenz (1891–1974) at his estate, Mariensee, near Danzig.

required all members of the SS who wished to marry to obtain permission, which was either granted or denied based solely "on considerations of racial and hereditary health." Members of the SS who married despite having had their applications denied could be expelled. Himmler founded a Rassenamt [Racial Bureau] of the SS under the direction of Richard Walther Darré to handle the marriage applications. He, however, reserved the right of final decision to himself in matters regarding marriages of SS members.

Himmler's goal was to accelerate the birthrate in the SS, and he expected his SS men to conceive at least four "genetically healthy" children.

The problem of the declining birthrate had concerned him for some time. In a letter of November 29, 1928, he had reported to Marga that he had just read something about the problem and found it "appalling." In 1924 he read the newly published book *Mehr Sonne: Das Buch der Liebe und der Ehe* [More Sun: The Book of Love and Marriage], by Anton Fendrich, in two days, and had praised it, saying that the book was "ideal," because it proposed "natural and unhampered procreation."

In 1931, Reinhard Heydrich (1904–42) joined the SS. This former naval officer, who had been a member of the NSDAP and SS since the summer of 1931, had had to leave the navy because of a broken marriage promise. He was looking for work and—through the influence of Karl von Eberstein, the SA-Oberführer [senior leader], who was active in Munich and whose mother was also Heydrich's godmother—got the opportunity to apply to Himmler. As Himmler later recalled in an anecdote, he misinterpreted Heydrich's training as a technical communications officer in the navy, surmising that communications officer actually meant intelligence expert, and he therefore hired Heydrich for the Sicherheitsdienst, SD [Secret Service] of the SS, which he planned to expand. At the time, this department consisted of no more staff than Heydrich himself, who had half an office and no typewriter at his disposal. But Heydrich understood how to establish the SD quickly and in doing so gained increasing influence. He was among Himmler's closest colleagues.

POCKET CALENDAR

For the rest of 1931, Himmler noted almost no more meetings. According to this calendar, he was in Berlin twice more, on November 28 and December 6. From there he returned to Munich on December 8. This can be extrapolated from a diary entry by Goebbels of December 9, 1931, which reads, "Group journey to Munich. Whole sleeping car full of Nazis. Discussed things until late at night with the Boss and Himmler."

No pocket calendars survive for the years 1932–34.

Hotel Deutsches Haus
Berchtesgaden 26.1.32

Dear good little wife!

I must quickly write a few lines to you from our Berchtesgaden. It is now 9:30. I woke up at 7:15 and could not get back to sleep, but I stayed in bed. Bathed, shaved, and got dressed. The hotel rooms are heated—wonderful! Going right off to breakfast with the others (Röhm, Seidl, Reiner, Eberstein, Hühnlein and Waldeck.[140] Yesterday we met with Hitler on the way and had coffee with him on Lake Chiemsee. On the trip, the weather in the half-open car was cold and wet. Today it is raining again already, but we are not letting that spoil our good mood. You must not let that happen either. Otherwise, have a stove put in your room.

At 11:00 we are driving to see Hitler on the Obersalzberg (Röhm and I) and will probably stay there with him all afternoon.

So, my dear, now you know what your husband is up to. Give little Püppi with her ducklings a kiss.

Many many loving greetings and kisses, you good thing,

Your husband

---

[140] Ernst Röhm (1887–1934), as the leader of the Bund Reichskriegsflagge [Imperial Battle Flag Group], had been Himmler's mentor through early 1924. From January 1932 on, he was the head of the SA. Siegfried Seidl (1911–1947) joined the NSDAP in Austria in 1930. Rolf Reiner (1899–1944) presumably knew Himmler from 1923 from Röhm's Bund Reichskriegsflagge. From 1931 on, he was Röhm's personal adjutant and his chief of staff. Baron Karl Friedrich von Eberstein (1894–1979) became the full-time SS-Führer in Thuringia in 1930. Adolf Hühnlein (1888–1941), *Generalstabsoffizier* [general staff officer] and SA lieutenant general; 1927 head of the *SA-Kraftfahrwesen* (SA director of transport); in 1931 he founded the NS-Kraftfahrkorps [NS Motorcorps, NSKK].

Hitler and his entourage lodged in the Hotel Deutsches Haus in Berchtesgaden (with its view of the Watzmann Peak) from 1926 on. It was here that he dictated the ending of volume two of his autobiography, *Mein Kampf.* In later years his staff would also stay here after Hitler himself had rented Haus Wachenfeld on the Obersalzberg in 1928. He bought that house in 1933 and had it transformed into the extensive complex called the "Berghof."

Reichstag Abgeordneter
Berlin, 24.2.32

Sweet beloved little wife!

Good little scamp, how are you? I hope there are not too many things bothering you.—On Monday I got to the station just fine and traveled with Reinhardt, Frank II and Rosenberg[141] to Berlin. Slept magnificently. Arrived Tuesday morning, went to the Hotel Kaiserhof, shaved, unpacked, talked with Dietrich.[142] At 11:00 went to a party committee meeting in the Reichstag, 12:00 back to the Kaiserhof. Reported to the Führer, ate lunch, back to the Reichstag. The session began at 15:00, very good speech by Dr. Goebbels. Terrible brawl with the Sozis. 18:30 back to the Kaiserhof. Conferences. 20:00 presented 20 men to the Führer. Conference until 21:30.—I telephoned Elfriede later and was able to get to the Reifschneiders' by 22:00. Herr R. was there as well, was also charming. Stayed for dinner. Elfriede is still hoarse, but otherwise she is fine again, and I think that goes for the clinic as well. The boxes of seed corn are harmless *Bomi* [barley seeds—Trans.]. Fräulein Else Lehmann has excellent references and, according to them and to Elfriede's stories, she is a true gem. I stayed until 1:00, we toasted you—could you tell?—and then I drove home.—

---

[141] Fritz Reinhardt, Hans Frank, and Alfred Rosenberg were also members of the Reichstag. Rosenberg (1893–1946), who had been editor in chief of the *Völkischer Beobachter* since 1923, wrote *Der Mythus des 20. Jahrhunderts* [The Myth of the 20th Century] (1930).

[142] Joseph ("Sepp") Dietrich (1892–1966), police officer; he and Himmler knew each other from their early days in the SS; in 1928 Dietrich had founded the first SS-Standarte [SS unit] in Munich. He also became a member of the Reichstag in 1930.

Got up today at 8:45, slept wonderfully. This morning chief of staff von du Moulin arrived.[143] Breakfast together, and had a wonderful conversation.

11:30 to Hedemannstr., which houses the whole Munich Propagandaabteilung [Propaganda Division], which coordinates elections.

[Continuation missing.]

———————

The year 1932 was, in modern German political jargon, a "super-election year," a term that designates a year in which several elections take place. When the Reich president had to be newly elected early in 1932, the NSDAP proposed Hitler as their own candidate rather than join an alliance in support of Hindenburg's reelection. The party styled him as *Führer des Jungen Deutschland* [leader of young Germany], in opposition to the "moribund system" of Weimar and the elderly Hindenburg. In the first round of voting on March 13, 1932, Hindenburg won with 49.6 percent. While he was clearly ahead of Hitler, who received 30.1 percent of the votes, he had nonetheless failed to achieve an absolute majority, which made a second ballot necessary. In the run-off election on April 10, Hindenburg garnered 53 percent of the vote, but Hitler's tally rose to 36.8 percent—an election result for the National Socialists that was twice as high as it had been in the Reichstag elections of 1930.

In the regional elections held during the following months in Mecklenburg-Strelitz, Bavaria, Hamburg, Oldenburg, Mecklenburg-Schwerin, Hessia, and Thuringia, the NSDAP emerged as the strongest party in all states except Bavaria. In Prussia, where a Social Democrat–led government had existed since 1919, the number of National Socialist seats rose from 9 to 162, which meant that the Social Democrats relinquished one third of their seats. Otto Braun, the Social Democratic *Ministerpräsident* [Prime Minister], stepped down in frustration.

The continuing economic crisis ensured that trust in Brüning's competence ebbed and that the intrigues proliferated against him in the circle around the Reich president. Early in June 1932, Franz von Papen of the DNP became the

———————

[143] Karl Leon du Moulin-Eckart (1900–1991), politician and SA leader who had known Himmler since 1924 at least; 1930–32 he was the head of the Nachtrichtendienst [Information Bureau] of the SA in the Brown House; also one of Röhm's adjutants.

new Reich chancellor. He immediately dissolved parliament and scheduled new elections for July 31. These elections—as Hitler declared to the NSDAP Gauleiter—would have to be "a final reckoning of the German people with the politics of the last fourteen years." The party propaganda machine under Goebbels designated the SPD as the main adversary. The primary election slogan was "Deutschland erwache! Gebt Adolf Hitler die Macht!" [Germany, awake! Give power to Adolf Hitler!].

The election campaign was characterized by extreme violence. In Prussia alone, during the ten days leading up to the election, 24 people were killed and more than 280 injured. On Sunday, July 17, in Altona near Hamburg, a parade of National Socialist demonstrators marched through the workers' quarter. Shots were fired, which then led to a full-fledged gun battle among police, demonstrators, and residents. Eighteen people were killed, mostly innocent bystanders. This so-called Bloody Sunday of Altona was the pretext used by the Papen government on July 20 to issue an emergency decree that ousted the existing Prussian government administration. In a coup d'état, Papen then appointed himself provisional Ministerpräsident. The opposition that was expected from the Social Democrats and the unions never materialized.

When the voting booths closed on the evening of July 31, 1932, one of the most embittered election campaigns of the Weimar years had ended. The decisive loser in this election was the liberal-conservative middle-class center; the German Nationals (DNP) also registered losses; the Social Democrats (SPD) received only 21.6 percent of the votes; the Communists (KPD) came in at 14.3 percent. The NSDAP, by comparison, was the conspicuous winner. Its 37.3 percent of the votes and 230 seats in the Reichstag meant that National Socialism had become by far the largest party in Germany.

"Der Bundschuh"
Waldtrudering, 5.3.32

My dear good husband!

You will be calling me from Munich!?

I arrived here safely and found a healthy, happy Püppi. I do not have the money from the post office yet, I telephoned them, and they said you had claimed you would collect it yourself—Lydia arrives tomorrow morning, Bastians is picking me up, we are taking Püppi along too. We were supposed to go to the Klussmanns' in the afternoon but I declined, saying it was too much for Lydia . . . —On Tuesday Bastians is supposed to pick up my hog casings and the meat.[144] You will be here then and can tell him yourself. We will not see each other until Tues. night, because I am not coming [into Munich] on Tuesday.—Everything here is just normal. Last night people plastered our entire fence with our [political] posters. As a result, a lot of people stop and read.—I have written to Dütz [?] and also ordered the rabbits.

Your suitcase is packed, I hope everything is in it.

All right then, see you on Tuesday.

    1000 greetings and kisses

    Your Marga

Unterwössen, 31.7. [32]

My dear Pappi!

    Püppi is never home, there are little girls next door and P. is beginning to make friends. It is just too cute. In addition to us, Frau Berkelmann lives here.[145] We slept wonderfully. I am sitting on a balcony. There's also a grandmother in the house, who looks after her now and then.

    The Unterwössen [river valley—Trans.] lies below us. I hope it does not rain, because everything here is indescribably primitive. You can only hold out until the end of the week here. How are you? I told Bastians that I shall be waiting for your telephone call tomorrow morning between 9–10:00. I am hoping. We are supposed to go to the Blösls' at noon, but we will be cooking

---

[144] Marga slaughtered her own pigs.

[145] Gabriele Berkelmann was the wife of Theodor Berkelmann (1894-1943), SA-Standartenführer [colonel—Trans.], Himmler's adjutant beginning March 1932. In July, Gudrun and Lydia were living at the Berkelmanns' at first, after the Himmlers' house in Waldtrudering had been shot at [*Childhood Journal* of August 14, 1932]. They subsequently stayed with Marga and later also with Heinrich for a while in the Chiemgau in places such as Gasthof Daxenberg, which belonged to an old party member, Hans Blösl. Later, the Himmlers would often take vacations at this inn.

in the Reichstag elections of November 6. In contrast to the July
he NSDAP lost 2 million votes and declined from 37.3 percent to
ent. It nonetheless remained the strongest party.

political situation, which had ground to a halt, was not changed by the
n results. The so-called Cabinet of the Barons under Franz von Papen
supported by no more than 10 percent of the electorate, whereas
percent had voted for parties that opposed the government in power. Papen's
disguised vote for a dictatorial solution intended to eliminate the parliament and failed in part because it collided with the military leadership. He
resigned in mid-November. At the same time, his successor, General Kurt von
Schleicher, (*Reichswehrminister* [minister of the army]) and influential politician in the inner circle around President Hindenburg, attempted to create a
third position with the unions and a portion of the NSDAP under Gregor
Strasser, the organizational leader of the NSDAP. In a secret meeting on December 3, Schleicher offered Strasser the offices of vice-chancellor and Prussian Ministerpräsident. Strasser, however, did not dare defy Hitler. A few days
later, when the party leadership declared allegiance to Hitler, Strasser resigned
from all offices and left Berlin. A year and a half later, in the purge of the SA
leadership of June 1934, both Gregor Strasser and Kurt von Schleicher were
assassinated.

The party crisis at the end of 1932 is also evident in Himmler's reading
matter. In September he read Hans F. K. Günther's *Platon als Hüter des Leb-
ens* (1928) [Plato as Defender of Life] and commented, "I hope we shall succeed, that we are not too late, the way Plato came too late for his people." In
October, furthermore, he noted, about Heinrich Bauer's *Oliver Cromwell: Ein
Kampf um Freiheit und Diktatur* (1932) [Oliver Cromwell: A Struggle for Freedom and Dictatorship]: "We can learn much from this."

Grevenburg, 5.1.33

My dear good little wife!

Our accommodations here are magnificent in an old (1540)
Westphalian moated castle, full of culture, with charming hosts, Baron [and
Baroness] von Oeynhausen. They have three boys.

our own supper. Otherwise things get t⸻
bed costs per day. And then everythi⸻
on 8 M a day.

I wonder what this evening will bring a⸻

Be well, my dear good beloved. I kiss you⸻

With my most affectionate greetings,

Your Marga

Waldi⸻

My dear good husband!

This letter has to go out today so that it reaches you in Danzig⸻
surely be staying in Danzig until Monday. And then you can relax a bi⸻
Mariensee.

There are surely still many more worries ahead of us, so much is
happening in politics.

My stomach is gradually getting better. If Frau Fürstin [princess—Trans.]
Weikertsheim is home on 5.9, I shall telephone her and say that we are not
buying the property. Then that will be an end to the entire matter. Otherwise
we shall just have to keep waiting.—Write and say whether you are coming
directly home or whether you have to stay in Berlin. Do not have any sad
thoughts, when you come we will be in a position to change many things, and
then we shall do so.

[Continuation missing.]

———

After his electoral victory in July, Hitler justifiably hoped that Hindenburg
would appoint him Reich chancellor. But the Reich president would not do
so, and offered Hitler the vice-chancellorship in a cabinet formed by Papen,
which Hitler declined. Hitler's refusal to be satisfied with merely participating in power led the NSDAP—a party already certain of victory, hungry for
power, and fed up with the opposition—into a major crisis in the winter of
1932–33.

This made new elections unavoidable. The disappointment in the general
public at the inability of the parties to find a solution to the political crisis expressed itself in the rise in the number of nonvoters from 7.0 million in July to

Yesterday was interesting but strenuous. After a 6 hour car trip from Cologne, we arrived in the Lipperland[146] at our quarters at 13:00 and got to bed at [?]:30. Slept wonderfully until noon today. Ate at 13:00. Conference[es, continuation missing].

With the support of Goebbels, Hitler focused on the National Socialist movement's ability to consolidate power and on gaining limitless authority. The regional elections in the small state of Lippe-Detmold on January 15, 1933, were exaggerated as proof of the unbroken strength of National Socialism. By virtue of its immense election campaign, the NSDAP was able to increase its share of the vote to 39.5 percent. By comparison with the election result of July 1932, the party had actually received fewer votes, but the stage management of this accomplishment was a triumph, and Hitler emerged from the election stronger.

Beginning in early January 1933, Hitler and Papen engaged in private negotiations behind the scenes. Papen believed he would be able to keep Hitler under control as Reich chancellor. In the meantime, the clique around Hindenburg had already been persuaded to support Hitler's appointment. After Schleicher's resignation on January 28, Hindenburg also showed that he tended to support a Hitler cabinet, especially since Papen had won over the German Nationals and their party leader, Alfred Hugenberg, for the new cabinet. On January 30, at 12:00 noon, Hitler was sworn in as the new Reich chancellor.

One day after this seizure of power[147] Himmler received numerous letters of congratulations, among them a letter from his parents. His father, Gebhard, wrote, "Dear Heinrich! We have just written to the Reich Chancellor, and to you, and today our sincerest congratulations also go to you for the success and victory of the Movement in which you have played such a great part. So then, finally, a foothold within the fortress. [. . .]" And his mother writes: "[. . .] We were so very pleased to get your card from Lippe containing Hitler's autograph, which we have wanted for such a long time. [. . .]" Both of Himmler's parents became party members in November 1933. Ernst Himmler had already

---

[146] Lippe is a district in the east of North Rhine–Westphalia. [—Trans.]
[147] The NS term for this "power grab" was *Machtergreifung*. [—Trans.]

joined the NSDAP in November 1931. In May 1932 Hilde Himmler, Gebhard
Jr.'s wife, became a party member by proxy for her husband, who was a civil
servant. In 1933 both brothers joined the SS.

Early in February 1933, Heinrich Himmler and his family moved into a spa-
cious apartment on Munich's Prinzregentenstrasse. Their house in Waldtrudering was sold.

Letters

1933–39

"Everything was very nice. The Führer *came.
[. . .] It was wonderful to sit at a table with him
in a small group."*
MARGA HIMMLER, JOURNAL ENTRY, MAY 3, 1938

After the National Socialists came to power in January 1933, Himmler's career did not progress smoothly.[148] Right after the Reichstag election of March 5, 1933, he had to be content with the office of chief of police of Munich. By April 1933, however, after the removal of the Bavarian government, he advanced to the position of *Commandeur der Bayrischen Politischen Polizei* [commander of the Bavarian political police]. His first official act was to establish a concentration camp in Dachau near Munich. The combination of SS, political police, and concentration camp proved to be very successful within the NS system. Hitler did not want to leave the suppression of political opposition in the hands of the established civic bodies, police, and the legal system. Thus the political police—which, after the Prussian model, were soon universally called Geheime Staatspolizei [State Secret Police, the Gestapo]—became the most essential

---

[148] Only one of Heinrich Himmler's letters from the first years after the party came to power has been preserved in its entirety. There are individual letters by Marga Himmler from the years 1937 and 1939. Other documents, therefore, have been used to supplement this material: Marga's *Journal* from 1937 on; Gudrun's *Childhood Journal* from the documents in Tel Aviv; and Lydia Boden's *Erinnerungsbuch* [Memoirs] and *Um und mit Gerhard 1933–1945* [Near and with Gerhard 1933–1945] (Berlin and Gmund am Tegernsee, 1955), which was written for Gerhard von der Ahé and graciously made available from his father's estate by Horst von der Ahé.

police apparatus for repression. Its formation was made possible by the State of Emergency Decree of February 28, 1933, following the burning of the Reichstag. Together with the concentrations camps, in which the inmates were imprisoned without due process or legal representation, this created a system of terror that swiftly crushed all political opposition.

Hotel Bristol-Britannia, 14.6.1933

My good, good sweetie!

It is too beautiful here. I am living on the Canale Grande and have a wonderful view.[149] I sleep well and am living as if I were in paradise.—Mami, I have bought such things, you just cannot imagine.

Yesterday we went swimming on the Lido. In the evening we took a gondola. Mami, you have to come and do this too and see it all.

Today we visited St. Mark's Church and the Campanile. Tomorrow the Doge's Palace.

Today (afternoon) it even rained here, and it is cool.

My beloved ones, I hope you are doing well.

Greetings and kisses to you, my dear ones, Mami, Püppi, and Bubi,
Your Pappi

Bubi is the pet name for the Himmlers' foster son, Gerhard von der Ahé (1928–2010), who came to live with them in March 1933. His father was an SS man who had died in street fights in Berlin in February 1933. Because his mother had difficulty caring for Gerhard and his elder brother alone, it must have been a relief for her that the Reichsführer-SS[150] took a personal interest in one of her sons. Heinrich Himmler had always wished for a son, but Marga could not bear any more children. The blond son of an SS man who had fallen in action must have appeared as the ideal foster son. Marga writes about their early days with Gerhard in her *Childhood Journal*: "He is a handsome, bright boy. Püppi has

---

[149] It is unclear why and with whom Himmler was in Venice in June 1933.
[150] Commander, the highest rank in the SS. As Reichsführer-SS, Himmler became the highest-ranking officer and commander of the SS.

been immensely happy, and she comforted him whenever he wanted to go home and when he cried. [. . .] I am expecting so much for her own development through this contact with another child. The boy is very obedient, let us hope Püppi soon learns to be so too" (10.3.33).

In the months following the NSDAP seizure of power in 1933, Himmler was able to assume leadership of the various political police units in the different German states. In April 1934 he finally also became inspector of the secret police (Gestapo) in Prussia, the largest and most important state. Hermann Göring, the Prussian Ministerpräsident, had taken over the state Gestapo directly. The fact that he approved Himmler's appointment relates to the power struggle within the NS leadership, which would culminate in the bloody purge of the SA in June 1934. The murderers' victims were not only countless SA leaders, but also conservative politicians and generals such as the last Reich chancellor, Kurt von Schleicher, and others who were persona non grata, such as Gregor Strasser. The perpetrators of these murders came from the ranks of the SS. They emerged stronger from this power struggle, finally separated themselves from the SA, and were designated by Hitler as an independent organization, especially obligated to him through their Treue zum Führer [fidelity to the Führer]. Himmler was proud of the intimidation tactics of the SS. In November 1935 he stated in a speech "that there are many people in Germany who are sickened when they see this black uniform; we understand that and we do not expect to be loved by very many."

In 1936 Himmler reached the pinnacle of his prewar power. In June Hitler elevated him to the position of chief of all German police. In other words, in addition to the Gestapo, he now led the Kriminalpolizei [Criminal Police],[151] the green-uniformed Schutzpolizei[152] [Security Police Force], and the Landgendarmerie [Rural Police]. Together with his function as Reichsführer-SS and commander of the concentration camps (which were centralized and expanded in 1937), Himmler was now one of the most powerful men in the NS system. Reinhard Heydrich, who was head of the Sicherheitsdienst [Security Service, SD] of the SS, took over the leadership of the Sicherheitspolizei

---

[151] The Kriminalpolizei (Kripo) designates the criminal investigation agency within the police.

[152] The Schutzpolizei (Schupo) were a branch of the Landespolizei [state police]

[Security Police], which combined the Gestapo and the Kripo. Kurt Daluege became the *Chef der Ordnungspolizei*[153] [Chief of Order Police], which included all other police units.

Himmler's appointment as head of the Prussian Gestapo in 1934 meant that he now had to be present in Berlin, which affected his private life. The Himmlers had lived in their Munich town apartment for just under a year because in 1934 they had already purchased Haus Lindenfycht in Gmund, on the Tegernsee. They had bought it from the singer Alois Burgstaller for 65,000 gold marks with the financial support of the NSDAP, thereby realizing their shared dream of a house on a lake. In the same year, they moved into an official apartment on Hagenstrasse in Berlin's elegant Grunewald quarter. In the following years, they commuted regularly back and forth between Gmund and Berlin. Marga complains about this repeatedly in her *Journal*: "All this packing nonsense. How many days a year are we on the road!" (8.1.38) and: "Gmund on the Tegernsee. Now we are back again, and how I wish we had never moved. Moving 8x a year! But H. thinks it is fine" (4.4.39). Several staff members came with each of the two households, including a servant, cook, and gardener. The staff changed frequently because, according to Marga, there was "nothing but friction" with them and they were, apparently, "disrespectful and lazy."

Haus Lindenfycht stood on an extensive property that offered sufficient room to raise ponies, sheep, pigs, and deer. There was a fish pond, a greenhouse, a private dock, and a meadow behind the house on which one could play croquet in summer and fill with water in winter to make a skating pond. In a separate building, the SS command post Gmund was located. Three or four SS members were always in residence there. In 1938, Himmler had a two-story guesthouse built on the property, using prisoners from one of the Dachau satellite camps as construction workers.

In spring 1937 Landhaus Dohnenstieg, a fourteen-room villa at 10 Dohnenstieg in Berlin-Grunewald, became available to Himmler. In addition, he later acquired three former customs buildings in the Valepp, an Alpine village on the Austrian border near Gmund; he had these buildings renovated as a hunt-

---

[153] The Ordnungspolizei (Order Police [ORPo]) were the regular police of the Third Reich, sometimes called "green" police because of the color of their uniforms. [—Trans.]

ing lodge. Himmler had known the Valepp region[154] since his childhood, and had spent time hunting here. After the renovation, the house was used primarily for summer vacations. Occasionally, foreign guests were received here, as in 1939 when the chief of the Italian police, Arturo Bocchini, paid a visit.

Marga's younger sister, Lydia Boden, a trained seamstress, a spinster, and a member of the NSDAP since 1932, gave Haus Lindenfycht as her permanent address from 1934 on. During the following years she frequently cared for Gudrun and the foster son, Gerhard, when the parents were either in Berlin or traveling for political or social reasons.

In her *Memoirs* she describes the frequent presence of the Himmler parents. She emphasizes the high esteem that the family had for her mostly absent brother-in-law. For example, she writes idealized descriptions of holidays and vacations spent together. "The parents came on vacation for a little while in the summer, then we took several trips. We went to the Valepp. We went by car through the Tegernsee Valley and into the mountains. We got up as far as the milking huts, then we drank coffee, then climbed higher to a hunting lodge. The last part we had to do on foot. In the mountain meadows we found many rare types of orchid, and through our binoculars, you could see far up to the mountaintops. It was always beautiful."

Once a year Marga and Heinrich Himmler took a vacation without the children. It was always for three to four weeks in November or December. For example, in 1936 they spent four weeks in Wiesbaden. In 1937, following an official visit to Italy, they later took a vacation in Sicily with a side trip to Libya. In 1938 they traveled to Salzburg and again to Wiesbaden.

The Himmlers kept in close contact with the Ribbentrop, Wedel, and Johst families. In 1920 Joachim von Ribbentrop (1893–1946) had married Annelies Henkell (1896–1973), daughter of the producer of sparkling wine, Henkell, who had made a fortune as a wine merchant. Both became members of the NSDAP in 1932. Ribbentrop advanced to the position of Hitler's foreign policy adviser. From 1936 to 1937 he was the German ambassador in London; in February 1938 he became Reich foreign minister. Annelies Ribbentrop was generally considered her husband's most important adviser and the driving power behind

---

[154] Valepp refers to a mountain valley as well as a stream and a village in the Bavarian Alps. [—Trans.]

his career. At official events, such as the Italian trip of 1938, or the annual party rallies in Nuremberg, Marga Himmler preferred to spend her time with Annelies Ribbentrop. During the 1930s they used to invite each other frequently to dinners or to tea. Yet this friendship was not free of rivalry. When Ribbentrop became foreign minister in 1938, Marga would write in her *Journal*, "Ribbentrop has become foreign minister. H. is very nervous. He had to collaborate on this day and night and was not promoted himself."

The Wedels were also good friends. The estate owner, Wilhelm Alfred Count von Wedel (1891–1939), was the police prefect of Potsdam from 1935 until his death in 1939. His wife, Ida von Wedel (1895–1971), was a close friend of Marga, who had joined the party before her husband. After his death, she would sometimes come to tea in the afternoon or drop in for evening bridge parties at the Himmlers'.

The author Hanns Johst (1890–1978) lived on the Starnbergersee [Lake Starnberg] with his wife, Hanne, and their daughter. During the 1930s, both families would often visit each other when the Himmlers happened to be in Gmund, and would spend the days swimming, fishing, or playing badminton together. Hanns Johst and Heinrich Himmler were personally very close. They shared imperialist, pan-German dreams and in 1934 took a trip to Pomerania together. Johst published many articles in the *SS-Leithefte* [SS guide booklets] and in the Schwarzes Korps [The Black Corps] and during the war visited Himmler several times at his headquarters in the occupied Soviet Union.

———

Berlin, 25.5.[37]

My dear good husband!

Now I am leaving tomorrow morning. Herr Böhmer (architect) told me that he had not yet received a reference number from Herr Bormann for iron and the like for Haus Dohnenstieg and in some places they were going to have to stop work! The interior decorator led me, actually directed me, to a Frau von Haustein, and presented me with the same swatches and paint samples as before. I was *beside myself*. I wasted almost 2 hours for nothing. It is so disrespectful to act that way. I shall give you all the details in person.—The gardener from Dohenstieg was here, his wife makes an excellent impression. Would you remember that somebody has to talk with them as soon as possible about the finances and prices, etc.?! We do not want to give the impression that nobody is paying any attention to them. Please do not forget!!

I told Maria that she could leave any time, then she wanted to stay because she had not found a new job yet, etc. The question is now still open. If she does not find a job, we are going to have to keep her for another month. But I do not think it makes much sense anymore. I am sticking to saying: "Stay until you have found something." And I will ask you to please do the same.

And now I've unburdened myself to you a little bit, my good husband, and now I can go to bed feeling calm. Write to me and forward the mail.

My good husband, your
Mami

Königsberg, 28.5.37
4 Regentenstr.

My dear good husband!

I have arrived here safely and I am very well. Martin got on the train back in Berlin and in Elbing so did H. v. Schade,[155] so I was hardly ever alone. It was indescribably hot. We went to the theater yesterday. Good, very good. How are you? Have a lot to do? When should I be in Danzig? Do I have to visit both women in D.? When are you coming to D.? I hear I am not allowed to take any money along to D., what am I supposed to do? Please write me about this soon, and forward my mail to me.

With warmest greetings and kisses,
your M.

Greetings from the Schades.
Telephone Königsberg 22025.

---

[155] Marga was visiting mutual friends in Königsberg, Hermann Baron von Schade (1888–1966) and his wife Erna (b. 1891). As *SS-Brigadenführer* [brigade leader], he led the SS unit Königsberg in 1936–37.

[Place and date are almost completely obliterated. Only "Königsberg" is
legible.]

My dear good husband!

The three of us are just about to have a large lobster dinner. You see how
well I am doing here. The terrible heat has subsided a little bit. I am sitting here
in peace and quiet, and you have to work so terribly hard. It depresses me.
Would it not be better if I came home and tried to take care of you a bit? You
know how I would like to do that. Your telephone call today made me very
happy, my good husband. I heard from Lydia once, they are well. The goslings,
I cannot stop thinking about them.—Everything is finally settled with the
gardener. I find it just too much that you are going to have to help out again with
this business with the interior decorator. Shouldn't I perhaps be talking to
Speer?[156] I can take care of the money situation right here. Then on Tuesday
8.6, you will be in Danzig; [Rest of this line obliterated.]

What, do you think, should I go to see Frau Prützmann?[157] Telephone me
and tell me what you think. Then I will do what you think is right, it makes
no difference to me.—Then on the 9th we are going to fly from Danzig. Can't
we then go to the Schmitts' on the 9th? They would really like to invite us.
The maid for Gmund will arrive in Gmund on 1.6. And I have a new one to
replace Maria too. So that settles the question for now.—It is too bad that I
have not found any good books to read, you know my taste. Have things sent
special delivery. It would also be so nice to have them for Danzig. You know,
people mostly read gothic novels.

Many affectionate greetings to you, my beloved,
Your M.

The Schades send their greetings.

---

[156] Albert Speer (1905–81), Reich minister for armaments and production from 1942 to 1945.
He had studied architecture and was Hitler's favorite architect. He spent the early war years
preparing plans for rebuilding cities. After 1942 he was appointed controller of armaments
and thus would have had to authorize the supplies for Himmler's house. [—Trans.]

[157] Christa Prützmann (b. 1916) was the wife of SS-Gruppenführer Hans-Adolf Prützmann
(1901–45), who became the Höherer SS- und Polizeiführer Nord-West (Hamburg) [HSSPF:
higher SS and police leader of Hamburg]. On April 28, 1935, the Himmlers traveled to the
Prützmanns' wedding.

Königsberg, 1.6.1937

My dear, sweet husband!

I thought that yesterday you were going to say that I should come home, I would like to have done so. It is not right that I am sitting here quietly while you are chasing around the world[158] and cannot even get supper at home. That depresses me greatly. I am doing very well here, I just miss you and the children, and my house in Gmund where I could be doing so much. Yesterday I was all upset. Our poor Führer. As a weak woman, one can do nothing about all these big matters.—I am doing so well here, peace, relaxation every day. I will not go visit Aunt Martha until Saturday. I just telephoned Frau Prützmann. It was fine with her if I come out there and visit her on Thursday afternoon with Frau von Schade, it is good hour's drive by car.—have you sent me any books? I write to Lydia almost every day. Are you going to telephone me again Friday morning!

With many, many affectionate greetings and kisses,

Your M.

Himmler expanded his travels increasingly during the 1930s. He cultivated intensive contacts with Italian and later also Spanish Fascists. At the same time, he maintained close relationships in Berlin with diplomats from different countries, especially those allied with Germany. This clearly led to a strong interest in learning English, as one can discern from the pocket calendar of 1936 concerning their vacation in Wiesbaden and from Marga Himmler's *Journal* about vacations in 1937 and 1938.

Himmler had been interested in Mussolini's fascism since 1929. At the time, he read *Der Schmied Roms* [The Smith of Rome], by Adolf Stein (published in 1929 under the pseudonym Rumpel-stilzchen), a book in which he found Italian fascism and its leader to be "brilliantly" described and evaluated. Before his trip to Venice in June 1933, Himmler himself had been in Rome for the first time in December 1932. He maintained his admiration for Mussolini for many years. When Marga and Gudrun were planning a trip to Rimini in 1941, he recommended that they visit the house where Mussolini

----

[158] On June 5–6, Himmler had meetings in different places in Bavaria; on June 8 he noted in his pocket calendar, "Picked up Mami, then to Danzig w.o. [without] Mami."

was born, and in his letter of September 19, 1943, he ruefully referred to the dictator as a "dying lion."

On April 1, 1936, a half year before negotiations about the alliance between the two countries (the Berlin-Rome Axis), Himmler forged a secret agreement concerning German-Italian police cooperation with his Italian counterpart, the chief of the Italian police, Arturo Bocchini. In November and December 1937, shortly after Mussolini's state visit to Berlin, the Himmlers took a fairly long trip to Rome, Naples, Sicily, and Libya. Marga kept a detailed journal of the trip.

On November 16, 1937, she wrote about sightseeing in Rome: "The day began at 10:00 with a visit to the Capitol. Then on to the forums. Mussolini was the one who first excavated all the magnificent buildings. H's historical knowledge on the subject was unbelievable. [. . .] Today the first news of the children arrived. They are well. This evening we are going to the Schaumburgs', it is at the German embassy to the Italian Empire. Magnificent flowers awaited me when I arrived, from Boccini [sic], the Bergens (ambassador to the Holy See), the Bergens (Ambassador to the Holy See), Ettel (*Landesleiter*),[159] etc."

From Rome they traveled south by car with a police escort. Marga was enthusiastic about everything in Italy: the food, the landscape, the classical buildings, the reception that was prepared for them everywhere, and the many children: "We meet lots of children everywhere, what a blessed land this is" (Naples, 19.11.37). In Taormina they spent two weeks swimming, playing tennis and bridge, and taking day trips to Syracuse, Palermo, and Catania. They visited countless churches, cloisters, catacombs, Greek and Roman excavation sites, and the museums where the artifacts were exhibited.

During a brief visit to the Libyan oasis of Ghadames, she reported that "everything [looked] just as it had 2,000 years ago, but it is all clean." Her conclusion after a further city tour of al Khums was in a similar vein: "In the Jewish quarter, terribly dirty, and what a stench! The Arabs are much cleaner!" On this trip the Himmlers consistently sought out Germanic artifacts, and followed the tracks of the Hohenstaufen Emperor Frederick II, for example, when they

---

[159] Erwin Ettel (1895–1971), member of the German Foreign Service and deputy at the German Legation in Rome.

visited a castle from the Hohenstaufen period in Cosenza (19.11.37) or, on their return trip, when they visited "the grave and site where Conradin, the last Hohenstaufen, was beheaded" (9.12.37).

In January 1938, Himmler issued the order to all Gestapo offices in Germany and Austria (which had been annexed in March) to arrest so-called "asocials" and to imprison them in the Buchenwald concentration camp. This move, which sent approximately fifteen hundred people to the concentration camp, was, however, only a prelude to a greater wave of arrests in June 1938. This time every headquarters of the Criminal Police was issued a specific quota—namely, to arrest at least two hundred able-bodied "asocial" men. The police filled the quota three times over. In total, approximately ten thousand men were arrested and sent to concentration camps.

Among the imprisoned "asocial" concentration camp inmates were countless Gypsies (Roma and Sintis). In 1936 several large cities had begun to build camps for their Gypsy populations and had interned hundreds in miserable, unhygienic conditions. A special report in the Criminal Police headquarters focused on the elimination of the "plague of Gypsies." In December 1938, Himmler ordered a report on all Gypsies in Germany based on racial biology.

In March 1938 the annexation of Austria was carried out as a first step in an aggressive expansion of the regime, which involved intensified anti-Semitic policies. In Vienna and elsewhere, Austrians gave vent to their anti-Semitic hatred. Jewish shops were looted, Jews were arbitrarily arrested, driven from their homes, and physically maltreated; plunder for personal gain was the order of the day. 1938 became the fateful year for German Jews. After they were deprived of their rights, they were then systematically robbed of their fortunes; their shops and businesses were "Aryanized" or liquidated. The German state demanded such high taxes and fees from those who could still flee abroad, that they were left with almost nothing.

The next target was Czechoslovakia. The Sudeten-German minority in that country demanded to be absorbed into the German Reich, and the NS leadership fanned the flames of hatred between Germans and Czechs in order to crush Czechoslovakia. The western powers attempted to defuse the conflict. The British prime minister, Neville Chamberlain, the French premier, Édouard

Daladier, and Mussolini traveled to Germany in September 1938 to negotiate with Hitler. The Munich Agreement forced the Czech government to concede the Sudentenland. Yet with that, the war that Hitler wanted had not been averted.

In October a diplomatic conflict with Poland that had been festering since the spring led to further massive police actions against the Jews. The Polish government intended to implement an anti-Semitic policy of denying citizenship to Poles living abroad (especially aimed at Polish Jews) and to designate them as such by requiring special notations in their passports to prevent them from returning to Poland. On October 26, 1938, in response to this, Himmler issued a blanket denial of residence permits to Polish Jews and ordered them to leave the German Reich within three days. On October 28, the Gestapo initiated a mass operation, rounded up about seventeen thousand Polish Jews, and shipped them to the Polish border. Because Poland denied these people entry, they were left to wander around in no-man's-land and the border towns without any help, food, or sanitation. Only after a few days, when Poland and Germany agreed to an extension of the three-day expulsion order, did Himmler call a halt to this operation. It was this coldly calculated, brutal operation that motivated the young Herschel Grynszpan, whose parents had been deported, to assassinate Ernst vom Rath, a German diplomat in Paris, on November 7, 1938.

What happened everywhere in Germany during the night of November 9, 1939, exceeded by far the brutality, vandalism, and bloodlust of all previous pogroms. In plain sight, the SA troops broke windows, plundered shops, beat up the Jewish owners, and forced their way into Jewish dwellings, where they destroyed the furnishings, abused the occupants, and did not restrain themselves from committing murder. In the public streets, countless people were literally beaten to death. In the following days approximately thirty-five thousand Jewish men were arrested, sent to concentration camps, and released only when they relinquished all their possessions and emigrated immediately with their families.

On January 30, 1939, Hitler gave his speech to the Reichstag in which he called upon the European powers to provide a "solution to the Jewish Question," and ended with the threat that, if it were to come to war, the result would not be the "Bolshevization of the earth," but rather the "destruction of the Jewish race in Europe."

No letters of Himmler's survive from the year 1938, but we have detailed journal entries by Marga instead, which reflect the most important political events of the year and make clear how closely she was connected to the social life of the politicians in power.

[February 21, 1938]
Yesterday the Führer's tremendous speech. H. was at home in the afternoon and again talked about expanding [the house]. I was incredibly exhausted, went to bed early. H. still had to go to Hess's for a beer evening. The invitation from the Ministry of Propaganda was on Saturday. It was very boring, we left early. H. was also too worn out. The poor Wedels. The Oswalds are arriving today. Tinchen is going to England and wants to say good-bye. Eden[160] left after the Führer's speech yesterday. H. is sitting downstairs having tea with some gentlemen. I was at the Bülows' with Püppi yesterday. There were many ladies there. Tomorrow I am going to play bridge with four ladies here at my place, Frau Attolico is one of them. In the morning I want to pay a visit to the wife of the Japanese ambassador.

[March 5, 1938]
I always lie in bed until midnight and wait for Heini. [. . .] H. is cheerful and brave, and I am trying to be cheerful too.

[March 13, 1938]
Trouble would not leave us alone anymore, every day something new happened. H. understood what it was about, naturally, was in a good mood and downright cheerful. But for me, who see nothing but the frantic activity

---

[160] Anthony Eden (1897–1977), British foreign minister.

of his job, and have to pack up the military uniform, it was too depressing.
[. . .] Austria is now part of the German Reich. H. was the first one in Vienna.
The celebration was indescribable when the Führer entered Braunau early on
Saturday. Now the triumphal parade continues on to Vienna. H. telephoned
today from Vienna, things are going very well for him, he is healthy, and
overwhelmed by it all. We women sit here and have to make do with the radio.

———————

All the same, Marga Himmler clearly enjoyed the new social life after the isola-
tion of the country years in Waldtrudering. Invitations and return invitations,
elaborate dinners, teas with diplomats' wives, and the emotional lives of the
most important politicians engaged her throughout the year.

———————

[May 3, 1938]
     Everything was very nice. The Führer came. Püppi was very
excited. It was wonderful to sit at a table with him in a small group.
Things are not going too well with Heini's health. Has an immense
amount to do [. . .]. I am having some clothes made for myself. The
political situation is unsettled. The Führer is on the mountain [i.e.,
Obsersalzberg—Trans.]. Göring does not look very healthy. Father may
have water in his lungs. [. . .]

———————

In her *Journal*, Marga writes enthusiastically about Hitler's official state visit
to Rome in May 1938, where special events were scheduled for the ladies in
the large entourage:

———————

[May 4 and 8, 1938]
     The trip was entertaining and nice. We were immediately received with
great ceremony. The next morning we took a sightseeing tour through Rome and
I could refresh my memories, be pleased about how well-informed I am. [. . .]
     Gymnastic-athletic spectacle by Italian youth. They were terrific. What a
people Mussolini has created!

[July 3, 1938]

I have been married ten years today. H. is away on a trip, but he telephoned. Despite the happiness of marriage, I have had to do without a lot when it comes to marriage. Because H. is almost never here and does not know anything but work.

———

Marga was regularly present at the annual party rally.

———

[September 20, 1938]

In Nuremberg it was especially nice this time. Many flowers, lots of presents and congratulations for my birthday. With Frau von Ribbentrop frequently. With SS women in the hotel. Frau Gravitz [*sic*] and von dem Bach. Very nice. I have now been there six times and I would surely miss it if I could not be there next time too. Saw beautiful buildings in Nuremberg. The days are now magnificent here. H. and I were in Berchtesgaden at the same hotel as the Ribbentrops for two days. H. has just driven off in order to travel to Godesberg in the Führer's train. [. . .]

[September 24, 1938]

The negotiations in Godesberg are now over.[161] [. . .] What will happen? Everybody's disappointed, because there's no fighting yet. Here in the house there's an awful atmosphere.

[November 2, 1938]

In Italy H. was received with incredibly high honors. A magnificent feeling to know that he is so respected.

———

[161] A week before the Munich Agreement, Hitler met with Chamberlain in Bad Godesberg at the Rheinhotel Dresen for negotiations about the handing over of the Sudetenland.

[November 14 and December 3, 1938]

Salzburg "Hotel Österreichischer Hof." We drove here right after 9.11. because H. has vacation. Weather wonderful. H. is all for doing something every day. On Friday, the city, on Sunday Gross Glockner [mountain— Trans.], Sunday afternoon: to Fridolfing to visit the Rehrls; very nice. Today H. went hunting (Krupp hunting preserve). I am sewing, reading, and writing the first report about Püppi. All's going along fine. This Jewish business! When will this rabble leave us so that one can take joy in life?—I am really quite tired. Slept poorly last night. My feet are not very pretty. That comes from all the work that I have had to do. Maybe when I was younger I used to complain a lot about work, but today I am of the firm opinion that all this—my place in the sun, my happiness and love—I have earned it all myself. That is why I advise all young people, if you ever want to make anything of yourself, then you have to do everything to make it happen. Nothing falls in your lap. [. . .]

We've spent some lovely days with each other and have talked a lot. As for me, I've been learning English again. H. read a lot. There was often something going on.

———————

When she looked back and took stock of the year, she was as grim as ever:

———————

[December 31, 1938]

The year is over. There has been a lot of trouble in the house and even more work. What I have experienced this year, absolutely unthinkable.

———————

In 1938, Marga noted about her foster son, Gerhard:

———————

[April 2 and 8, 1938]

Gerhard is a criminal personality. Once again he has stolen money from somewhere or other. Indescribable how he lies. We have to send him to a reform school. [. . .]

I have written this to his mother. She was quite upset but of course does not want to have him back. She won't even take him for Easter.

————————

Before 1936 Marga's entries about both children in her *Childhood Journal* were for the most part favorable, even though their behavior continued to be an issue. Bad behavior was punished immediately. Marga obviously enjoyed delegating this punishment to her husband. In 1935 she noted about Gudrun, "Once when she was naughty she begged so long, until she was promised that Pappi would not be told."

In her own *Journal*, the tone shifted increasingly after 1937. Whereas Gudrun was always described as "sweet and charming" and Marga regretted "that one does not have six more like that who is so sweet" (26.1.38), she hardly ever mentions Gerhard anymore—and when she does so, it is only to complain about him. In 1938, when he was nine years old, the Himmlers actually sent him to a boarding school in Starnberg, where he was beaten by the other boys and, despite his fear of water, pushed into the lake so often that he was forced to learn to swim.

Gerhard himself remembered many years later that he was always afraid of his foster father's visits to Gmund because he was regularly beaten by him, once even with a riding crop. In Lydia Boden's *Memoirs*, she makes light of violence as necessary punishment for his escapades. In hindsight, she prefers to emphasize idyllic everyday life far from the war, or the modesty that Heinrich Himmler retained despite his political power, for example, when she describes their simple meals or emphasizes his solicitude toward the children: "Pappi loved it when his family sat around him at a meal. Pappi would eat just a single roll for breakfast, but half of it was divided and given to the children. Pappi cut small slices, which he would carefully make into little open-faced sandwiches, and then stick them into the children's mouths as if they were little birds."

After the "education" that Gerhard got at the Starnberg boarding school, his foster father sent him to the Nationalpolitische Erziehungsanstalt (NPEA) [National Political Institute of Education, or "Napola"] at Berlin-Spandau in the spring of 1939. Marga writes about this on March 15, 1939: "Gerhard has passed the entrance exam for the National Political Institute of Education in Spandau. I am happy, let us hope everything will continue to go well." But he had to leave this elite school after just half a year: "Gerhard must leave the Napola, he cannot keep up with the classes, but otherwise he has become nice and sweet, if it only stays this way" (16.10.39). Looking back on the Christmas holidays of the first winter of the war, she writes, "Gerhard left on the 7th, I have found that he's become nicer. He is very attached to us" (14.1.40).

Lydia's *Memoirs* confirm that the boy had a difficult position within the family, that Gudrun was treated more lovingly, and that the two children often quarreled. She herself found his pranks normal for a lively boy of his age, and also emphasized Gerhard's solicitude. She seems to have had a most loving relationship with him. It is clear from her writings how, on the one hand, Gerhard is begging for attention, which he temporarily found—more from the SS members of the Gmund headquarters than in the family—and on the other hand, the violence and humiliation that he constantly experienced and also inflicted on those weaker than he by torturing animals. The family obviously never recognized this connection, but simply punished him relentlessly.

On February 18, 1939, Marga noted in her *Journal*, "Life is taking its normal course, many invitations. I am awfully tired again."

————————

26.9.[6.] *39.*[162]

My dear good husband!

I am distressed about the Schades. Isn't there something one should be able to do about it? Eberstein should also leave someday. Or do you suppose intrigue, maybe even against you, is behind all this? I just spend my days with Püppi and all I can do is think about it. I am going to stand by her and show her my friendship. I do not dare write, maybe it will all come out all right. I am going to write in my journal and someday when I am no longer here you

---

[162] Marga has apparently recorded the date incorrectly and written 9 instead of 6. The entry in her *Journal* of June 26, 39 shows this: "We are in Kühlungsborn, Hotel Kaiserhof. It is nice and tidy here. [. . .] On Sunday, H. wants to come here for a few days so that we can spend the 3rd of July together."

should read it. Püppi is playing with another child and her mother on the beach and I have some quiet time. I want to offer Aunt Schadi the "du" form as soon as I get there.[163]

H. will now have to bear the consequences of the silly mistake he made. Can't this happen to any human being? All the best for these three days. We are all looking forward so much to having you here for supper on Sunday.

> I greet you most affectionately my beloved
> Your M.

The same day, Reich leader Martin Bormann communicated the following about the Schade incident to his "dear Party Comrade Himmler": "The Führer has instructed me to inform you that, in the presence of the Italian delegates, representatives of the Wehrmacht, of the State, and other onlookers, the SS-Führer Baron von Schade made 'such a sloppy' report to the Führer that 'the whole assembly was embarrassed.' [. . .] The Führer stated many times that he was ashamed for the entire SS! He wishes Baron von Schade to be disciplined by them. He has stated that Schade will never be considered as a successor to Lieutenant General von Eberstein, nor as chief of police in a different town, but only for office work instead."

Following this, Schade became a manager of a factory in Thuringia. Himmler apparently disciplined him less severely than Hitler had demanded, for he continued to receive a salary as a member of the staff of the Reichsführer SS and an inspector of the SD Düsseldorf. In 1942 he was reinstated as leader of the SS unit Elbe.

---

[163] Marga plans to express her friendship by offering her the informal—*du* ("thou," as opposed to *Sie,* or "you") form of address. The *du* is customarily used only for family and friends. "Aunt Schadi" was Gudrun's pet name for Frau von Schade. [—Trans.]

Temporarily Wewelsburg, 7.7.[39][164]

My dear good husband!

We arrived here safely, and I immediately saw your beautiful new room (dining room) and also the lovely green room downstairs.

When I wanted to pay my bill at the Hotel Kaiserhof I was asked: And the bill for the Reichsführer as well? I did not do it. You can imagine how terribly embarrassing that was for me. We were thinking of possibly going there again next year. I gave the chambermaid and the servant each 5 M. Maybe you can send a little money for Frau Wenkstein, the housekeeper, she will take money, I inquired. Püppi is asleep. Tomorrow morning you will telephone. I greet you affectionately,

      your Mami

In 1931, Himmler had inspected the Marienburg in East Prussia, the erstwhile seat of the Grand Masters of the Teutonic Order, successors to the chivalric order (see letter of 6.11.31). From the beginning he wanted to fashion his SS on a similar model—as the "Schwarzer Orden" [Black Order]—and to do this, and to establish a "Reichsführer Schule" [Reich Leadership School] for the SS, he sought an administrative and spiritual center. During the election campaign in Grevenburg (Lippe) in January 1933, Baron von Oeynhausen had proposed the nearby Wewelsburg Castle, a triangular Renaissance palace, as a potential site. Himmler was so taken with the castle that he purchased it immediately. In the following years the castle was gradually transformed into an isolated top-secret gathering place for SS officers, to which hardly anyone could gain access. The stucco covering the exterior walls was removed and the moat was deepened in order to give the castle a more martial aspect. The interiors were then decorated with ornamentation of a Nordic-Germanic style. In 1938, Himmler ordered an annual "Gruppenführertagung" [group leaders' assembly] to be held at Wewelsburg, during which the initiation ceremony of all new SS group leaders would be held. In addition, family coats of arms were to be

---

[164] This letter, which bears an incomplete date, is most probably from 1939, for in her *Journal*, Marga writes on August 13, 1939, "I have not yet written about Püppi's and my trip to the Baltic via the Wewelsburg [Castle] and to Düsseldorf [to the Schades']."

displayed there, and the death's-head rings of deceased SS leaders would be preserved there.

The site of Wewelsburg Castle held great symbolic significance for Himmler: the monument to Hermann, which commemorates the victory of the Cherusci leader Arminius over the Roman general Varus, was situated in the immediate vicinity. The remarkable geological formation called the Externsteine was also nearby. This sandstone formation, which Himmler revered as a Germanic cult site, could never really be proven to have spiritual significance for Germanic culture, yet Himmler's "SS-Forschungsstätte Ahnenerbe, e.V." [Research and Teaching Group for Ancestral Heritage, Inc.] tried actually to connect the two.[165] Furthermore, this region was the land of the Saxon king Heinrich I, whom Himmler particularly admired for his expansionist eastern politics. He saw himself as the reincarnation of this leader. Himmler stayed at Wewelsburg several times a year, either alone or with guests.

The construction plans for remodeling the castle and its surrounding village to create a central site for SS ideology and assemblies were monumental. The realization of the building plans required that prisoners be used after 1939, and in 1941 a concentration camp dedicated to the project was built on the site.

On March 30, 1945, shortly before the end of the war, Himmler ordered the demolition of the castle [which was never carried out—Trans.].

Gmund am Tegernsee, 26.8.39

My dear good husband!

The bill from Rösner and Seidl is from the hunting lodge.

The bill from Reiser is from both our house and the guesthouse. For our house it was things that were ordered last year. They should come out of our bank account.

We live on quietly, peacefully, and industriously here, and we wait. The radio is turned on every day.

---

[165] The research center Research and Teaching Group for Ancestral Heritage, Inc. was headed by Walther Wüst. Himmler put the hundreds of scholars in the group to work researching Germanic prehistory and anthropology in order to establish the "spiritual world domination" of the "Aryan race." During the war, the "Ahnenerbe" was also responsible for fatal experiments on prisoners as part of its mission to study the practical application of science to military defense.

I am so happy that you telephone me every day.

Püppi is studying.

> We greet you most affectionately thousands of times.

> Your Mami

Despite all promises of peace, Hitler held firmly to war plans. On March 14, 1939, German soldiers marched into Prague. Slovakia became a puppet state of Germany; the Czech region was designated "Protektorat Böhmen und Mähren" [Protectorate of Bohemia and Moravia]. In a secret memo of April 11, Hitler ordered the Wehrmacht to prepare the war against Poland.

In this situation the Soviet Union now assumed a key role, as both the Western powers and the NS leadership vied for its support. Time was of the essence, and finally Foreign Minister Ribbentrop himself flew to Moscow on August 22, 1939, with Hitler's absolute mandate to put the finishing touches on the treaty. That same night, the Hitler-Stalin Pact was signed, which, in a secret supplementary addendum, provided for the destruction of Poland and the occupation of that country by Germany and the Soviet Union.

While Ribbentrop was clearing the path to war in Moscow, on the Obersalzberg, Hitler explained his ideas about the impending war against Poland to his Wehrmacht commanders. One participant noted phrases from Hitler's speech. "Harden the heart against pity"; "brutal tactics. 80 million people must get justice. Their existence must be secured. Right belongs to the stronger. Greatest severity."

In the early morning hours of September 1, 1939, the Wehrmacht marched into Poland. Two days later, on September 3, Great Britain and France declared war on the German Reich.

[Marga's *Journal* of August 24, 1939]

Ribbentrop arrived in Moscow yesterday. It hit us like a bomb. Heini was able to witness the Führer's joy on the Berghof, He was very happy about it.

[August 28, 1939]

We are still waiting to see whether England will decide for war or not. [. . .] There are rationing cards. This all makes Schick (my servant) quite pale. Everybody is quiet and reasonable. We are surely going to have to economize a little bit with the soap, otherwise we have plenty of everything. [. . .] H. calls daily and is quite happy. I finally did have to tell Püppi that I would have to join the Red Cross in case of war. Of course she cried terribly and cannot calm herself down.

[September 4, 1939]

Now there's war with England and France. I am in Berlin. [. . .] The field hospital is gradually being set up, I am delighted to be part of it. If everybody really pitches in, the war will soon be over and England will remember us forever.

Letters

1939–45

"[. . .] I am enclosing a couple of little pictures
from my last trip to Lublin—Lemberg—
Dubno—Rowno—Luck."
HEINRICH HIMMLER, JULY 14, 1941

Nikolsburger Platz 5 13.9 [39]
(Received 15.9.39, written 15.9.39)

My beloved good husband!

I have not written for quite a few days now, but here in the field hospital there is so much to do and think about. We shall soon be finished setting things up, then it will all be better. I was just so happy to be able to speak with you on the telephone. Professor Gebhard[166] [*sic*] is doing better. Püppi is coming on Friday and Gerhard comes today. He has to go straight to Spandau because school has started.

I send you countless greetings and kisses.

Your M.

From the very beginning, the war against Poland was waged with particular ferocity. The Luftwaffe bombed Polish towns and flattened them. Warsaw, too,

---

[166] Karl Gebhardt (1897–1948), a friend of Himmler's from his youth and the "highest-ranking clinician of the SS," was, from 1933 onward, the head of the Heilanstalten [clinics] Hohenly-chen near the women's concentration camp in Ravensbrück, which he transformed into a surgical clinic. When the war began, a field hospital of the Waffen-SS was established here.

was so badly damaged by air raids that the military leadership capitulated on September 27, 1939, in order to save the city from further devastation.

Four Einsatzgruppen[167] of SS and police followed the German army and, working with armed militia of the German-speaking Polish minority, killed Poles by the tens of thousands. The Polish professional class—doctors, clerics, civil servants, journalists, teachers—was, in the words of Reinhard Heydrich, to be "rendered harmless to the utmost extent," meaning arrested, taken to concentration camps, or shot. In addition, SS commandos systematically emptied institutions for the mentally ill and murdered approximately 7,700 patients so that the buildings could be used by the SS. For this mass murder, one SS group used a van with its storage area converted into a mobile gas chamber. On December 12 in Posen [Poznan], Himmler himself observed the process of killing people in such a gas chamber. The Polish historian Bogdan Muisial accepts the fact that before the end of 1939, more than 45,000 Polish civilians were killed in the German occupied territory, among them around 7,000 Jews. The Wehrmacht sometimes participated in these murders.

Whereas central Poland fell under German occupation—the "General Gouvernement" [General Government]—western Poland, which contained around ten million people, primarily Poles, was slated to be annexed and "Germanicized" by the German Reich. The treaties with the Soviet Union had stipulated that the German minorities in the Soviet Union, especially those from the Baltic and the Ukraine, should be resettled in Germany. Several hundred thousand people would now receive their new Lebensraum [space to live] in those annexed western Polish territories. On October 7, 1939, Hitler assigned this task of resettlement to Heinrich Himmler, who had turned thirty-nine that day. On October 16, Marga noted in her *Journal*, "This birthday brought him such great joy. The Führer appointed him *Siedlungskommissar* [commissioner of resettlement] for all of Germany. A crowning achievement of his work. He works day and night. He often visits the Führer in the evening."

According to Hitler's decree, Himmler was now responsible for "the

---

[167] *Einsatzgruppen* were "task forces" or "deployment groups," euphemistic labels for the paramilitary death squads of the SS. [—Trans.]

repatriation of all *Reichsdeutsche* and *Volksdeutsche*[168] to be considered for ultimate resettlement within the Reich," and for the "elimination of the harmful influence of the foreign elements in the population that present a danger to the Reich and the German *Volksgemeinschaft*,"[169] and for the "creation of new German settlement areas through resettlement." As "Reichskommissar für die Festigung deutschen Volkstums" [Reich commissioner for strengthening of the German folk character], as he styled himself, Himmler now acquired new comprehensive authority, which should not be underestimated for his radicalization of violence. He was now responsible not only for the resettlement of German minorities, but also for the expulsion of "alien elements."

Before the end of 1939, approximately 88,000 people, Poles and Jews, were deported from the western Polish regions to the General Gouvernement under unspeakable conditions, often in unheated cattle cars without provisions, often even without drinking water. Hans Frank, the governor-general, summarized with brutal candor the German attitude that dominated at the end of November: "The winter here will be a hard one. If there is no bread here for the Poles, I do not want to hear any complaints. [. . .] In the case of the Jews, that goes without saying. It is a joy finally to be able deal with the Jewish race physically. The more who die, the better."

In early 1940, Himmler took several trips to occupied Poland. On January 15–16 he was in Lodz; on January 25–29 he traveled to Przemysl, Radymno, Cracow, where he met Hans Frank. In Zakopane he visited the Gorals (Górale), a west Slavic ethnic minority that Himmler considered to be of Germanic origin, and therefore eligible to be integrated into German culture. Marga wrote about this in her *Journal*: "H. returned today from his big trip. He met with the Volhynia Germans on the border of Prycemisl [*sic*] at the very end of their trek. I read this to Püppi and explained what it means: trek and homecoming to the Fatherland. It is an incredible achievement. People will still be talking about this after thousands of years."

---

[168] *Reichsdeutsche*, "Germans of the Reich," denoted ethnic Germans residing within the German state; *Volksdeutsche* denoted ethnic Germans living outside the borders of Germany. [—Trans.]

[169] NS term roughly equivalent to "community of people" or "population," based upon the notion of a common ethnic heritage. [—Trans.]

Marga herself profited from her husband's new position as young Volhynian-German women were assigned to high-ranking SS officials as domestic servants. Actually, they were placed in response to specific requests. In the summer of 1940, Rudolf Brandt, Himmler's personal aide, wrote to the Höherer SS-und Polizei Führer [senior SS and police chief] in Posen (Poznan) that Marga was "very satisfied with the girls," but said that she needed "another girl because one of the girls wants to marry soon." Furthermore, according to Brandt, Himmler needed "a second girl who could begin working for a well-known family as soon as possible."

Berlin, 9.6.40
(Received 11.6.40)

Dear Pappi

Your sweet package arrived this morning. I opened it and found the scarf, which I shall use as a head-scarf.

I used the shells as a nest for my wooden wagon and the four [chocolate] bars will taste good, but I have already eaten one of them. We are alone all day until the evening, when Fräulein Görlitzer arrives along with Aunt Edit [*sic*] and Uncle Franz Boden to play bridge. We are having beautiful weather here and I thank you heartily.

Many sweet kisses,
Your Püppi

My dear good husband!

We sent you tomatoes. You did not telephone today, we waited all day. Thank you so much for the beautiful things for Püppi. She was very happy. Tomorrow afternoon we have been invited to Frau Jöns's and we are going to accept.

I hope you do not have to see too many horrible things. I keep thinking about the war every day.—I want to write to Herr Koppe myself about the maids. We are planning to go to Gmund at the end of the month. Tomorrow the decision will come whether Kalkreuth gets drafted. I will probably have to leave one of the girls here, otherwise everything in the garden will die

it is a divine command to obey the Germans and to be honest, industrious, and well-behaved. I do not consider reading a requirement." Himmler acknowledged that in individual cases the "racial filtering" might be "brutal and tragic." He stated, however, that "even if you reject the Bolshevist method of the physical extermination of a people, out of an inner conviction that it is un-Germanic and impossible, it is, nonetheless, the kindest and best method." Himmler hoped to see the concept of the Jew "completely erased by the possibility of a large emigration of all the Jews to Africa or some other colony."

With that thought, Himmler breathed new life into an old anti-Semitic plan: the deportation of European Jews to Africa. Anti-Semites had been promulgating this idea since the end of the nineteenth century. In the 1930s, even European states such as Poland considered deporting its Jewish citizens to Madagascar. In the year 1940 the Reichssicherheit [State Security] and the Foreign Office were working hard on plans to move all Jews within the German sphere of influence to Madagascar. Whether the millions of people in question had a chance of surviving there does not seem to have bothered the planners. Yet the success of this plan depended upon defeating Great Britain so that it would no longer dominate the seas. The air war against Britain that Germany carried out starting in 1940 destroyed many cities and inflicted serious damage on the civilian population, but Great Britain did not surrender.

Germany was, however, successful against France, Belgium, and the Netherlands. Once German troops had occupied Denmark and Norway in early 1940, on May 10 the western campaign began. Within a few days the Netherlands and Belgium had surrendered. It was possible to evacuate around 338,000 English and French troops across the English Channel from Dunkirk before they could be captured by the Germans, but the now superior German Wehrmacht defeated the French army decisively and entered Paris on July 14. A great portion of France came under German military occupation; unoccupied France was ruled by a collaboration government in Vichy under Marshal Henri Philippe Pétain.

Along with the rest of the NS leadership, Himmler followed the advance of the German troops in a special train. In May and June he met with Hitler daily in his various headquarters and, in between, visited Antwerp, Brussels, Rotterdam, the Hague, Rheims, and Paris with his staff. He himself prepared a brief report about the first stations in Belgium and the Netherlands, which includes the following:

because of the drought. Are you getting a lot of rain where you are? I often play solitaire in the evenings, it stops me from thinking too much.

Have you thought about Edit [*sic*]? What can we still send you? Before I leave, I still want to send you a lot of laundry. I will return in fourteen days, I cannot leave Resi here alone any longer than that.—In times like this, one feels how terrible it is to be alone.

Many affectionate greetings and kisses,
Your M.

Please say thank you from me.

———

The planned "Germanicization" of the annexed regions of western Poland stalled due to the simple fact that not as many Poles and Jews could be deported to the General Gouvernement as Himmler wished. It was Frank, the governor-general, in particular who did not want any further influx, which would create additional problems for his administration of the occupied territory. Frank prevailed in a conference with Göring on February 12, 1940, where Himmler was also present. Göring spoke out against further "haphazard resettlement," and six weeks later, forbade "all evacuations until further notice" to the General Gouvernement. As a result, the Jewish population was placed in large ghettos, especially in Lodz (which the Germans called Liztmannstadt) and in Warsaw. They would later be deported.

Himmler, nonetheless, remained firmly attached to his deportation plans, and in May 1940 handed Hitler, with whom he often met in this period, a memorandum about the treatment of foreign elements in the east. Himmler noted that Hitler found it "very good and correct." In the memorandum, Himmler called for dividing the "foreign elements in the East [. . .] into as many parts and fragments as possible. [. . .] Nothing must float to the top, for only by separating this broth of peoples (15 million in the General Gouvernement and 8 million in the eastern provinces) will it be possible to carry out the racial filtering that must be fundamental to our deliberations—namely to fish out of this broth those who are racially valuable, bring them to Germany, and assimilate them there."

Himmler declared that the non-German population should amount to no more than five hundred, who can write their own names, and who know "that

"All Dutch cities made an excellent impression, the population is friendly and of good racial stock. [. . .] They represent a great prize for Germany."

In October he traveled to Spain, visited San Sebastián, Burgos, and Madrid, spoke with Franco, and on his return trip via Barcelona, made a detour to the cloister of Montserrat where he suspected the Holy Grail might be.

From the beginning of the war, Marga Himmler was seldom at home. She often spent weeks working with the Red Cross in Berlin, where, among her other duties, she looked after field hospitals and later distributed relief supplies to bombing victims. As in her earlier experience in the clinic, in this work she also had difficulties with the doctors, whom she found "arrogant," while they apparently disliked working with her just as much. As Oberführerin [female senior leader] of the Red Cross, she took extensive trips through occupied territories in order to assess the need for supplies in field hospitals and military infirmaries and to inspect schools for nurses' aides.

She was in Poland twice in 1940 and noted, "I have now been in Pozen, Lodsch [sic] and Warsaw. This Jewish rabble, the Polacks, most of them do not even look like human beings, and the indescribable filth. It is an unbelievable task to create order here" (7.3.40). And on March 23, 1940: "I was in the East again. Pozen, Bromberg at the Foedisches'. Everybody very nice, much to do there. These Poles will not die so easily from communicable diseases, they are immune, hard to understand. Bromberg at his wits' end. Mühlenkawel[170] and its region all terribly dilapidated [. . .] Not a single thing has been done in this entire country for as long as Poland has existed."

At the end of 1940 she traveled to Yugoslavia with the "most senior clinician of the SS," Professor Karl Gebhardt, and a delegation of the German Red Cross: "On 27.10.40 Frau Hermann, Prof. Gebhard[sic][171] with his adjutant, Mens, and I traveled to Belgrade to see the Bessarabian-German resettlement. [. . .] Big turnout there. Representatives of the party, of the resettlement, Foreign Office, and from the Yugoslavian minister of the interior. [. . .] In the

---

[170] Marga had lived in Mühlenkawel from 1910–1912 (*Journal*, 1909–16).
[171] See letter from Nikolsburger Platz 5, 13.9.[39]; Marga and Heinrich consistently misspell this name.

morning: village of ethnic Germans. Very instructive. Very good clean impression" (17.11.40).

In March 1941 she took another two-week trip through the occupied western countries: "to inspect military sanatoriums and German Red Cross *Verpflegungsstellen* [field kitchens]."[172] This time she was accompanied by Frau Ilse Göring, *Generalführerin*,[173] and her friend Nora Hermann. She visited numerous military sanatoriums in France and Belgium and praised the ones run by Germans ("very clean," "especially nice"). She also judged the French negatively ("population very bad, sloping foreheads," "hotel very filthy"). In Paris she stayed in the elegant Ritz Hotel. There she met with a representative of the Foreign Office and Kurt Lischka, the Deputy Commander of the Secret Police and of the SD in Paris. In the evenings she was a guest of the ambassador, Otto Abetz. Besides all that, she had enough time to visit Versailles, the castles on the Loire, and the Cathedral of Chartres, and to purchase lace from Brussels. "The trip went very agreeably. We saw a lot and were able to get a good impression of the presence of the Red Cross, and I am very satisfied."

By 1940 at the latest, Heinrich and Marga Himmler no longer seem to have had a good marriage. One can see from the detailed entries of 1940 in his pocket calendar that they continued to participate in each other's lives, but that they hardly ever saw each other. When Himmler was in Berlin in this year, he spent almost all his days in the office, the evenings either "with the Führer," "in the office," or, rarely, at home. The many "office evenings" suggest that he was frequently with his mistress, Hedwig Potthast, twelve years his junior. She had worked in the Reich Security Head Office since 1935 and had been his private secretary since 1936. On October 7, 1937, for the first time, she accompanied her employer to the Gmund office with other colleagues from the staff on his birthday. "Fräulein Potthast" appeared on Marga's Christmas gift list for 1937.

---

[172] In 1942 there were more than six hundred military sanatoriums, with approximately two thousand women and assistants from the German Red Cross. Most of these were in France. In Versailles there was a school for women leaders and assistants of the field kitchen units; in Malmaison there was one for the staff of military sanitariums. The staff quarters of the German Red Cross were in Neuilly and were frequently visited by prominent party members and state functionaries.
[173] Frau Ilse Göring held the rank in the German Red Cross of Generalführerin (general), whereas Marga Himmler held the rank of Oberführerin (colonel) [—Trans.].

Like Marga, Hedwig Potthast was blonde and blue-eyed, but in many other ways, she represented her opposite, with her friendly, warm-hearted, and happy personality. Her friends, acquaintances, and colleagues called her Häschen [Bunny], a nickname that Himmler and the entire personal staff adopted. In the early summer of 1940 during the western campaign, she accompanied Heinrich Himmler to the front. In her function as his private secretary, she necessarily came into contact with Himmler's policies, for example, through the "Denkschrift über die Behandlung der Fremdvölkischen im Osten" [Memorandum on the Treatment of Non-Aryan Peoples in the East"].

A draft of a letter that Hedwig Potthast wrote to her sister Thilde in November 1941 gives us a clue to how she and Himmler got together: "Christmas 1938 we had a frank conversation during which we confessed that we were hopelessly in love. For the next two years we considered every day whether there was an honorable way for us to be together. It was out of the question that he would simply get a divorce. In a few years, the only child will have grown up and will then surely leave her parents' house, so that I would not be taking anything from her. His wife, however, cannot help it that she was not able to have more children, and at age 48 is beyond the time when it would be possible in the normal way."

Marga then writes in her *Journal* on November 28, 1940, "Since I have been in Berlin I have been almost entirely alone. H. never spends an evening here anymore."

In 1940 limits were placed upon the deportation plans in western Europe. Yet where the Jewish minority could be driven out, this was accomplished with the greatest possible force. In Alsace-Lorraine, the SS and police rounded up the Jews and deported them into unoccupied France. At the end of September, Hitler demanded of both Gauleiters responsible for Alsace-Lorraine that they would report to him in ten years that their areas were "German, absolutely German," and that he would not ask "what methods they had employed to make the area German." By November 1940, 105,000 people from Alsace alone and about 50,000 people (all local Jews) from Lorraine were deported.

In a speech to the assembled Reichsleiter and Gauleiter [Reich leaders and regional leaders] of the NSDAP on December 10, 1940, Himmler took stock of the resettlements. He characterized the action as a "great 8[00?—Trans.]-year

migration of peoples" [*sic*], which, with all its immigration and emigration, affected nearly 1.5 million people. When measured against the original plans, however, the results were modest. Himmler now alluded to a new possibility: in
the region of the General Gouvernement, where "ruthless German authority"
applied, the Poles were to be used solely as a pool of seasonal laborers and for
other short-term work. In the same vein, a little while later, Hitler assured Hans
Frank that the General Gouvernement was the first region to become *judenfrei*
["free of Jews"].

In the meantime, once Great Britain showed it could not be conquered,
Hitler changed his strategy. The war against the Soviet Union, which was
originally to be waged after England's defeat, was now moved forward. On
December 18, Hitler issued the directive for Operation Barbarossa, the war
of aggression against the Soviet Union.

German troops first invaded Yugoslavia and Greece in April 1941 in order
to prevent a defeat that threatened the invading Italian troops; they set up a reign
of terror there from the start. Early in May 1941, Himmler traveled to Greece,
flying first to Sofia, and from there, on May 7, on to Athens. He made trips to
the Peloponnesus and Corinth and visited German troops in Larissa. Exactly
thirty years earlier, his father, a classicist who had introduced his sons to the
ideals of the classical world, had been in Athens. On May 8 Marga noted in
her *Journal,* "H. is now in Athens and we hear nothing from him. Normally
he would have telephoned every other day."

———————

Sofia, 7.5.41[174]

Dear Mami!

I spent the night here and toured the city. Now I am off to Athens. I am
very well. To you and Püppi many affectionate greetings your Pappi.

———————

With full knowledge and intent, the NS and Wehrmacht leadership planned
an unlawful war on the Soviet population. The so-called Commissar Order,
according to which all political officers of the Red Army were not to be cap-

———————

[174] This postcard bears the stamp "SS-Feldpost" [military mail] and is addressed to "Marga
Himmler—Deutschland—Gmund am Tegernsee."

tured, but rather executed immediately, contravened all accepted conventions of warfare, as did the order that German soldiers guilty of violent attacks on the civilian population were not to be subject to military justice.

Because the NS and Wehrmacht leadership calculated that the attacking army of three million German soldiers would advance rapidly and thus not be able to be fed by traditional military supply lines, the directive stipulated that the soldiers would have to rely on whatever provisions they could find in the countryside for themselves. In May 1941 a State Secretaries Conference in Berlin recorded literally that "countless millions will doubtless starve if we can take what we need from the land." Hitler himself declared that Moscow and Leningrad should be razed to the ground "to prevent people from staying there whom we would then have to feed in the winter."

The Wehrmacht leadership did not bother about providing care for Soviet prisoners of war. Tens of thousands died while marching to the camps; the camp inmates had inadequate housing, often in open fields where the soldiers themselves had to dig holes in the ground, and where they were left to die of starvation and disease. Nearly two million Soviet soldiers who were captured in 1941 died in the Wehrmacht prisoner of war camps before the spring of 1942.

From the very beginning, National Socialist policy was aimed at the complete subjugation and permanent domination of the eastern region. Thus the conquest of the Soviet Union proceeded with an ideology based on "blood" and "racial hygiene," which required the murder, expulsion, and starvation of whole population groups. Heinrich Himmler and the SS received "special orders from the Führer" that proceeded from the "struggle to be waged between two opposing political systems," as directives from the Wehrmacht High Command stated. In addition to the infamous Einsatzgruppen of the Secret Police and the SD, countless units of the Ordnungspolizei and the Waffen-SS were set up. These groups were all subordinate to higher-ranking leaders in the SS and the police, who commanded and coordinated the death squads.

In the first weeks of the invasion, the SS death squads targeted primarily Jewish men, but women and children were not spared either. In Bialystok, for example, on June 27, 1941, members of a police battalion forced approximately 2,000 Jews (men, women, and children) into the local synagogue and set it on fire, burning all inside. In the course of the summer, the destruction expanded to include whole Jewish communities, including women, children, and old people. In the Ukrainian town of Kamenez-Podolsk, at the end of August, units commanded by SS-Obergruppenführer and Polizeiführer [SS lieutenant-general and chief of police] Friedrich Jeckeln murdered more than 26,000 Jews; in just two days at the end of September, SS and police shot more than 33,000 people in the ravine at Babi Yar, near Kiev. By March 1942, SS, police, and the Wehrmacht had murdered nearly 600,000 people in the occupied regions of the Soviet Union—Jews, Gypsies (Roma), Communists, and Russian civilians.

On June 19, 1941, Heinrich Himmler was in Gmund where he spent a day in the Valepp taking walks and picking flowers with his wife and daughter. His driver, Franz Lucas, who was also an SS war reporter, took several photographs of the excursion. On this day Himmler apparently told his wife nothing about the impending attack. She merely "suspected" something, as she had in 1938 just before the German troops marched into Austria. On June 21, 1941, Gudrun writes to her father, "I am very sad that you are going to the front again. I hope you are well? Take good care so that nothing happens to you. [. . .] It is just awful that we are waging war against Russia. They were our allies, for heavens' sake. Russia is sooo big. The fight will be very hard if we conquer all of Russia."[175]

A month before, when he was on a short visit to Gmund, her father wrote in her *Friendship Album*, "In life one must always be honest and brave and kind. Your Pappi."

———————

22.6.41 (received Berlin 23.6.41)

My dear good husband!

Now we are at war again. I suspected it, I slept so poorly. Look after yourself. Do not eat the stuff that you have received from R. [?].

There is another tin of caviar in the icebox, take it.

You will soon be telephoning.

Many affectionate greetings and kisses,

Your M.

———————

[175] Numerous spelling errors have been corrected here, as well as in Gudrun's other letters and journal excerpts.

Gmund am Tegernsee, 27.6.41
(Received Headquarters 1.7.41, 12:00)

My dear good husband!

Today we are driving to Munich and picking up Edit.[176] Then I am driving to Innsbruck tomorrow. You see I am absolutely healthy.

The heat was terrible, we have just now had thunder and rain.

Püppi is fine, except that she too suffered a lot from the heat.

Dr. Fahrenkamp and his family were here.[177] We talked about the Valepp region and invited Frau F. and the children to the other house. I hope that is all right with you.

Herr Hammerl[178] suggests that a policeman ought to live here on the ground floor?

What do you think? The three policemen would absolutely have enough time. Or do you think that might attract too much attention? A cable arrived yesterday saying a spot for Gerhard had been found. Lisl is here.

My dear husband, you know Herr Hammerl has just told me the following. Yesterday afternoon the district administrator Dr. Pelikan from Miesbach paid a call on Weber in order to take an inventory of all the things that he delivers to us. He only delivers butter, and he continues to do so. He brought some today. H.[ammerl] immediately asked the mayor whether he had invoiced it. The district administrator received a telephone call from the mayor and he claimed that his superiors had instructed him to do so. The superiors can only be the Reichsnährstand.[179] The centrifuges are now being taken away from the farmers, so they cannot make butter. Now they are keeping the two liters of milk they are allotted, and now there will be less butter. Please authorize at least four guest cards for us, that would be best,

---

[176] Gudrun writes in her *Journal* on July 23, 1941, "Edith, our vacation playmate from Klagenfurt, 9 years old, who has visited us every summer for 4 years."

[177] Dr. Karl Fahrenkamp (1889–1945), an internist and the Himmlers' family doctor; both families were also friends. Himmler sent numerous SS leaders and civilian colleagues from his personal staff at the Reichsführer SS office to him for their physical examinations. Fahrenkamp would later inform Himmler of the results.

[178] Sebastian Hammerl (b. 1894) SS-Oberstürmführer [first lieutenant] with the Reichssicherheitsdienst [Reich Security Service] of the SS took over the administration of the SS command post in Gmund in June 1934. Gudrun was a friend of his daughter's.

[179] The Reichsernährstand (RNS) (Reich Ministry of Nutrition) regulated food production and distribution.

and it is ours by right. I wonder whether Richard can get along on the 400 grams of meat per week? Are things really so bad in Germany, the good people are asking. But I know myself what the others have.

           With many affectionate greetings and kisses,

           Your M.

Many thousands of kisses. I cannot write any more, there is no time. Your Püppi.

                                        Führer *HQ, 7.7.41*

       It is too bad that the connection was so bad twice today. I was so sorry that for the first time I neglected our wedding anniversary; but these days an awful lot has been happening. The battles, especially for the SS, are very tough.—I hope you got some pleasure today from the flowering plant.

       You are both two poor little things because Püppi was so sick. I hope that everything is all right now. I am sending you a couple of photos, one of the tennis game in Berlin, and the little ones of Lukas from our lovely day in the Valepp.

           To you and dear Püppi 1000 greetings and kisses,

           Your Pappi

Greetings to Aunt Lydia and little Edith.

                           8.7.41 (Received Führer *HQ 11.7.41)*

      My dear good husband,

       It was so hard to understand you yesterday during that second telephone call.

       Herr Schnitzler[180] came later with your flowers. Many, many heartfelt thanks. They are so beautiful. Püppi is doing well again. But I really did have a scare. That was especially during the night from Thursday to Friday.

---

[180] Erich Schnitzler (b. 1901), SS-Führer on Himmler's personal staff (Reichsführer-SS), headed the duty station of SS adjutants, Munich office, after 1939. He frequently ran personal errands for the Himmlers and was also responsible for bringing Marga her monthly household stipend of 775 RM (reichsmarks, see letter of 25.7.41). Their actual monthly expenses were

We are having magnificent weather here, we were outdoors all day. Yesterday the guestbook arrived from Mayr, pretty as can be, leather bound. We must not be disappointed, Püppi's report card is almost certain to be bad. She was absent too much. Affectionate greetings to you my good husband, Your M.

———————

On July 5, 1941, Marga noted in her *Journal*, "We often hear things from H. [. . .] The war is moving forward magnificently [. . .]."

In large so-called *Kesselschlacht*[181] battles in the beginning of July, several Soviet armies were defeated and hundreds of thousands of Red Army soldiers were taken prisoner. The resistance of the Soviet soldiers was, however, fiercer than the Germans had expected, and the German advance stalled. Among the members of the Army General Staff, the first voices were heard suggesting that the concept of "Blitzkrieg" did not apply to the Soviet Union and that the war would last longer than predicted.

———————

Gmund am Tegernsee, 13.7.41
(Received Berlin 14.7.41, written 20.7.41)

My dear good husband!

Yesterday evening Anneliese Ribbentrop telephoned me and talked about the death of Mops.[182] I told her that Beer was going to be recalled. But I added immediately that I wouldn't tell that to Ida because she certainly would not want it.

Ida just telephoned, completely distraught, she kept saying I should tell you that it is impossible for Beer to be called up again. She could

---

usually in the region of 1,000 RM. All the Himmlers' larger expenses were paid from the business account of the Reichsführer-*SS*.

[181] *Kesselschlacht*, or "cauldron battle," refers to a military maneuver involving encirclement, in which an enemy is surrounded, as if in a soup kettle. [—Trans.]

[182] Ida Wedel's son, Wilhelm, called Mops, had just been killed at Ternopil as an eighteen-year-old *SS-Untersturmführer* [second lieutenant]. Marga writes about this in her *Journal* on July 13, 1941: "Mops Wedel has been killed in combat. Eighteen years old, SS, this boy. Racially superb, clever, and nonetheless modest and boyish. Poor mother, and one cannot comfort or help her."

not endure both deaths (husband and Mops). It was hard for me to explain to her that this kind of thing is often done (for example, Hermenau) and that it was nothing special. She clung to that thought, and told me that she had just gotten a card from Mops, from 3.7, and the last one from Beer was on 2.7. They just did not know what could have happened after that. I do not want to write to her until tomorrow, I have to calm down a little bit.

I am enclosing a letter for you from Gauleiter Hofer,[183] I have not sent any kind of answer yet. Gauleiter Dr. Reiner [*sic*—Trans.] Salzburg[184] has invited me to the festival, I declined for the whole war.

Frau von Teermann,[185] Buenos Aires, writes that she is sending me coffee for the SS field hospitals and for you, woolen underwear for children of the SS. I hope that both will arrive.

Blösl Hans writes to me that there is no hope for his wife, he says thank you for all the help. Frau Kalkreuth writes that her husband is in the field hospital in Warsaw again. Can anything be done? The money for the carbon dioxide machine has been transferred to me. The heat is really terrible. Today we are going swimming. Püppi is very well again. She was quite sad and upset that you did not write to her. The pictures are beautiful. I am having them enlarged.

> With 1,000 affectionate greetings and kisses,
> Your M.

Dear Pappi, 1,000 kisses, Your Püppi

                                                              Führer *HQ, 20.7.41*

My good Mami!
    Another short letter in haste before I depart. First I want to thank you for both your letters of 8 and 13.7. Mami, you have to do something about your stomach, warmth and greatest regularity are certainly good.

---

[183] Franz Hofer (1902–1975), Gauleiter of Tyrol-Vorarlberg.

[184] Friedrich Rainer (1903–47), whom Himmler had known since 1930, was the NSDAP Gauleiter and Reichsstatthalter [Reich governor] of Salzburg and Kärnten [Carinthia].

[185] The correct spelling is Thermann.

Otherwise, you are really going to have to ask the doctor. I am happy that you are going to the Valepp, I think that is where you will really be able to get better.

I still have to write to Countess Wedel, I have not gotten to it yet. There is so much work. But I am doing very well.

The coffee and underwear from Frau Hermann have not yet arrived.[186]

Enclosed find Püppi's report card, which was sent to me. Of course it could be better and next year I am hoping that our good Püppi will do better. In German she has to get a 2, and in history, geography, and biology, also a 2, in math and English first a 4, but then it must be a 3.[187]

Now say hello to our sweet little mischief-maker! To you and Püppi 1000 affectionate greetings and kisses,

Your Pappi

I have to leave now, enjoy your visit in Dachau and say hello to everyone from me.

————————

Heinrich Himmler often complained about his daughter's poor grades; one can conclude from her *Journal* that he had always been a very good pupil himself. His sister-in-law, Lydia, regularly gave him reports about Gudrun's efforts: "Dear Heini! [. . .] I work with Püppi regularly on her schoolwork, she really is trying hard. When it comes to written work in school, she has indescribable anxiety and as a result, of course, writes worse than she does at home. How can one help her here?" Gudrun was, however, raised more indulgently than Gerhard. Gerhard had been going to Hitler Youth meetings for a long time. Gudrun registered with the *Bund Deutscher Mädel* (BDM, [girls' branch of the Hitler Youth—Trans.]) but apparently did not attend regular meetings of the *Jungmädel* in Reichersbeuern [for girls aged 10–14—Trans.] until she was ten years old.

On July 20, 1941, Himmler traveled to Lublin, where he oversaw the establishment of a forced-labor camp and the construction of a large SS and police

————————

[186] Here Himmler is apparently confusing Frau Thermann with Nora Herrman, who sometimes sent him packages.

[187] In the German grading system, 1 is the highest grade and 5 the lowest. [—Trans.]

complex to manage the permanent resettlement of ethnic Germans in this eastern territory. On the previous evening, he had ordered the deployment of two SS cavalry regiments to Baranowitschi (Baranowice) for the purpose of "the systematic combing" of the Pripet Marshes. In so doing, he launched the extensive executions of Jews, which these units would carry out together with other SS forces.

Himmler traveled on from Lublin to Lemberg and there visited Karl von Roques, the commanding officer of Army Sector South, and presumably also of the SS-Einsatz command located in Lemberg.

———

Gmund 19.7.41 (Time of receipt missing, written 25.7.41)
My dear good husband!

We are all well here. Frida [*sic*] and Röschen are here. Monday is Frieda's birthday and on Tuesday we shall drive to Dachau to the "magic garden," as Herr Pohl writes. Is there a rank of *Hauptmann* [captain] in the Waffen-SS?

I am enclosing the letter from Frau Thermann. If I am to answer it, then I would like to have it back. I am also having a new pair of glasses made for myself. Today we are both driving to Tegernsee. Aunt Martha and Ella have arrived safely in Danzig.

We live here lonely and quietly. The presents for Püppi arrived yesterday. She is already looking forward so much to her birthday.

With affectionate greetings and kisses, your M.

———

Dachau was not only the site of the first concentration camp built by Heinrich Himmler in 1933, but also the site of an early SS training camp set up on the extensive grounds of a former powder and munitions factory. Himmler also established several SS businesses, with which he hoped to achieve at least partial economic independence for the SS.

Oswald Pohl (1892–1951), former navy bursar and early confidant of Himmler, directed the growing business empire. In 1935 he became the chief administrator of the SS and in 1939 was made director of the SS Headquarters for Budget, Building, and Administration. From February 1942 on, he was also head of the SS Business Administration Headquarters and thus responsible for all business regarding the concentration camps.

In 1937 the SS venture Deutsche Versuchsanstalt für Ernährung und Verpflegung (DVA) [German Experimental Institute for Nutrition and Provisions] was also founded at Dachau. The project began with the cultivation of spices and medicinal herbs. For this purpose, prisoners had to drain an immense area of marshland near the camp under inhumane working conditions, following which herbs were planted and processed on a large scale. Greenhouses, drying and storage rooms, a modern spice mill, a teaching and research institute for medicinal plants and the study of nutrition, and an apiary were all set up as part of this undertaking. While the SS euphemistically referred to the site as the "herb garden," the camp inmates feared being assigned to any work detail for the "plantation" (another SS term for it). At times as many as a thousand inmates were put to work there. Many of them died of exhaustion, and others fell victim to arbitrary executions.

Like her husband, Marga Himmler had a long-standing interest in medicinal plants. In June 1938 she had noted a visit to Dachau in her *Journal*. Now she was planning another visit to the SS operations there. On July 22, 1941, Gudrun writes extensively about the excursion to Dachau with her mother, Aunt Lydia, Aunt Frieda Hofmann, her daughter Röschen, and Gudrun's friend Inge Hammerl: "Today we drove to the SS concentration camp in Dachau. There we then toured everything with Hanns Johst and his family, the large nursery, the mill, the bees, saw how all the herbs were processed by Fräulein Dr. Friedrich.[188] Then the books from the sixteenth century onward, all the pictures that the prisoners have made. Magnificent! Then we ate, then everybody got a present. It was lovely. A very big operation."

⚜

---

[188] Dr. Traude Friedrich, pharmacist, headed the laboratory of the Lehr-und Forschungsinstitut für Heilpflanzen- und Ernährungskunde [Teaching and Research Institute for Medicinal Plants and Nutrition], opened in 1940 in Dachau. She supervised experiments in plant breeding, nutrition, and the healing properties of plants, among other things.

Führer *HQ, 25.7.41*

My good Mami!

Many dear thanks for your sweet message of 19.7. I hope that your days in our Vallepp have been nice and relaxing for you both, but especially for you; have thought of you both so often.

Enclosed are the enlargements from the Vallepp, etc., which really came out beautifully, such nice pictures.[189] Mami, in the next few days Schnitzler will send you the monthly allowance of 775 M. The bills from Italy turned out to be more expensive than 500 M, around 800 M. I suggest that I contribute half of the balance. Do you like that? I shall send it (the bill) to you next time.

A captain of the Waffen-SS certainly does not exist in this form;[190] good that you sent it to me.

Have your eyes gotten worse? (because of the new glasses). I am enclosing a letter from Frau Hermann and a couple of little pictures from my last trip to Lublin—Lemberg—Dubno—Rowno—Luck.—I do very well under a heavy workload. I get treatments every day and sleep very well.

The struggle goes well, but it is *unbelievably tough*. The enemy defends himself *tenaciously*.

Pohl told me about your visit.

Many sweet greetings and kisses,

Your Pappi

Do not forget Grandma's name day on the 26.7.

[Letterhead cut away, Valepp]
(Received Führer *HQ 28.7.41, written 29.7.41*
In the airplane to Kowno)

My dear good husband,

we are now in the Valepp valley. The weather is magnificent and we are enjoying it greatly. Püppi is very happy. This evening we plan to go see the

---

[189] See his letter of 7.7.41.
[190] See Marga's letter of 19.7.41. [—Trans.]

deer with Herr Heiss. People go without a lot here, but you do not notice it until you live here in the country.

Frida really wanted to take a drive in the car, and so we found a source, it was just too good. Well, so much for reticence?

We are so curious about Püppi's report card. Frau von der Ahé sent birthday presents for Gerhard, we sent them to him. A silver bracelet for Püppi was included. She took it, we can't just send it back. She writes, Horst is with the SS, he apparently did very well in the training.[191]

Many affectionate greetings and kisses, your M.

My beloved Pappi.

I am so lazy about writing. It is magnificent here. At home I write you a lot.[192]

I love you sooooo much. 1000 kisses,

Your Püppi

Dear Uncle Heini!

Mother and I send you the most affectionate greetings. It is wonderful here. Such beautiful, good air that at first we all had headaches,[193] but now we have all gotten used to it!

Your Röschen

On the airplane to Kowno [Kaunas],
29.7.41

My good Mami!

Many thanks for your sweet letter from the Vallepp. I believe that there is still a lot that has to be done there. But the main thing is that everything

---

[191] Horst von der Ahé was four years older than his brother, Gerhard, who turned thirteen on July 21.

[192] During this summer she actually wrote a long, wistful letter to her father every second day. On the letterhead is, as usual, the date of receipt noted in his own hand, and sometimes the date when he wrote back to her, which was significantly less often. His letters to his daughter do not survive.

[193] See footnote to letter of 14.10.[1930] from Marga to Heinrich, which also mentions headaches.

went well for you there.—Of course one cannot send back the bracelet from Frau von der Ahé, but Püppi should not wear it. I will write to Frau Ahé about Gerhard sometime. Yesterday I wrote to Countess Wedel.—I am enclosing the bill for Italy. My trip now takes me to Kowno—Riga—Vilna—Mitau—Dünaburg—Minsk.

To you and our sweet little mischief maker, many dear greetings and kisses.

Your Pappi.

In Riga Himmler met with Hinrich Lohse, Reichskommissar [Reich commissioner] for the Ostland [Baltic States], and with Hans-Adolf Prützmann, senior SS and police leader–Russia North. Among other things, they discussed the possibilities for the Germanicization of Lithuania. In Himmler's eyes, only 10 percent of the population was eligible for this policy. Right after Himmler's visit, Prützmann's men expanded the mass murders of Jews in Lithuania and Latvia. Men, women, and children were indiscriminately shot in ever greater numbers.

On this trip he was apparently not in Vilna and Mitau. Instead, he took a side trip from Riga to Segewold (Sigulda) on July 30, 1941. The castle in the Latvian town of Sigulda had once belonged to the Teutonic Knights. On July 31 he flew on to the Lithuanian Düneburg (Daugavpils) and drove by car through the city. The previous day, the *Lettische Zeitung* [Latvian Times] of Düneburg had reported that as of July 28, after a "thorough, final purge of the 14,000 Jews [in the city]," Daugavpils was "free of Jews." On the same day, Himmler met with senior SS and police leader of Russia Central, Erich von dem Bach-Zelewski in Baranowitschi (Baranowice). The next day, the following radio message was broadcast to the SS cavalry regiment stationed there: "Express order of the Reichsführer-SS. All Jews must be shot. Drive the Jewish women into the marshes."

On July 31, Himmler flew back to his base. The planned visit to Minsk was postponed from August 14 to 16.

❧

Gmund am Tegernsee, 29 July 41
(Führer HQ 1.8.41, 22:00, written 2.8.41)

My dear good husband!

Just after you telephoned yesterday Prof. Gebhard [*sic*] telephoned. He wanted to take a look at my wounds.[194] Because I am already a patient of Fahrenkamp, he was present at this examination as well. I am supposed to apply compresses. He said the wound will calm down by itself. He said it was an inflammation of the periosteum,[195] I am not anemic. Then we took a look at the research Fahrenkamp was doing, the Höfls were there too. Hugo [Höfl] wants to come visit me too.

But it is still raining. Frida wants to leave this week. Röschen left yesterday. We have not heard anything from Herr Deininger.[196]

The professor looked very well, he said he did not have much to do. Make sure you do not work too much, you are going to need your strength later.

Last evening we received your letter with the many pictures, which we like very much. We were not able to congratulate your mother on the 26th.[197] Püppi, however, wrote a card and got an answer today. She wants to telephone today.

Many affectionate thanks for your sweet letter.

Yes, the poor soldiers, and they have to fight in Africa, of all places, in this heat.

Because I did go to the eye doctor, I had my eyes examined. He just prescribed glasses and said they would be perfectly fine for me. And now I can see through them just fine. Many thanks for the 150 M. Where shall I send the check for 150 M? Put it in the letter? Or deliver it to the office in Berlin? I want to drive to Berlin after Püppi's birthday. Maybe that is too bad, because she does have a vacation. But I want to get a massage, and I want to go back to the Red Cross.

---

[194] Early in June, Marga was injured when a carbon dioxide machine exploded. (*Journal* of 11.6.41)

[195] Fibrous membrane, connective tissue covering the bone surface. [—Trans.]

[196] The reference to "Herr Deininger" suggests the SS-Führer Johann Deininger from Burtenbach, near Günzburg, Swabia.

[197] See letter of July 25, 1941, from Heinrich to Marga.

On Friday I want to visit the art exhibition with Frau Bouhler,[198] Lydia, and Püppi.

Püppi could not grasp that you wrote you could no longer laugh as you used to in 1936. Maybe it is a good thing that she cannot imagine the war. She is just turning twelve. She talks about her birthday every day.

> With many affectionate greetings and kisses,
> Your M.

———

Karl Fahrenkamp was not only the family doctor and friend of the Himmlers, but from 1933 to 1944, was also the staff doctor of the Waffen-SS in the SS training camp at Dachau. He was also the head of "Department F" on the personal staff of the Reichsführer-SS. Prior to 1939 he had his own garden on the grounds of the Experimental Research Institute in Dachau, where he conducted diverse experiments with glycosides. Following Himmler's order, he at first treated seeds in order to increase productivity. Later he expanded his experiments using glycosides into the area of prolonging the life of flowers, fruit, and vegetables. He even planned to mix them into baked goods in order to achieve a general improvement in the health of the population. He implemented this last idea in a six-month series of experiments on prisoners in Dachau. Later Fahrenkamp advised Sigmund Rascher in his fatal vacuum chamber experiments, also conducted on prisoners. On the side, he managed his private cosmetics firm in Dachau, which was financed by the SS.

———

Führer *HQ, 2.8.41*

My good Mami!

Many thanks for your sweet letter of 29.7—I am very glad that Fahrenkamp and Gebhard [*sic*] examined you and that it is nothing serious.

---

[198] Helene Bouhler (b. 1912) was the wife of Philipp Bouhler (1899–1945), one of the earliest party members. In his role as business manager of the NSDAP, he had known Himmler for many years. With Hitler's authorization, Bouhler, an SS group leader, was responsible for tens of thousands of murders of the sick and handicapped ("Aktion T4"). Now and then Marga came into contact with Frau Bouhler at receptions in Berlin or Munich, but she found the woman too flighty and did not especially like her.

Gebhard telephoned me today; he will arrange for a physical therapist for you in Berlin. I think it is very good that you are doing the right thing for this.

I am enclosing a very decent letter[199] from Countess Wedel for you and such a nice picture of Mops. Return them to me when you have a chance! I have written to her again. It is too bad about this boy and about many others.

You are right that it is good that our Püppi does not *completely* comprehend the war, but you have to tell her about it now and then.

I shall be with the Führer tomorrow, Sunday, at noon and in the evening. The trip to the Baltic was extremely interesting. We have *huge* tasks ahead of us and, as far as the distances are concerned, this is just the beginning.

Many sweet greetings and kisses,

Your Pappi

———

On July 16, 1941, the most important conference about future occupation policies in the Soviet Union took place in Hitler's headquarters. Göring, Lammers, Rosenberg, Bormann, and Keitel were present—but not Himmler. Hitler explained to those present that their task was to "divide the giant cake into manageable portions so that we can first of all rule it, second administer it, and third, exploit it. [. . .] From these newly won eastern regions, we must make a Garden of Eden; they are vital to us."

The reason for Himmler's absence is unknown, but it could be related to the capture of Stalin's son, which took place the same day. Although Hitler had confirmed in that meeting that, after victory, the administration of the occupied territories should be transferred to civilian agencies, Himmler was left enough latitude to expand his authority by "using police to secure the eastern territories." In 1939 Hitler had given Himmler, as Reich commissioner,

———

[199] Himmler often sent Marga letters from widows or mothers of soldiers who had fallen at the front, provided that they were written in a "decent" or "proper" tone. The women had to display "courageous" and "heroic" behavior and accept the death of their loved one as a necessary sacrifice for Germany.

specific authority to plan the "Umvolkung"[200] of Poland, but Himmler none-theless interpreted this assignment as applicable to the Soviet Union as well.

Just two days after the attack on the Soviet Union, Himmler instructed the agronomist, SS-Oberführer [Colonel] Konrad Meyer (1901–73) to draw up the "General Plan East." The first version that he submitted on July 15, 1941, connected racial, ideological, and economic goals. These goals called for ethnic restructuring, permanent "Germanic" settlement, and the economic exploitation of occupied regions in the East. In order to make it possible to move the "ethnic German frontier" farther east—secured by a "wall of Germanic blood" that was to stretch from the Baltic to Crimea—approximately thirty million Russians, Poles, Czechs, and Ukrainians would have to be forcibly resettled in Siberia. Following that, the region would have to be populated by German "Wehrbauern" ["soldier-peasants"—Trans.]. For Himmler an important prerequisite for German settlement and permanent domination of the previously "emptied" eastern territories, was the marshaling of all Germanic peoples. According to this plan, Norwegians, Danes, Belgians, and Dutch would expand the population of the Greater Germanic Reich by about thirty million people. He calculated, furthermore, that a maximum of 20 percent of Poles, 35 percent of Ukrainians, and 24 percent of White Russians could be Germanicized. The long-term goal was that the eastern territories should be almost completely Germanicized by the "return of German blood" within thirty years. For this purpose, the SS stole and transported at least fifty thousand Polish children "of good blood."

Although Himmler's enormous resettlement project in Poland had by no means achieved his original ambitious goals, he decided to grapple with the ethnic cleansing of the East immediately, rather than after the war as planned. He considered this to be most quickly attainable through a systematic expansion of the mass murders of Soviet Jews in the summer of 1941—people who, in the eyes of the NS leadership, represented the pillars of the Bolshevist system. Hitler's propaganda proposing a struggle between two worldviews—national socialism versus "Bolshevism and World Jewry,"—was something that Himmler interpreted as the ultimate battle in a centuries-old conflict between Europe

---

[200] NS term roughly translated as "ethnic transfer"—in other words, replacing an indigenous population with a different one. [—Trans.]

and Asia. His "soldier-farmers" were not only meant to resettle the conquered territory and produce children there, but also "occasionally to engage in military expeditions into the still-unconquered expanses of Asia, where they would seek booty and also become tougher and experience racial culling." According to Himmler's vision, in four hundred to five hundred years, five hundred to six hundred million Germanic people would inhabit the eastern territories.

———

Gmund am Tegernsee. 2.8.41
(Führer HQ. 5.8.41, 20:00, written 9.8.41, 20:00)

My dear good husband!

Yesterday you asked me what we do all day. There's enough work if everything is to be tidy and clean and if anything is to grow in the garden.[201]

Too early! We get up between 8:30–9:30. Before that we read—Püppi too. Then there's a lot to do in the kitchen, canning, and Anna is not independent yet, cleaning up. Walking through the garden, discussing all the jobs. Sewing. It is mostly quiet in the afternoon unless fruit or vegetables are delivered or Dr. Fahrenkamp visits. We rarely get visitors and we love our peace and quiet. After 8.8.[202] I'd prefer not to travel to Berlin, but that is just the way it has to be.

Otto said yesterday that his father had now settled in and was sick, which was why he needed to go home. But he himself said that of course it was not going to be possible right away. Now we are waiting to see how everything will develop with Otto, and then we (rather Herr Baumert) will have to find us someone new. Because Herr Tannberger is still "sick" Frau T. does nothing, even though Herr Hammerl has asked her to several times.

---

[201] It is typical of the correspondence of this married couple that, throughout the years, each assures the other of how busy he or she is, even when the actual daily routine does not suggest a very strenuous life.

[202] August 8 was Gudrun's birthday.

Püppi is quite delightful, and that is another reason why I am sad that I have to leave. She has vacation now. She has been helping me with the canning for hours.

There are Christmas presents included in the bill. The intelligent man plans ahead. I cannot comprehend that fruit is so expensive. I do not find the other things so bad. I am enclosing the check.

Frau Bäumel wanted to visit us for two days, and Frau Stang has also gotten in touch. Frida and Röschen have gone. F. was very depressed.

It would certainly be a good idea if you were to write to Frau von der Ahé. It could be that Horst is making progress, and we shall see the same with Gerhard.[203] When I write to him should I sign it "Mother?" When I write to him, I shall tell him he should write to his mother.

I really liked the picture of Heydrich at the exhibition.

Professor Gebhard will probably already have reported to you about my wounds. It is taking a long time, but I have the feeling that things are improving. Furthermore, one gets used to pain.

   With most affectionate greetings and kisses, your M.

———————

They divided the task of buying Christmas presents. While Heinrich Himmler's secretaries were responsible for the presents for his SS-Führer colleagues and their relatives, Marga provided for the private staff and their families, colleagues at the Red Cross, her own relatives, and friends. These amounted to between sixty and eighty people per year. The presents consisted mostly of soap, stockings, stationery, books, and porcelain from the factory in Allach owned by the SS. During the course of the war years, this involved ever-greater logistical difficulty, so that they usually began to assemble their presents early in the year. Nonetheless, during the war, the Himmlers had ready access to consumer goods of which the normal population could only dream.

⚜

———————

[203] On June 11, 1941, she had noted, "Terrible things just keep on happening with Gerhard."

Führer *HQ, 9.8.41*

My good Mami!

I have been sitting here from noon today until this evening in Hegewaldheim, a lakeside restaurant that we have requisitioned. Arnold, the chef from Wewelsburg Castle, is cooking here.—The sun shone occasionally today. I did a little walking, otherwise I worked in a dining room. I am feeling well again, but these intestinal problems are pretty disgusting and really wear you out. In some places at the front, people have this by the dozens. Our victories are wonderful, we are now proceeding *very* well in the South. Last night Ribbentrop and I dined together, it was very nice and went smoothly.[204]

Once again, many thanks (this time in writing) for your letter of 2.8 and the check for 150 M.—With Otto, we shall just have to wait.—I will write to Frau von der Ahé. Next time I am going to send you the carbon copy. With Gerhard I would not sign with "Mother" for the moment; if he really does improve, then we can think about it later.

You are clever to be planning for Christmas already! I am so glad that at least everything is better with your stomach and your bowels! I am sure the wounds will certainly heal as well. You have had to endure a lot of pain, my poor Mami! It is very sweet that Püppi is so nice, our little scamp!

Now a little bit about my daily routine. Up at 9:00. Then the "Fat Man" comes for an hour. 10:00, get dressed and eat breakfast. Then shave, and while I do so, Dr. Brandt reports on the morning mail.[205] Then comes work and "governing" by telephone, radio, and teletype. Every other day, 13:00, trip to the Führer; 14:00, there. Meal. Between 16:00 and 17:00, return. More work on the train. On the rare nice days, I am in the Hegewald Forest by the lake. 20:00 dinner, work, and reading until 23:00 or 24:00. In the afternoon, 13:00 and evenings at 20:00, a courier arrives with new mountains of mail. Then come trips of three or more days in between. I have the mail forwarded to me, if at all possible. After that, lights out.

---

[204] During the war years there were frequently tensions between these men.

[205] Rudolf Brandt (1909–48) was Himmler's personal aide from 1936 to 1945, and since the end of the 1930s, had been his liaison officer to the Ministry of the Interior.

Every other day I eat with Lammers.[206]

I now wish you and Püppi a lovely Sunday, and to you, have a good trip to Berlin.

> To you and Püppi many dear greetings and kisses,
> Your Pappi

After the invasion of Russia, Himmler spent most of his time in his "Sonderzug Heinrich" [Special Train Heinrich], which was located mostly in the vicinity of Hitler's headquarters, the Wolfsschanze [Wolf's Lair], near Angerburg, in East Prussia. The letters to Marga confirm the entries in his *Official Appointment Book* from the period, namely that he visited Hitler every second day for lunch and thereafter would stay through the afternoon or evening.

The "Hegewaldheim"—approximately an hour's drive from Hitler's headquarters—gradually became Himmler's permanent headquarters if he was not away for a trip of several days to visit his SS units at different sectors of the front and to give them orders or make sure that orders were being carried out.

The "Fat Man" was Himmler's masseur and physical therapist, Felix Kersten (1898–1960), an Estonian by birth, with Finnish citizenship, who treated Himmler for years for his chronic stomach pains. In 1952 he published his memoirs and presented himself as someone who used his proximity to power to save human lives by persuading Himmler to release Jewish prisoners shortly before the end of the war.

[206] Hans Heinrich Lammers (1879–1962) was the head of the Reich Chancellory and SS-Gruppenführer. In his capacity as state secretary, leader of the Reich Chancellory (from 1933), he shared the special train with Himmler and Foreign Minister Joachim von Ribbentrop during the war against Poland and France.

Gmund am Tegernsee, 9.8.41
(Received Führer HQ 11.8.41, 22:00
Written 13.8.41, 19:15)

My dear good husband!

Wölffchen and Nüsschen have now arrived, and they have brought me a present from their father, tell Herr Wolff many thanks from me.[207] On Thursday I am off to Berlin. Herr Pohl telephoned me. H. will not be there himself.

Püppi was very sweet yesterday. Yes, she is our good little monkey! She was just so overjoyed with the things, especially with your pencil case. We lit the Yule light.[208]

Herr Dr. Fahrenkamp just telephoned, he said that his children will not be visiting Püppi because Inge is quite sick and his wife is also in bed. Intestinal flu. And how are you really? Better? You really did not tell us how bad it was, but from your language I could see how bad things were, I thought you had caught a cold, which would not have been strange in this weather.

I am enclosing the letter from Countess Wedel.

Herr Schnitzler will see to it that we get a replacement for Otto, who is now leaving us. His father does not really seem to have settled in. He is supposed to be working as a day laborer on an estate in Pomerania and to have received ten *Morgen*.[209]

Is such a thing possible?

Professor Gebhard wrote me a long letter—very calming. I am also doing much better now. Things are now gradually getting back to normal.

With many affectionate greetings and kisses, Your M.

---

[207] Wölffchen (b. 1930) and Nüsschen (b. 1934) were the two oldest daughters of Karl and Frieda Wolff. Wölffchen was half a year younger than Gudrun and were friends of her and Gerhard from Munich. She was in the same class as Gudrun in Gmund, Berlin-Dahlem, and later in Reichersbeuern; the children often visited each other.

[208] The *Julleuchter* [Yule light] is a pyramidal ceramic candleholder of rustic design used by hard-line National Socialists at the de-Christianized Yule festival during the Third Reich. Himmler gave these as presents to members of the SS. [—Trans.]

[209] A unit of land measuring from 0.6 to 0.9 acres. [—Trans.]

Gmund am Tegernsee 13.8.41
(Received Führer *HQ 16.8.41, 14:00,*
Written 27.8.41, 20:00)

My dear good husband!

Your sweet letter arrived today; many, many thanks. Tomorrow it's off to Berlin for me. If there are air raids there every day, I do not want to stay there very long. Maybe you can speak to Professor Gebhard and ask whether I can take Frau Seeger, the physical therapist, along with me.

Two letters enclosed. Dr. Rühmer[210] wrote to me as well, which made me happy. I have had luck so far with people I have recommended to Herr Pohl. I do not know what to say about the other letter, I did not like Steinmeyer, the nurse who was with him at the time; that was the only reason I went there. I preferred our old Dr. Setzkorn,[211] I hope he is doing well.

You will be phoning soon. This afternoon, Frau Stang and her husband will visit. Frau Bäumel was here, it was very nice, she is such an intelligent person.

A small inflammation has appeared around my wound, and I have been hoping to apply compresses more often, because the chill has done such good.

All day long Püppi just talks about the fact that I am leaving. She keeps saying you are not in favor of it, please tell her that you are when you telephone.[212]

Otto is leaving, it is such a shame, he worked out so well with us, our piglets are the proof of it. In the garden we have harvested around 175 pounds of red currants, but have also given some to the policemen, and also to Herr Laur who is again doing well.

You asked what we do all day. I stand in the kitchen almost every morning. We have put up so many preserves, how I would like to show it all

---

[210] Karl Rühmer (b. 1883), expert on fisheries at the SS-Wirtschafts-Verwaltungshauptamt (WVHA) [SS Main Economic and Administrative Department]. Established an SS-Fischereiabteilung [SS Fishery Department] in Unterfahlheim. Beginning in May 1942, prisoners from Dachau had to work there. In July 1941, Rühmer apparently moved to Pohl's WVHA, on the strength of Marga's recommendation. Now and then she would order fish from him.

[211] Dr. Setzkorn was a general practitioner and naturopath in Berlin. For years he treated not only the family, but also Heinrich's brother.

[212] On this day Gudrun wrote to her father, "Tomorrow my good Mami is off to Berlin and I will be all alone. It makes me cry."

to you, and our garden is in good condition too. We have no news from Kalkreuth. It has been raining every night for almost 3 weeks.

Strangers are here, indescribable. They are buying up everything. And they stand right at our gates. One can barely go into the garden.

With many affectionate greetings and kisses,

Your Marga

Berlin, 15.8.1941
(Received Führer HQ 16.8.41, 14:00,
Written 27.8.4, 20:00)[213]

My dear good husband!

Gertchen [i.e., "Little Gertrude"—Trans.] is standing right here and entertaining me. When I arrived here I found everything very nice because Liesl had gone on ahead. The trip was magnificent, our beautiful German Fatherland. Of course it could rain a bit less. Today I just stayed around here in order to organize things, make telephone calls and set things up. Frau Hermann will visit tomorrow, then Nurse Friedl comes in the evening. I was able to comfort Püppi at the last minute because Inge Jarl will visit. Unfortunately, she does not get along so well with Lydia anymore. I am enclosing some crumb cakes.

With many affectionate greetings and kisses,

Your Marga

———

Himmler found both letters waiting for him when he returned from Minsk. He had been accompanied on that trip by Hans-Adolf Prützmann and Karl Wolff, as well as Hitler's photographer, Walter Frentz, who documented the journey of August 14–16, 1941, in color photographs. In the White Russian town of Minsk, 1,050 Jews had been shot on July 13; on July 19 a ghetto was established, from which more Jews were rounded up every day. On August 15, near Minsk, Himmler watched an execution of "partisans and Jews."

❧

———

[213] His response dated 27.8.1941 has not survived.

Berlin, 28.8.41

My dear good husband!

I hope that you are really better and that you are not just acting that way on the telephone.

There's a little bit of excitement today. Kalkreuth is in a bed in the Reserve Field Hospital 106.[214] It would have to be 106! I shall go there tomorrow. Shrapnel in his foot.

Enclosed is a letter that came yesterday. I hope that not everything in it is accurate, the poor children. On Saturday I am traveling to Gmund to my little Püppi.—Hammerl is in bed, he is said to be very sick.

True of Herr Karl as well,[215] he is said to have pneumonia. Everything is pretty much normal around here, peaceful and beautiful. There's a lot of fruit, especially plums and pears. "Gmund the Garden" looks magnificent with so much fruit.

When we are in Rimini and have a hotel I am going to send a telegram to Herr Baumert, that is what we agreed.

I keep telling myself we cannot help you even if something were to happen. We cannot leave until the 4th, because the others did not get sleeping car tickets.[216] I shall bring you a pair of pajamas. Anything else?

With many affectionate greetings and kisses,

Your M.

---

[214] Kalkreuth was one of her employees in Gmund. The Reservelazarett 106 was the first field hospital in Berlin-Wilmersdorf, and where Marga began working in 1939.

[215] Josef Karl (b. 1910) became a Führer on the staff of the SS Headquarters in 1937; in 1941 he was promoted to SS-*Sturmbannführer* [major].

[216] "The others" were Hugo and Friedl Höfl and their daughter, Irmgard Klingshirn, from Apfeldorf, who were traveling to Rimini with Marga and Gudrun. Hugo Höfl, SS-Obersturmbannführer (SS lieutenant colonel), had worked as a volunteer for the Sicherheitsdienst [Secret Service] of the SS since 1935. The Himmlers were the godparents of Irmgard Klingshirn's new baby son.

29.8.41 *(Received* Führer *HQ 30.8.41,*
Written 31.8.41, 20:00)

My dear good husband!

I would have thought that the children could have walked the five kilometers from Gmund to Tegernsee. Right away I ordered cars, and they are coming on Tuesday. Their companion too, who's supposed to be with them. Frau Johst and her daughter too. Hanns Johst is supposed to be in Berlin.

Many heartfelt thanks for your letter, I received it last night. I am leaving tomorrow morning and am really looking forward to seeing our little scamp.

Today when I went to the field hospital 106 to visit Kalkreuth, everybody was pleased, and that made me very happy too. Kalkreuth's wound should take four weeks at the most.

With many affectionate greetings and kisses,
Your M.

Führer *Headquarters, 31.8.41*

My dear Mami!

I visited the Führer this noon and afternoon and took a walk with him. He is doing fine again. Dinner is in one-half hour, and so I am writing to you from the actual Führer Headquarters. Everything is going very well. After all, when you stop and think about it, tomorrow on 1.9, we will have had 2 years of war. Just think of all we have achieved!

My loving thanks for both your sweet letters from 28 and 29.8. I really am better; I can safely say, very well. But these things are all boring and tedious, and we have so much to contend with in the East at the moment. I am pleased that your visit to your old field hospital was so nice and that Kalkreuth is doing so well.

I received your enclosed letter, I am going to have it checked very precisely, and if anything is missing, I will help. Please tell Hammerl and Karl from me to get well soon.

I am so happy for you that you can recuperate a bit in Rimini. Other than that I would not do much driving around, but you do have to see Ravenna. You must tell Püppi everything. The mausoleum of the Gothic king Theodoric the Great—the man who is named Dietrich von Bern in the saga—is there. This word "Bern" is the German name for Verona, just as "Ravenna" means Raben. The mausoleum is one of the oldest Germanic structures; two years ago I had the "Ahnenerbe"[217] survey it again. Theodoric's body, however, no longer lies in the mausoleum, nobody knows where his body is.—Enjoy the sea and the sun, and really take it easy! You will send me a telegram with your hotel!

And now all good wishes and many affectionate greetings and kisses,

Your Pappi

Give the Höfls my very best!

Gmund, 3.9.41 (Received Führer *HQ 6.9.41)*

My dear good husband!

Many thanks for the beautiful carpet, it made me very happy. Püppi really had me looking forward to it. We are leaving tomorrow in the hope that we can catch some magnificent weather. When we return, we will hear whether you are coming, otherwise I shall go on to Berlin. We plan to stay around 10–12 days. On Monday the 22nd Püppi has to start school again. Herr Dr. Fahrenkamp wrote that to us. Unfortunately Püppi does not seem to be losing much weight.—

I did not find your mother looking too bad. But she feels so exhausted. The magnificent weather that we have today—and let us hope it hangs on—will surely help her somewhat.

Herr Schnitzler arrived and brought me the money for the trip. I had no idea how much money one gets for a trip. When Püppi travels next time she is going to have to have her own passport. Herr Schnitzler says that would be the only thing anyone could challenge. Maria is going on vacation, her mother had someone write and tell us that she was not going to return because they need her there themselves. Maria claims that she is definitely coming back. Herr Tannberger is still sick. Otto's successor cries and does not want to stay. Always alone and so little money. What that means is that we—actually Herr Schnitzler—are looking around for a new one. We have

---

[217] *Ahnenerbe*, is short for Forschungs- und Lehrgemeinschaft das Ahnenerbe e.V. [Research and Teaching Group for Ancestral Heritage, Inc. [—Trans.]

wonderful fruit and the vegetables are coming along well. All this will be put up as preserves. Enclosed find the book by Hanns Johst. Be well and just stay healthy.

Many greetings to you from my heart and many kisses your M.

Gudrun writes in her *Journal* that on September 4, 1941, she had traveled by train to Rimini, where SS-Oberführer Eugen Dollmann, Himmler's liaison officer to Mussolini, awaited her and where she was "driven to the best hotel that was still open." "Of course the police chief of Rimini was there too. [. . .] Naturally nobody speaks a word of German but the porter, but Friedl speaks Italian, thank God." They spent the mornings at the beach. In the afternoons they visited, among other things, Mussolini's birthplace, Dante's grave, and as Himmler had recommended, the Mausoleum of Theodoric.

In 1926 Himmler had noted in his personal *Leseliste:* "This Dietrich von Bern must have lived, otherwise he would not be so deeply engraved in the hearts of his people." The equation of the mythical Dietrich von Bern with the Gothic king Theodoric had been popular for centuries, but the correlation is historically uncertain at best. In July 1938, Himmler had successfully requested permission from the Italian minister for national education, Giuseppe Bottai, to have Theodoric's mausoleum in Ravenna resurveyed by an archaeologist and an architect from the SS-Ahnenerbe. For Himmler this was "for Germany, one of the most awe-inspiring monuments of classical history." Himmler's researchers believed they could prove the "Germanic character" of the structure, and they registered it as "the oldest work of German architecture in stone."

Marga and Gudrun had to break off their Italian vacation early because Heinrich Himmler's mother, Anna, died on September 10, 1941. Gudrun wrote regretfully that she was not allowed to attend the funeral, and that now she had no more grandparents.

Berlin, 17.9 [1941]

My dear good husband!

We spoke yesterday, and I was so happy about that. Today the Russians marched after all. That is going to change everything. As I have already told you, we have 50 (critical cases) here, really only fairly trivial ones. Püppi is delightful and plays so nicely with her houses. We took these pictures in Gmund. Frau Foedisch[218] is alive and has written, with great joy, that Werner was with the Hilfspolizei 7 [auxiliary police] of the SS and has been discharged so that he can work his land. The notice of the probating of the will arrived. After Grete's death[219] Lydia is going to inherit 30,000 M, or rather the interest from that amount. The housekeeper and Anni are very tidy, Schick is the only one who is unacceptable. We really should give him his notice soon.—I weigh 131 pounds, so am really not as fat as I look in the pictures. There was horrible weather here yesterday; beautiful today. You have no idea how I enjoy going to my field hospital. In times like this I want to be of help. I have an invitation from Frau Foedisch.

But I am not leaving right away. We are waiting for you with so much longing my good husband.

With many affectionate greetings and kisses,

Your M

Berlin, 21.9.41
(Führer *HQ 23.9.41, 19:20, written 28.9.41*)

My dear good husband!

Yesterday evening just as I arrived, Herr Baumert showed up with your lovely roses and the coffee. Many, many heartfelt thanks. Also to Herr Wolff. The weather was magnificent today, let us hope that "they" [the RAF—Trans.] will not visit us again. Püppi was very sad when I left. She said, "Do not forget me." After the long vacation, school is hard for her. It is also too bad that she

---

[218] Old friend of Marga from Bromberg. Her son Werner was an *SS-Scharführer* [staff sergeant] and a member of the Rasse- und Siedlungshauptamt [Central office for Race and Resettlement] and, later, of the Waffen-SS.

[219] Second wife of Hans Boden. During the final years, Marga apparently did not have good relations with her. After the death of her father in July 1939, she wrote in her *Journal*, "Let us hope we will not be hearing much from Grete, I am almost afraid" (24.8.39).

cannot make a real friend at school. Herr Burgstaller would really love to have an autographed photo of you. Both of them made a good impression.[220] We have so much caviar here, shouldn't I give it away? I do not find any boots of yours to give to the boot collection drive. Can't we send you anything?

With 1000 greetings and kisses, your M.

Berlin, 24.9.41
(Received Friedrichsruh 26.9.41.
Written 28.9.41)

My dear good husband

As you can see, here are the walnuts from Frau Hermann. I hope you are better. I have high hopes for the fact that you are now living in a house and not on a train. At the end of the week we are planning to bake crumb cakes. I shall telephone Püppi today. This evening I shall visit Frau von Ribbentrop. She was in Hohenlychen for just 3 days. At the Red Cross things are running according to plan.

An affectionate greeting and kiss your M.

Berlin, 24.9.41
(Received Friedrichsruh 27.9.41, 24:00, Written 28.9.41, 12:00)

My dear good husband,

Enclosed is a letter from Püppi, please send it back. Because there is probably no chance that you will be here for your birthday, I want to go to Gmund (by train) for 3 days. I do not think one should leave her alone. In addition, a letter from a Major Nolte to me is enclosed. He is in charge of the railroad stations here and is very responsible (on top of that, 8 children). Maybe you can do him this favor. Then he would surely be more inclined to do one for us here.—I am also enclosing Püppi's Christmas wish list, maybe you could put a check by the things that you will buy her and then send the paper back to me. I also have a woolen jacket and gloves (lined) for her. Or just write me what I should buy from the list. I have also bought the H.J. and

---

[220] Alois Burgstaller received the desired framed picture of Himmler for Christmas.

the B.D.M. girl from Allach.[221] I can give them to her too. Frau Foedisch writes that Werner could be drafted by the army before 1.12. He would rather join the SS, can you do that? Then he can be deployed nearby. S.D. [Secret Service] or something similar? His estate has been made into an agricultural training site. We are having magnificent weather here. I hope that holds true for Gmund as well so that my plums can still ripen.

After hearing back from Herr Pohl's office, I am now buying Christmas presents for the SS men, and also some things for myself, on credit. 10,000 bars of chocolate for the SS. Kalkreuth told me that everyone got a bar a day in the field hospital. I am so happy that there are also some there for the SS, and that there are socks there too. We still do not have any books. It is hard to get any.

He brought 50 kilos of coffee and some tea, among other things for me. I am paying for that privately. I shall give most of the tea to the SS and take the coffee as Christmas presents. Who knows whether there will be any geese? Should I also give anything to the old people in the 106? Cleaning ladies, etc.? I am not receiving any sweets or *Pfefferkuchen* [gingerbread]. Have you got a solution to this? Dümig in Haar[222] does not have any people to do the baking. I have about 60 people to give gifts to, and then no gingerbread.[223]

With many affectionate greetings and kisses, your M.

Frau von Schade's father was buried on Friday.

Führer *HQ, 28.9.41*
Freidrichsruh

My dear Mami!

First off, many thanks for your three sweet cards and letters from 21, 24, and 27.9.

Convey my thanks to Frau Hermann, then I will not have to write a separate letter to her. [The cookies] are very good.

---

[221] The Hitler Youth and the BDM girls were part of a series of porcelain figurines produced in the factory at Allach belonging to the SS. Prisoners from Dachau were used as labor there.

[222] The Dümig Bakery in Munich-Haar remains a family business to this day.

[223] This year she actually had about eighty people to give gifts to. After her husband had arranged sugar for her (see letter of 28.9.41) she apparently baked the gingerbread herself (letter of 23.11.41 and *Geschenkebuch* [*Gifts Record*]).

The letter from our Püppi is lovely. She wrote to me so sweetly. The day before yesterday I sent her some candy.

I am also sending back the wish list, I think I will take care of the scrapbook and frames for our travel photos.—-I have approved the petition from Major Nolte's aunt.

I am sending back the description of Födisch [*sic*]. I do not want to do anything about Werner. Let that take its normal course.

By the way, Paula's brother (Ernst's wife), Walter Melters,[224] was killed in combat in the SS.

The monthly allowance is enclosed.—The branch is not for display. It is a plant called "Porsch" that I cut in Latvia, and it is supposed to help against moths. You have to lay in in among your woolens.

It is wonderful that you are buying Christmas presents for the SS men. It goes without saying that I would give something to the old people in 106.

Is it of any use to you to get sugar for sweets?

I am now driving over to see the Führer! I hope you do not get as many bombers this week!

    1000 greetings and sweet kisses,

    Your Pappi

The German Reich, which had devastated cities such as Warsaw, Belgrade, and Coventry with its massive aerial bombings, now became the target of Allied air raids itself. In May 1940, British planes first bombed Dortmund, Mönchengladbach, and other towns in the regions of the Rhine and Ruhr. In August the first bombs fell on Berlin. In comparison to what would follow, the losses were relatively minimal, yet they demonstrated that the city was inadequately defended. Improvised air-raid measures were put in place far too late. In the letters between Marga and Heinrich Himmler, these aerial bombings are a

----

[224] Walter Melters (1913–41), SS war correspondent, was the youngest brother of Himmler's sister-in-law Paula Himmler. He was killed on the Russian Front on September 14, 1941. Himmler was apparently the first to learn of his death. In order to report this death, he telephoned his brother Ernst in Munich on September 16. Ernst was in Munich with Gebhard and Hilde, after the death of Anna Himmler, in order to settle their late mother's estate and dispose of the contents of her apartment.

constant theme, with the bombers referred to as "beasts" who pay them a "visit" in the night and "drive" Marga out. At this time, she was often spending nights in the bunker in Berlin—which was the reason Heinrich forbade his daughter to visit her mother in Berlin during the war.

———

Dahlem 2.10.41 (Friedrichsruh 5.10.41, 23:00,
Written 17.10.41, 23:00)

My dear good husband,

My affectionate, my most heartfelt good wishes on your birthday. Just always stay healthy, so that you can continue to bear all your responsibilities. Püppi could not comprehend that you are not able to celebrate your birthday. We should be so happy that she loves us so much. I am leaving on Saturday morning, and very much looking forward to seeing her.

I have had a couple of things bought for you because I think you need them. Everything here is running its normal course.

We often get a "visit" during the night, and that is what I am waiting for right now.

On Tuesday afternoon you will be phoning us in Gmund, am I right?

If you do not like the crumb cakes please say so, and we shall make something else.

I hope you come back safely from Kiev, I cannot stop thinking about it. [. . .]

All good wishes to my Pappi.

Greetings and kisses, your M.

———

Lydia also writes to her brother-in-law on October 2, 1941, from Gmund: "Dear Heini! I want to send you many heartfelt good wishes on your birthday! Most of all stay healthy so that you can weather all storms. [. . .]"

From October 1 to 5, Himmler traveled via Slovakia to the Ukraine. On October 2 he met with Friedrich Jeckeln, the Höherer SS- und Polizeiführer [senior SS and police chief] in Kiev, who, a few days before, had organized the massacre of Kiev's Jews in the ravine of Babi Yar (see commentary to the letter of 7.5.41). On October 4 Himmler ordered the Sonderkommando [Special Detachment] Lange to be sent immediately to Novgorod to murder the inmates of three mental institutions there because their quarters were needed to billet German troops. The unit had already gained experience at murdering the sick in mobile gas chambers in Poland. On the same day, he gave a speech in Nikolaiev to members of Einsatzgruppe [death squad] D in which he declared that the war against the Soviet Union would serve to destroy Bolshevism and gain space for resettlement. He stated that the mass shootings of Jews and political opponents was a difficult task, but one that had to be achieved in order to reach the stated goal. After his return on October 5, he reported about his trip to Hitler on the evening of the same day. During the meeting he explained that the population of Kiev made a bad impression, so that one could "do without a good 80–90 percent of them."

Dahlem, 14.10.41 (written 17.10.41, 23:00)

My dear good husband!

    I enclose some letters that were sent to me. I have just heard that Ilse Göring's second son has been killed in action. He was her darling.—I am doing very well here, we haven't had a late-night "visit" here for a long time. The envoy Ettel[225] with his wife and sister were planning to visit me in the next few days. Funny things are happening again at the Red Cross. I will have to tell you about it face-to-face. We are still hoping you will visit on Christmas. (Kalkreuth will be here on vacation.) Püppi would be so unhappy. I do not know how on earth I would comfort her. For now, I am not going to say anything. I have gotten a clock. Do you know what I want you to give me for Christmas?

    With many affectionate greetings and kisses, Your M.

On October 26, 1941, Marga noted in her *Journal*, "H. often telephones. He is healthy. The war is progressing magnificently. We owe everything to the Führer."

---

[225] Erwin Ettel (1895–1971), from 1936 a high-ranking official in the Foreign Office, and beginning in 1941, SS-Brigadeführer [SS major general].

The war was by no means "progressing magnificently." The attack on Moscow, which the army group had begun in October, remained mired in mud and hampered by the early onset of winter. The German troops had reached the city borders, but on December 5 the Soviet counterattack began. The retreat of the exhausted German army resembled a rout, and it was only with great effort that the front could be stabilized one hundred kilometers west of Moscow. On December 19, Hitler personally took over high command of the army. The Japanese attack on Pearl Harbor on December 7 brought the United States, the largest economic power in the world, into the war against Germany. That, combined with the defeat at Moscow, made it clear that the war was unlikely to be won.

———————

Dahlem, 31.10.41
(Received Friedrichsruh 1.11.41, 19:00
Acknowledged verbally, Gmund, 9.11.41!)

My dear good husband!

I am finally writing to you again, mostly to say thank you for all the many things you have provided for my wounded soldiers and also for the staff.—Frau Foedisch was supposed to visit today. This afternoon the countess [Wedel] will visit. She seems to be in bad shape. Her husband also died this month. I am spending this morning at home. My household duties require my presence. We have already made some quince jelly and will send you some. Don't you want to have anything from us here? We would be so happy to send you something.—I have not heard anything from the Red Cross, and Dr. Brekenfeld[226] has been here since Monday.—Yesterday Captain Abt asked me whether I could arrange a meeting between him and Herr Pohl. I am so happy that we can help this extraordinarily decent man. Thank you very much for this.

With affectionate greetings and kisses, Your M.

———————

[226] Dr. Friedrich Wilhelm Brekenfeld (b. 1887) *Oberstabsarzt a. D.* [chief staff surgeon, ret.] and *DRK-Generalhauptführer* [general director German Red Cross].

On November 7, 1941, Himmler took his Sonderzug [special train] Heinrich from Rastenburg (East Prussia) to Munich in order to participate in the annual commemoration of the anniversary of the Hitler Putsch. On the evening of November 8 he was in the Löwenbräukeller [beer hall] for a rally, and following that, at a meal with the SS (Ober-) Gruppenführer and Gruppenführer [lieutenant-generals and major generals]. The next day there was a ceremony in which SS-Führer [SS officers] were promoted. A brief meeting of all Reichsleiter and Gauleiter followed.

During this time, he stayed in Gmund for two nights and spent his free time with his wife and daughter. On November 10, 1941, Gudrun wrote about the visit in her *Journal*: "In the evenings we played rummy and dominos and did jigsaw puzzles together. He left again early this morning. It is such a shame."

Berlin 23.11.41

My dear good husband!

Many thanks for your sweet letters. Last evening I was at Anneliese Ribbentrop's with the Countess [Wedel]. She really does not look well. Working with Frau Hofmeister is still sheer pleasure. Tomorrow a courier leaves for Gmund, so I am giving him a lot of Christmas things to take with him. Will you tell us soon when you can visit? Püppi was so proud that she can type. She has only done it in bed.

The pictures of the models from Speer[227] unfortunately are not labelled to explain what they show. I have to go to the kitchen, we are doing a lot of baking.

With many affectionate greetings and kisses,
Your M

What do you say to the letter I have enclosed? Please return.

---

[227] See note to earlier undated letter from Königsberg.

2.12.41
(Received Friedrichsruh 4.12.41)

My dear good husband!

Tomorrow would be Mother's birthday.

Püppi is well, in the meantime you will be talking to her on the telephone.

Enclosed are two letters. I can recommend Kalkreuth to you very highly.

Frau Hofmeister has just left me.

Frau von Schwöder [?] telephoned me, she is enthusiastic about your idea.

Many thanks for the chocolate. In my office it is only 8 to 10 degrees, terrible. Since yesterday it has been very cold outside. I am making a lot of progress with my Christmas preparations.

With affectionate greetings and kisses,

Your M

In the airplane, 21.12.41

Dear Mami!

I forgot something else. The little box belongs to you. It comes from our family (Heyder).

Again, all best wishes to you and our dear little scamp,

Your Pappi

———————

Heinrich Himmler had just celebrated the Yule festival with his family on 20 December, rather than celebrating Christmas on December 24.[228] The next day he flew back to the Eastern Front. Gudrun writes about these days in her *Journal*: "Mutti arrived on 13.12 from Berlin. Gerhard came on the 19th from his new boarding school in Gotha. Pappi arrived here on the morning of the 29th after he had visited the grandparents' graves. We celebrated Christmas at 5 o'clock. [. . .] I wonder if the war will still be going on next Christmas? God preserve Pappi for us."

---

[228] The pocket calendar from 1940 suggests that in the prior year the family had still celebrated Christmas on December 24.

Gudrun's aunt Lydia provides a more detailed description of the Christmas celebration in the Himmler family:

"It was especially beautiful and festive, in a space as big as the hall. The days leading up to it were very mysterious and exciting for the children, especially because they were not allowed to enter the hall. [. . .] A large fir tree almost covered the second window. Colorful balls—red, yellow, and blue—alternated with the rich assortment of Christmas tree decorations. They represented symbols of the colors of stars in the sky. Old Germanic symbols were baked from a certain kind of dough: fish, the Yuletide boar, the three Norns, the swaddled child, and Wotan on his horse Sleipnir. A lot of tinsel hung on the branches, and we couldn't do without sparklers. In recent years we added the emblems of the Winterhilfe.[229] You children helped prepare the fir tree. Among the many candles, a blue one shone brightly, to remind us of ethnic Germans abroad. [. . .] In the hall there were places set up to include the entire staff. [. . .] After a bell was rung, everyone gathered in the hall and sang Christmas carols by candlelight. Then everyone exchanged presents. The children recited verses that they had written on beautiful sheets of paper. They each had a present for their parents. Gerhard had made some pieces of fretwork and Püppi embroidered little doilies. [. . .] Everyone ate dinner together, including all the residents of the house. A true traditional German Christmas celebration.[230]

In 1936, Himmler explained in a speech to his assembled SS-Gruppenführer the meaning that the old "Germanic festivals," especially the Yule festival, had for him. There he stated, "The winter solstice is not only the end of the year, the Yule, after which come the twelve *Rauhnächte*,[231] the time when the New Year begins, but more important, it was the festival when one contemplated one's ancestors and the past, a festival that made it clear to the individual that he is nothing without his ancestors, and without honoring them, he is nothing but a tiny atom, extinguished at any moment. But when he is connected to this

---

[229] The NSDAP Winterhilfswerk was an annual charitable drive to provide food, clothing, coal, and so on during the winter months. [—Trans.]

[230] From Lydia's *Memoirs,* from the posthumous papers of Gerhard von der Ahé.

[231] The twelve nights after Christmas, literally "harsh nights," which have special significance in European folklore and are commemorated in the Christian twelve days of Christmas. [—Trans.]

infinite chain of his people in true humility, the ancestor and descendant are everything.

Himmler introduced an obligatory new ritual for all SS units. He specified twelve "Yule sayings," each to be recited upon the lighting of a candle, and ordered that these be "used now and forever for the Yule celebrations." The main points were the "struggle for freedom," "reverence for one's ancestors," comradeship, and duty. The last Yule saying was an oath to the Führer: "We believe in him because he is Germany, because he is Germania." In 1944, Himmler had these sayings revised. The new version, written at a time when Germany's defeat was inevitable, was marked by strong religiosity. Thus the first and last sayings address the "All One, eternally prevailing mind and God of the world," who is the "sacred goal," the "incorporation of our Germanic life into the meaning of the earth and, with that, into the will of God the All One."

Gmund 25.12.41[232]
(Friedrichsruh 31.12.41, 17:15,
Written 1.1.42, 13:00)

My dear good husband!

My heartfelt thanks for the beautiful lilac that arrived yesterday. Toward evening we looked at our things again and lit the tree. And later played games with the children. How beautiful the other celebrations always were.—

Many more flowers are still arriving, I am enclosing the cards. And beer for you too.

I sent two bottles over to Herr Burgstaller. Would you like some? Who else is going to drink it?—A goose arrived from the Oswalds. We have kept it here, I do not feel good about sending it off with this kind of mild weather.—A terrible storm raged all night. In the bedroom the drapes were blowing around like crazy, even though the wooden door and windows were closed. Gerhard had a high fever, he is now better again. Seidel has

---

[232] This is the last letter written by Marga that has survived.

gone to visit his stepfather, who is deathly ill. I hope he comes back. I am enclosing the letter from Herr Hofmeister for you. I think it may be of interest to you. Please return. I am out of cigarettes, that is to say, good ones. How about you? He [?] always receives the packages because they are sent by courier.

Tomorrow we are going to clear out the Christmas room, just because it is so cold and we cannot heat in there anymore. The tree will stay fresh longer too. We want to light it again on New Year's Eve.

We are really hoping that you will call us soon.

Heartfelt greetings and kisses,

Your M

Friedrichsruh 1.1.1942

My dear good Mami!

First off, from the bottom of my heart, all good wishes for you and our dear little scamp. I have just gotten off the telephone with you.

Thank you so much for your sweet letter. The beer just arrived here.—I have told you almost everything on the telephone. The address for Kiss is: "Hauptmann u. Abteil.[ungs] Kommandeur [captain and section commander] Kiss, Fp. [Feldpost, military postal service] No. 20 088." You will have to ask him about a soldier for Püppi.[233] I am including a brief note I have written for Hofmeister.

Get a really good rest during these days in our peaceful, beautiful Gmund! The little scamp is going to get a letter from me next time.

Many greetings and kisses to both of you from your Pappi

Go ahead and leave the tree up for a few more days, it is just so pretty.

I am sorry this letter is so short, I have to run now.

---

[233] Gudrun apparently wanted the military postal address of a soldier in order to be able to send mail to him at the front. On March 7, 1943, she noted in her *Journal*, "I am corresponding with two SS men."

After writing this letter, Himmler drove to Hitler's headquarters around noon, where he spent the rest of the day before his conference with Hitler in the late evening. During their discussion he reported, among other things, on his inspection tour of the SS divisions "Leibstandarte[234] Adolf Hitler" and "Wiking," which had taken place at the end of December. He also cancelled his visit to Army Group North and the SS divisions stationed there, which had been scheduled for January 3–6, 1942.

———

3.1.42

Dear Mami!

In great haste, am enclosing the note I wrote for Hofmeister plus letter and documentation from Gotha.

Many greetings and kisses to you and Püppi

Your Pappi

Friedrichsruh, 19.1.42

My dear Mami!

Just quickly, time for a brief note to you before the courier leaves with the beautiful amber box of Gauleiter Koch and his wife (belated Christmas present).—I am glad that you are better again, control yourself and do not go out too early!

Enclosed are the 125 M, and then a very interesting report in which our Gerhard is mentioned. I probably cannot do anything about it, but his tendency to tell lies is typical. Send the report back to me sometime.—The magazine is from Caschina Castle,[235] but it is not this nice anymore. It is a remarkable and rather spartan military bivouac near Leningrad. I stayed there.

———

[234] The First SS Division Leibstandarte SS-Adolf Hitler (SS-LAH) was originally his personal bodyguard regiment, but evolved into a separate unit of the Waffen-SS. [—Trans.]

[235] He refers to the Neoclassical Gatchina Palace near St. Petersburg. [—Trans.]

In addition, another letter from Italy and a postcard from Leissinin, where we were in beautiful peacetime.[236]

Many greetings and kisses and get well.

Your Pappi

In the former villa of the industrialist Ernst Marlier (at this time the guesthouse of the Chef der Sicherheitspolizei und SD [chief of the Secret Police and the Security Service] on the Grosser Wannsee [Lake] in Berlin), a meeting took place on January 20, 1942, that would go down in history as the so-called Wannsee Conference. In addition to Reinhard Heydrich, the chief of the Gestapo; Heinrich Müller and Adolf Eichmann from the Reichssicherheitshauptamt [Reich Security Headquarters]; several other high-ranking representatives of the state and party apparatus took part in the meeting. They included Staatssekretär [secretary of state] Dr. Wilhelm Stuckart from the Reichsinnenministerium [Ministry of the Interior]; Martin Luther, the leader of the Germany Section in the Foreign Office and *Unterstaatssekretär* [undersecretary of state]; the *Staatsekretär* [secretary of state] in the Ministry of Justice, Dr. Roland Freisler; and Erich Neumann.

Contrary to what has been assumed in earlier historiography, the Wannsee Conference did not confirm the "final solution of the Jewish question," but rather, as seen from Heydrich's notification of the meeting and in the later minutes of the meeting, the goal was to agree upon the "Parallelisierung der Linienführung" [parallelization of the chain of command]. In other words, the participants coordinated a master plan for mass murder. In the literal wording of the minutes of the Wannsee Conference, which discuss mass murder in euphemistic terms, "The evacuation of the Jews to the east" was to take the place of emigration, "in accordance with the previous permission of the Führer."

---

[236] On April 28, 1935, they had been together on the estate of Leissienen in East Prussia at the wedding of the Höherer SS-Führer [senior SS leader] Hans-Adolf Prützmann and his wife, Christa (see note to Marga's undated letter from the end of May 1937 from Königsberg). On January 17, 1942, Gauleiter Erich Koch had arranged a hunt in Leissienen in which Himmler participated. At this time he probably received the belated Christmas present from Koch.

In the days preceding the conference, Himmler had spoken to several participants, for example, Dr. Josef Bühler, the Staatsekretär [State Secretary] of the General Gouvernement in Krakow. He also spoke with Dr. Eberhard Schöngarth, the commander of the Secret Police and the Secret Service in that city, and with Heydrich himself. In addition, a high-level meeting of all the chiefs of the SS Headquarters took place at Himmler's field HQ on January 14–15. On the day after the Wannsee Conference, Himmler had Heydrich telephone him to report on the proceedings of the meeting.

———————

Friedrichsruh 17.2.42

Dear Mami!

Enclosed are five double chocolate bars that I promised you for the children; in addition the cheese that you so badly need.—The white stuff is honey with almonds, tastes very good, you should eat it (if you like it). I recently sent Püppi some. I am told the Ovosport[237] is very good.

Many fond good wishes and kisses,

Your Pappi

———————

On February 15, 1942, two days before this letter was written, Hedwig Potthast gave birth to their [Heinrich's and her] son, Helge, in the SS clinic at Hohenlychen. Not only did the head of the clinic, Karl Gebhardt, personally attend the difficult birth, but he was also made the child's godfather. This is stated in a letter that he wrote to Hedwig Potthast at Christmas 1942. There one reads, "My dear Madame! [. . .] When I think back to the hour of the birth of your little son, my godchild, and on all the responsibility and joy that we felt at that time, then I am at a loss for words to express myself. [. . .] I can only give you the assurance that I will endeavor to be an absolutely faithful follower of the Reichsführer, and that I shall always be glad to stand by you and your child in friendship, as doctor and comrade. [. . .] In loyalty and devotion, Heil Hitler! Your Karl Gebhardt."

———————

[237] A brand of candy bar with malt extract and chocolate, still manufactured today. [—Trans.]

In November 1941, Hedwig Potthast had told her sister Thilde about her pregnancy for the first time, in the hope that she might convey this news to their parents diplomatically. She wrote to her, "My last vacation marked the end of my official duties, and since then have been without a profession. [. . .] After my vacation I was then given a half-year leave without salary, and after that I no longer showed up for work. In February [1941] I began to set up a little apartment for myself [. . .]. It is located in a house on Caspar-Theyss-Strasse,[238] which stands empty; in peacetime its downstairs rooms are used by the SS for receptions of foreign guests or for specific meetings. I have been living here since the beginning of May [1941] [. . .]. We have decided to have children and to be together as often as possible without robbing his wife of her rights. They have talked about his reluctance to accept the fact of having no more children, and understand that he will seek a solution to the problem. She must not discover that the way has been found until ours has arrived, and then represents the justification for its own life by its very existence. [. . .] Neither I nor the child will suffer financial need as long as he is alive. The Führer, Bormann, and Wolff know of our secret; Jochen and Sigurd [Peiper], Erika Lorenz, Brandt, Baumert know [. . .]."

Thus Heinrich Himmler and Hedwig Potthast's decision to have children secretly had been carefully planned and long prepared. It was no accident that this coincided with Himmler's Kinderzeugungsbefehl [Edict to Propagate] of 1939–40, in which he publicly called for the conception of illegitimate children and for second marriages, so-called Friedelehen for the SS.[239]

In November 1941, Hedwig Potthast wrote about the way "K.H."[240] imagined the future in a further letter to her sister: "As soon as the war is over he wants to buy us a house in the country on a piece of land which will remain my home and refuge forever. He has the idea of using the land either for a small tree nursery or for breeding small animals, or for cultivating berries in order to

---

[238] The villa owned by the SS was located at 33 Caspar-Theyss-Strasse in Berlin-Grunewald. For a time, Himmler's "Rasputin," the occultist Karl-Maria Wiligut (alias Weisthor), lived there.

[239] See introduction, section III, for discussion of Friedelehe.

[240] "K.H." stands for König Heinrich [King Henry], which is what Hedwig Potthast and other members of the personal staff called Himmler, based on his conviction that he was a reincarnation of the Frankish king Heinrich I (c. 876–936). His mistress continued to do this after the war.

make the land profitable." She herself does not seem to have been very enthusiastic about the idea: "The idea is not bad—I have not quite decided about it yet. It would certainly be a huge adjustment, and I would have to learn so much."

Heinrich Himmler's ideal of the National Socialist "soldier-peasant," who would relocate to the East certainly fit Marga better than Hedwig. Marga was knowledgeable about agriculture, while Hedwig was an educated city-dweller. On the other hand, his mistress was apparently the person in whom he could confide. While Marga's *Journal* entries and the report of her interrogation in 1945 suggest that her husband hardly ever spoke with her about his murderous activity, he seems to have been more open with Hedwig. Besides, as a secretary on his personal staff, she had far greater access to his work.

On February 24, 1942, a few weeks after Helge's birth, Heinrich Himmler went to Munich for the anniversary of the founding of the party. As one can gather from Marga's and Gudrun's journals, he spent three evenings and one morning in Gmund with his family before flying back to Berlin with his wife. Although she noted on March 1 that "Püppi was blissful" about their time together and that the "flight was very beautiful," one can assume that Himmler used their time together finally to inform his wife about his second family. One of Marga's *Journal* entries from the same day suggests this: "Frau Berkelmann wrote me today that she is getting divorced. Her husband is apparently having children with another woman. That does not occur to men until they are rich and respected. Otherwise, older wives have to help feed them or put up with them."

In no place in her *Journal* does she explicitly mention her husband's infidelity or the name of his mistress. During her interrogation in Nuremberg on September 26, 1945, Marga indicated that she had known about her husband's infidelity and about other children, but that she had not known how many other children he had or with which women.

On May 27, 1942, two British-trained Czech resistance fighters carried out an assassination on Reinhard Heydrich, *Chef des Reichssicherheitshauptamtes* [head of the Reich Security HQ] and deputy *Reichsprotektor* in occupied

Czechoslovakia. The assassination took place as Heydrich was driving into the city from his residence outside Prague in order to fly to a long-planned meeting with Hitler about German policies in Czechoslovakia. A week later, on June 4, Heydrich died of his wounds.

Himmler reacted swiftly to the assassination. He conferred with Hitler on May 27 and discussed the new situation with him. Hitler's lust for vengeance knew no bounds: at the beginning of June, in the Czech town of Lidice all the men were shot, the women taken to concentration camps, and the children deported and placed with German families.

On the morning of June 4, when Himmler learned of Heydrich's death, he left for Prague at noon, paid a condolence call on the widow, conferred with the local SS leaders there, and flew back to headquarters that evening to discuss further steps with Hitler.

The state funeral for Heydrich took place in Berlin on June 9. The entire SS leadership participated. Himmler's speech not only expressed the feeling of discontinuity caused by Heydrich's death, but tried to convey a sense of renewed confidence and direction to the SS leadership. He spoke several times of despondency, to which one must never succumb, and of pessimism, which had no place in the SS. He told the men that the war could last for years. For that reason, every workplace had to be systematically combed through and every able-bodied man enlisted in the fight. "The word 'impossible' must not exist, and with us it never will." In view of the high losses among young (and, in Himmler's view, racially valuable) men, he stated that the rebuilding of the SS and the police should be given top priority after the war. Finally, he saw the third great mission as being the German settlement of conquered territories in the East. Himmler's decision to take over the leadership of the Reichssicherheitshauptamt personally shows just how seriously he took the situation.

During the long interval between his last letter of February 1942 and the following one from July, Heinrich Himmler paid several visits to Gmund. His daughter mentions in her *Journal* that a few days after Easter, April 10 to 13, he was in Gmund, and that he came back again on April 30 for a short visit.

On June 7, Gudrun wrote in her *Journal*:

On 20 [May] Mutti finally arrived in the morning. In the evening we sat on the terrace and played Pulok[241] and suddenly we heard a loud car horn and we thought to ourselves, who has the nerve to do that, and it was Pappi (8:30 p.m.). He had just come from Holland and had [brought] a lot of fruit, vegetables, and 150 tulips. [. . .]"[242] Unfortunately, Mutti left again for Berlin on the 29th, then on 1.6., on to Riga, to take charge of a military sanitarium there while the head nurse is on vacation (1 month). On May 4, Reichsprotektor Heydrich died of his serious injuries (assassination). He will be buried on 9.6. It is a state funeral. Pappi is speaking, he was very very sad.

[June 27, 1942]

Pappi arrived on 13 [June] at 7:00, later we played Pulok. In the morning we played Äffi, that was nice. Long ago I once saw Pappi in civilian clothing, now he finally is wearing it again. We two went alone to the Waller Hunt,[243] everyone had binoculars, we walked through the woods, I picked flowers and moss. It was so lovely. In the afternoon we went rowing on the lake. [. . .] It was a wonderful day. Unfortunately, he left the next day at noon again.

———————

A week later, on June 20, Himmler visited Gmund again for an evening during his wife's absence. The reason for his visit was the state funeral of Korpsführer [corps leader] Adolf Hühnlein on June 21 in Munich. Meanwhile, after having been vaccinated, Marga came down with smallpox and spent fourteen days in a field hospital in Mitau (*Journal*, 4.8.42). On July 4 Himmler traveled to

---

[241] Sag nix über Pulok! [Don't Say Anything About Pulok] was a favorite game at the time. A parlor game for two to five players, involving letter tiles, the goal of which was to form the sentence "Sag nix über Pulok!" [—Trans.]

[242] Himmler was in Holland May 16–20, 1942. There he met with Reichskommissar Arthur Seyss-Inquart, and with both of the two adversarial leaders of the NS movement in the Netherlands (NSB), Anton Mussert and Meinoud Rost van Tonningen. He had landed in Munich at 18:00 and driven from there to Gmund.

[243] A hunting ground on the nearby Wallberg Mountain.

Tilsit and accompanied his wife to Berlin on the train. She stayed there until July 20 before traveling on to Gmund.

On July 11 Marga noted in her *Journal*, "Such a pack of lies, I can't stand it anymore. Püppi not here. I am always alone, I would like to go there but Frau Hermann is not here and I just cannot get away. H. is beside himself about this. I just cannot manage in this world. [. . .] Why am I always supposed to go to Gmund? I do not work here much at all, at most 3 or 4 hours in the Red Cross office."

The following letter from her husband, however, does not betray any of these tensions between the two.

———————

Berlin, June 1, 1942, with Nora Hermann.
15.7.42

My good Mami!

Before I leave here, I want make sure you get a quick note from me, and also a couple of flowers. The next time I write, it will be from Russia.

Thank you so much for your sweet letters of 6, 11, and 12.7.—As I told you on the telephone, the business with Werner Födisch has already been taken care of. I think the next time I see him, he will be on duty, either for me or on a *kolkhoz* [collective farm—Trans.].

I was not able to send Püppi any crabs, I would gladly have done so for our little gourmet. She is happy that she has vacation now and is so looking forward to your arrival. But Mami, you really do have to stay in Gmund for 2 or 3 months so you can truly get some rest, that was necessary even before your trip east, and now after you've gone and gotten smallpox, definitely.

—So, be *very sweet to yourself* for a change and do it.

In the coming days I will be in Lublin, Zamosch, Auschwitz, Lemberg, and then am moving to new quarters.[244] I am curious to see how, and whether, our telephone conversations will work. It is roughly 2000 kilometers from Gmund. Now all my love, have a good journey, and really

———————

[244] The "new quarters" were his new field command post "Hegewald," near Schitomyr (Zhytomyr, Ukraine), which he inspected on July 26, 1942.

lovely days in Gmund with our little daughter. Many affectionate greetings
and kisses

      Your Pappi.

————————

Once German troops began to kill Jews systematically within the Soviet theater of war, beginning in the summer of 1941, the Polish Jews were also threatened with mass murder. After the option of deporting Jews from the occupied
regions in western Poland to the General Gouvernement had been eliminated,
the German occupiers were uncertain about what to do with the ghettos. There
were 140,000 people crammed into the ghetto in Lodz, which created cata-
strophic malnutrition and disastrous hygiene, which led in turn to devastating
epidemics. This gave the Germans a fresh opportunity to portray the ghettos
as "cauldrons of pestilence" that had to be ruthlessly cleansed.

In October 1941, Gauleiter Arthur Greiser asked Himmler for permission
to kill one hundred thousand Jews who had been classified as incapable of working. Following this, an extermination site with mobile gas chambers was set up
in nearby Kulmhof (Chelmno), where people were methodically murdered from
December onward. Among the first victims were Gypsies (Roma) from the Austrian Burgenland who had been deported to Lodz.

In mid-October 1941, Himmler ordered Odilo Globocnik, SS- and Police
chief in Lublin, to establish a regional extermination camp in Belzec for Polish Jews in the General Gouvernement. At the same time, T4 experts from the
death squads that had specialized in eliminating the handicapped and the sick,
were transferred to Lublin. It would be their task to build the new extermination camps where gas would be used in the murders. In contrast with Kulmhof (Chelmno), now for the first time large-scale gas chambers were built in
Belzec with powerful engines attached for the sole purpose of killing people
with their exhaust.

The "clearance" of the Jewish ghetto in Lublin and nearby towns began
directly after Himmler's visit to Kracow and Lublin. By the middle of April,
in Belzec, approximately forty-four thousand people classified as "incapable of
working" had been murdered. In the beginning of May, Sobibor was added,
and in the second half of July, Treblinka, to which the inhabitants of the Warsaw Ghetto were brought to be murdered immediately in the gas chambers.

Himmler met almost daily with Heydrich between April 26 and May 2, and on April 23 and May 3 he had long meetings with Hitler. He apparently wished to have the executive powers in occupied Poland placed under his control. The governor general, Hans Frank, had been politically weakened in an extensive corruption scandal; Friedrich-Wilhelm Krüger, Hitler's deputy in the region and the higher SS and Police leader, was named state secretary for security in the General Gouvernement on May 7.

On July 17, 1942, Himmler flew to Kattowitz and from there drove on to Auschwitz. According to the descriptions given by the camp commandant, Rudolf Höss, during this two-day visit Himmler focused on all aspects of Auschwitz, inspecting laboratories, nurseries, rubber trees, and animal breeding operations. In Birkenau, according to Höss, he viewed "the entire process of extermination" with precision: the arrival of a transport from Holland, the "selection of those able to work," and the murder of several hundred Jews with gas. On July 19 Himmler gave the order that there should be no more Jews left in the General Gouvernement by the end of the year.

Now began the most terrible period of the mass murders. In just a few months, between July and November 1942, well over 2 million people fell victim to methodical genocide. Under the direction of German police, it was mostly local people who drove the Jews from their houses and into the ghettos. Sick and handicapped people, or young children who had been left behind, were shot on the spot. The other victims were collected in a central place where selections then followed accordingly; those who could work were initially spared deportation and certain death. All the others were driven to the railroad station and taken by train to the extermination centers. In the three camps of the Aktion Reinhard alone, more than 1.4 million were gassed. About 435,000 people died in Belzec; in Sobibor, between 160,000 and 200,000. In the extermination camp at Treblinka, around 850,000 people were killed.

The name Auschwitz in particular has become synonymous with one of the most horrible crimes in human history. Although it was first established in 1939 as a camp for Polish political prisoners, it was expanded in 1941 for thousands of Soviet prisoners of war. Prisoners had always been murdered during these years, but two crematoria were included in the planning for the new camp at Auschwitz-Birkenau in September 1941. The first murders using Zyklon B [gas—Trans.] were carried out on Soviet prisoners of war in September 1941. From July 1942, trains filled with deported Jews from all of western Europe were running regularly. At the platform in Birkenau, SS doctors divided victims into the categories of "able to work" and "unable to work." Those classified as unable to work (primarily old people and mothers with their children) were murdered immediately in two renovated farmhouses in which the rooms functioned as gas chambers. Later, in the spring of 1943, two large new crematoria were finished, each of which was fitted with its own gas chamber. A third camp, Monowitz, was built in Auschwitz when the chemical firm of IG Farben sought a site for its new factory, which was to manufacture synthetic rubber, important for the war effort. In Auschwitz, however, not a single kilogram of synthetic rubber was ever produced, but plans for a German model city with a gigantic forced-labor camp took shape. Visions of settlement and extermination policies went hand in hand.

———

Hegewald 28 July 1942

My good Mami!

I shall soon be flying from here to Finland. I have just spoken with you both on the telephone, now you are going to get a few more lines from me. Enclosed is Püppi's report card. True, it could be somewhat better.

In Finland I am hoping to relax a little bit outside of my official duties. Officially, of course, there's a lot going on. Visit with the president, foreign minister, Marshal Mannerheim, then to the north to see Dietl and visit the division.

I am enclosing a pamphlet about drying techniques; perhaps it will interest you.

In a great hurry now, much love and *get better.*

Greetings and kisses,

Your Pappi

Helsinki, 30.7.42

My dear Mami and dear Püppi!

I was greeted here most pleasantly and cordially by the Finnish government.

Now I am off to the North. I am very well.

Enclosed a couple of little things for Mami and the scamp.

Many loving greetings and kisses,

Your Pappi

Himmler's unofficial trip to Finland lasted from July 29 to August 5, 1942. There he met with the president, Risto Ryti; the premier, Johan Rangell, Foreign Minister Rolf Witting, and Field Marshal Carl G. E. von Mannerheim. Afterward he flew to Rovaniemi, in the North, where he spent two days with General-Oberst [colonel general] Eduard Dietl and the SS-Division Nord. He had known Dietl since their time in the Freikorps Epp. From 1942 to 1944, Dietl was commander in chief of the Twentieth Army Mountain Corps in Norway; in 1944 he died in an airplane crash.

Following the advice of Felix Kersten, Himmler spent one day on the island of Petäys, to rest there with the help of the "healing and magnetic powers of sunbathing." During a subsequent meeting with Rangell on August 4, Rangell refused to condone the marginalization and persecution of local Jews, with the justification that they were completely assimilated. According to the record kept by Rudolf Brandt, Himmler responded "that one can only solve the social question by killing the others and taking their fields."

Hegewald, 10.8.42

My good Mami!

I want you to have a brief note from me along with the package—the little basket is for you, it is very practical and made out of birch bark.—I have sent you all kinds of paper: tissues, wax paper, toilet paper; two little lamps for you and Püppi, two wash cloths for you and Püppi. In addition, a wooden tray and wooden bowl, then laundry bag for Mami's trip.—Two Finnish dolls, the wooden dish for the scamp.—Some scouring powder, an old toothbrush of mine (maybe you can use it for polishing shoes or something similar), otherwise a couple of Finnish coins and two little bags to snack on for Mami and little daughter, and letter paper for Aunt Parre.[245]

I am enclosing a letter from Gertrud von Patom for you.

Many thanks for your nice little package from the pharmacist and the charming photographs and both your letters from 24.7 and 4.8!

I have lots of work and meetings. I will write Püppi soon and will tell you a bit about Finland and here. I am very glad that Frau von Schade and Fräulein Görlitzer are visiting you, give them my best.—There are *30* eggs from this region waiting for you in Berlin from me.—Paula's[246] fourth child is their *third* girl, her name is Ute. Why don't you send them a telegram from you and Püppi.

I have to close now. Do not be so terribly industrious, relax a little bit too!

Many affectionate greetings and kisses to you and Püppi,
Your Pappi

———

After July 1942, Hegewald, near Schitomyr [Zhytomir], was Himmler's Ukrainian headquarters. The same name that was used for his headquarters in East Prussia was transferred to the new one, while the expanded command post in East Prussia was renamed Hochwald. Whereas the former command post accommodated approximately five hundred people, the new quarters, which were on a small former Soviet airfield between Schitomir and Winniza, were markedly larger. More than one hundred SS officers and a force of one thousand SS police were stationed there. The facility included an airfield, a cemetery, bunkers, banquet rooms, elegant houses, and an office and private quarters for the Reichsführer-SS. Himmler was frequently stationed in Hegewald through the summer of 1943. In November and December 1943, the facility was destroyed by retreating SS police forces.

During this time Hanns Johst stayed at Hegewald, as he did so often during

---

[245] This is what the family sometimes called Lydia. Old Parre is a character from the novel *Rulaman* (see letter of 5.5.29). In that context, she is the wise old ancestress. The nickname probably derives not only from the fact that Lydia used to write fairy tales, but also because, like her brother-in-law, she loved "ancient Germanic" traditions and customs.
[246] Ernst Himmler's wife.

the war years. Rudolf Brandt's minutes of Himmler's table talk of August 11, 1942, record, "SS-Gruppenführer Hanns Johst arrived here on 8 August and, in accordance with the wishes of the Reichsführer-SS, will stay circa four weeks, in order to join various trips. SS-Gruppenführer Hanns Johst is more or less the bard of the SS."

Johst and Himmler spent a great deal of time together; they ate together, amused themselves by fishing in the afternoons, and in the evenings, engaged in extensive conversations.

———

On September 6, 1942, Marga wrote in her *Journal*:

Tomorrow I am going to Berlin again. I have been here for seven weeks. Püppi and I were in the Hotel Vier Jahreszeiten [Four Seasons] in Munich for almost 8 days; Lydia spent 2 days with us.[247] We waited for H. He arrived, visited his parents' graves, the exhibition, then we went to the Scharfes' in Starnberg and were in Gmund by Friday evening. H. stayed until Monday after dinner. He just telephoned and is quite surprised that I already want to go to Berlin.

[September 29, 1942]

I went to Berlin on 7.9. There is much to do here with the Red Cross. But it satisfied me completely. I could not be in this war if I did not have work outside of the house. [. . .] H. has been here since yesterday. There is a lot that is new and interesting. In the evening I am almost always alone. Ladies will visit this afternoon.

[November 29]

There is much to do before Christmas, but it all makes me happy. If only it did not have to be done in such a rush. I went to the theater 2x.

---

[247] Gudrun writes about this in her *Journal*: "On 24 August we went to Munich (Mutti, Aunt Lydia, I). We stayed in the Hotel Vier Jahreszeiten in Pappi's apartment" (3.9.42). According to Marga's household budget accounts, the hotel bill for these days came to 241 RM.

1x to the Staatstheater [State Theater]. Content: outrageous. Theater des Volkes [People's Theater]: very good. I went to a fashion show 2x. [. . .]

According to Gudrun's *Journal*, Himmler was in Gmund October 8–9, 1942, with his family for a late celebration of his birthday. He then traveled on to Italy, and on October 15, on his return trip, spent another night in Gmund. Later, when Gudrun looked back, she also noted that he had "been there 2 or 3 times in November."

December 16–19 Himmler again stayed in Gmund and Munich. In Munich he met Erich Schnitzler, the head of the SS office there. He also visited his parents' graves both on the way there and upon departure; and on December 17, celebrated an early Christmas with his wife and the children. Gudrun writes about this: "Christmas was wonderful, I got so many things, 14 books, place settings, things for my doll house, a fur outfit, and a 1000 other things" (entry of January 19, 1943).

During this year of the war, Himmler visited Gmund with remarkable frequency.

26.12.42

My good Mami!

I spent yesterday and today moving, and have very nice quarters in a new, very livable barracks, large workroom, bath, bedroom, and breakfast room.[248]

I have a *huge* amount of work, but that does not matter; the year is going to be difficult and will demand more of us than all other years.

Enclosed is a late Christmas packet of coffee from the Führer, a picture of the Hegewaldheim here in East Prussia (the one that corresponds to the other Hegewaldheim in Gmund), a little package from the Zipperers[249] for Püppi, book and letter from Gauleiter Hofer (please excuse the fact that it was opened by mistake, I am just searching for the little piece of [*handi?*]work,

---

[248] On December 25, 1942, in East Prussia, Himmler moved from his old quarters, "Friedrichsruh," and into the field command post, which was immediately renamed Hochwald.
[249] Falk Zipperer received his doctorate in 1937, and following that, was a legal adviser at the "Deutschrechtliches Institut [Institute of German Law] in Bonn, which belonged to the SS-Ahnenerbe (see commentary on the letter of 7.7.39).

and I shall send it along then), marzipan, flour, and sugar from Gauleiter Koch.—
The chamois trophy with the horns is from the hunt in the Steiermark (Styria).
I think it is best if we put it in a cupboard in the library at first. You should
have a look at the album and the books, some of them are very beautiful, and
then keep them for me. Especially nice is the book *Ein menschlich Land* [A
Humane Country]—very obviously Bavaria!!

The courier is already leaving. Get better, both of you—you and our dear
little daughter.

And now many sweet greetings and kisses,
Your Pappi

My best to Lydia and Frau Albers[250]

After the National Socialists came to power, persecution of the Roma and Sintis increased. They were interned, and a great many of them were deported in
the spring of 1941 from Reich territory and into occupied Poland. On December 16, 1942, Himmler gave the order to send "all those of Gypsy blood, Roma
Gypsies, and members of Gypsy clans of Balkan origin and non-German blood"
from Germany, Austria, and Czechoslovakia to the concentration camps. A so-
called "Gypsy Camp" was established in Auschwitz, to which around 23,000
people were brought. In the spring of 1944 there were only about 6,000 of them
still alive; they were then killed in the gas chambers in August 1944. According to estimates, up to a half million Roma and Sintis were murdered in German-
occupied territories.

5.1.1943

My good Mami!

My most affectionate thanks for both the letters from 24.12 and 2.1. I am
so glad that you and our dear little daughter are having a restful time in beautiful
Gmund. Eat and sleep well! I think it is wonderful that you have gained three

---

[250] Frau Albers, a native Englishwoman, gave Marga English lessons and tutored Gudrun in
English (Gudrun's and Marga's *Journal*).

pounds. Thank God that your recent "car adventure" ended so well. I was actually a bit nervous afterward. Enjoy the days in our dear Munich and go to the theater. Please be so kind as to take Püppi to visit her grandparents' graves!

Two packages enclosed: gingerbread, a little piece of fruitcake, the belt for you, the beautiful Bohemian glass vase, a book for Gerhard, books I have read for storage; 2 are nice to read and look at (about Danzig and Schobert).— I am thinking over the matter concerning Födisch and Schönthaler. I am also sending two little calendars, one for Mami, who should choose, and the other for our little scamp. Enclosed is a letter from Maria Wendler.[251]

It looks bad for another visit.

All my love, many greetings and kisses,

Your Pappi

In the beginning of January 1943 the situation of the Sixth Army had become hopeless. This fighting force had set out to conquer Stalingrad and with that clear the way for the conquest of the Caucasus and the important oil fields on the Black Sea. Soviet soldiers defended Stalingrad with unexpected tenacity. By November 22 the Red Army had successfully established a defensive position that encircled the whole city. It was possible to supply the German soldiers only by air, which became ever more difficult.

For Hitler, the siege of Stalingrad had become an issue of prestige, a question of his personal victory over his adversary, Stalin. He therefore gave Paulus an order to stand fast and refused to let him break out of the cauldron.[252] Thus 250,000 soldiers were trapped in the largely destroyed city during the winter, and could receive only the barest minimum of supplies from the Luftwaffe. On January 18, German troops had to give up their last lines of defense and retreat completely into the city. Despite Hitler's expectation that his army should fight to its "heroic death," Paulus surrendered on January 31 with his remaining troops in the southern part of the cauldron. The northern sector did the same two days later.

---

[251] In 1934 Maria Wendler became the third wife of Himmler's brother-in-law, Richard Wendler. She lived with her husband in the General Gouvernement.

[252] See note to commentary following Marga's *Journal* entry of July 5, 1941, regarding the "Kesselschlacht" at Stalingrad.

2.4.43

My dear Mami!

A quick and sweet hello before I fly off. Enclosed you will find Gerhard's report card, three copies of the essay "Kämpfer für eine Weltaunschauung" [Fighters for a Worldview] (for you, for Püppi, for the nieces), the money, the lecture by Dwinger.[256] Also six packets of [yerba] maté.

Baumert is sending bobby pins, they are coming from Denmark.—All my good wishes. I will call you again on Wednesday.

Many sweet greetings and kisses to you and our beloved little daughter,

Your Pappi

On March 30, 1943, Himmler was present at a "meeting with the Führer" on the Obersalzberg, and from there he flew back to the Eastern Front.

Himmler's nieces, the daughters of his brother Gebhard, had been living in Gmund with their mother since March. Gudrun writes of this in her *Journal*: "Because of the many attacks in Berlin, Aunt Edith Boden with 2 children and Aunt Hilde Himmler with 3 children arrived in mid-March. Both families are living at the inn" (entry of 7.6.43). Gudrun, who was then thirteen years old, went to school in Reichersbeuern with her two oldest cousins (who were fifteen and twelve years old).

At the beginning of March, Gudrun had noted, "If only the war were over, Pappi says we still have to fight and sacrifice a lot" (entry of 9.3.43).

[256] Edwin Erich Dwinger (1898–1981), agronomist, folkish writer, war correspondent. After 1942 he increasingly criticized German policies in the East, and as a result was forbidden to publish and was placed under house arrest. Himmler apparently continued to appreciate his writing.

The capitulation of the Wehrmacht at Stalingrad was the decisive turning point of the war. Approximately 150,000 German soldiers had died in the fight, or from hunger and cold. Around 90,000 were taken prisoner by the Russians, of whom very few survived. Most important, this defeat had grave consequences for German certainty of victory. Doubts about the "Endsieg" [Final Victory] increased, despite the attempts of the NS leadership to represent the demise of the Sixth Army as a heroic epic, and despite Goebbels's call for "total war" in his speech in the Sport Palace on February 18, 1943. The mobilization of all personnel and material resources was ordered for the "final victory:" all German men between the ages of sixteen and sixty-five, as well as all women between seventeen and forty-five, could now be drafted to defend the Reich. The labor shortage that this caused in turn brought about an increased recruitment of forced labor.

According to Gudrun's *Journal* (19.1.43), she was with her mother and Gerhard in Munich January 7–9, where they again were living in the fashionable Hotel Vier Jahreszeiten. During this time, she went skating, attended several theater performances, met the Fahrenkamps and other friends, and ate star chef Alfred Walterspiel's cuisine in the hotel's elegant restaurant.

Hochwald, 9.2.43[253]

My good Mami!

Thanks for your little letter and the beautiful smoked things. I am sending you two magazines. One of them, *Germanische Gemeinschaft* [Germanic Community] is especially good; I am also including a good essay about the SS. Do you like the Königsberg marzipan? Püppi got some too.—In summer, things will be easier when it comes to alcohol and eggs.—Our little imp is also getting the magazine, and also a map of Mami's home region.

Lots of loving greetings and kisses,

Your Pappi

[253] Postcard with the printed legend "Der Reichsgau Warteland, Bildreihe das Schöne Posen (Poznan)" (The Reich District Warteland, Picture Series: Beautiful Posen").

Two editions of the series *Germanische Gemeinschaft* appeared, one in 1941 and the second in 1942. The publication was a large-format magazine with full-page glossy photographs of soldiers, workers, and farmers—idealized Nordic types playing sports or folk dancing—and Germanic kings. The texts on such themes as *Germanisches Erbe* (Germanic heritage], *Wanderzug nach Osten* [migration to the east], or *Sippe und Heimat* [clan and homeland] were short and pithy, mostly quotations from sources such as speeches by Hitler or Himmler. In addition there were short poems and excerpts from letters by Waffen-SS soldiers. The major theme of both editions was the community of all Germanic peoples: "the 20th century is the century of the rebirth of the Germanic idea. The awakening is coming from all German and Germanic peoples. Wherever men of Germanic blood have joined the fight for a new Europe of their own free will, we greet them as comrades and brothers." These words were accompanied by corresponding portraits of Dutch, Flemish, Norwegian, and Danish volunteers.

9.2.43[254]

Dear Mami!

Enclosed find the tea for Frau Göring.—How can you even think such a thing, my good Mami!

Lots of loving greetings and kisses,

Your Pappi

At the Red Cross, Marga had made friends especially with women from a higher social class who, like her, were also volunteering and whose husbands were playing significant public roles—women such as Ilse Göring, Frau Hofmeister, and Frau Hase. Frau Hofmeister is named several times in her and Gudrun's journals. Her husband, Georg Hofmeister (1892–1959), held the rank of *Generalmajor* [major general]. After the arrest and execution of the *Stadtkommandant* [city commander] Paul Hase in connection with the at-

---

[254] Military postcard showing Gruppenführer der Waffen-SS [group leader of the Waffen-SS].

---

tempted assassination of Hitler of July 20, 1944, Hofmeister became Stadtkommandant of Greater Berlin, a position he held until the end the war.

19.2.194?

My good Mami!

Just a short note in haste, so the courier can take it all with him. Lamp and electric plug for Countess Wedel, marzipan and sweets plus ½ lb. of coffee for you. (We are starting to run out of that) then the vials [of oil or ointment?—Trans.] for rubbing in. G [goes] onto one arm, A onto the other; each one should be good for a couple of applications.

I will look into the palaces of the Prince of Hessen. The courier for Gmund leaves tomorrow.—I will send you the Cinzano from Berlin. At the moment I cannot place any orders with the firm of Verporten.—

Many great thanks for your sweet letter of 12.2.—Enclosed find two little flowers, and in the envelope, an interesting report by Dollmann,* a letter from [Frau] Attolico, and the *Totenfeier* [funeral service] for the Prince of Hessen.[255]

Now get well really soon, my good Mami, and lots of greetings and kisses,

Your Pappi

*please return this

---

[255] Ludwig von Hessen. His wife, Margaret, was surely known to Marga in her role as an official of the Red Cross. During the war, she placed at least one family palace at the disposal of the Red Cross for use as a field hospital, possibly in response to a request from Marga Himmler. ("I will look into the palaces of the Prince of Hessen.") The Totenfeier was presumably a printed memorial service for Ludwig's brother, who had died with his family when their airplane crashed in 1937.

Bergwald,[257] *11.4.43*

My good Mami!

I have just heard that a car is leaving for Munich, and I do not want to let it go without a little letter and couple of things.—I have read the things, some are quite good, you should have a look.

Shampoo and the hair clips are for our little scamp, as are the WHW [Winterhilfswerk] flowers. The bobby pins and cards with sweets are for you. Furthermore, two photographs from Angoulême for Püppi's collection. Many thanks for your sweet letter of 3.4! I continue to be worried about the matter concerning Werner Födisch. It would be good if the Födisches did not take this thing quite so dramatically. Nobody is going to kill Werner; he just tried to do that himself.[258]

I will have the bills from Spree paid.

I am enclosing a very good *Leitheft*[259] and an interesting essay about the Prussian military doctors and a booklet of postage stamps.—Our little scamp will soon be getting a letter.—Get some good rest, my good Mami.

And now many loving greetings and kisses to you and the little scamp!

    Hoping to see you soon!

    Your Pappi

Reichenhall,[260] *22.4.43*

My good Mami!

I want to write you a few lines before I fly off tomorrow. I hope you like the box of assorted candies and that the scamp likes the ones with the candied almonds.

---

[257] Himmler's headquarters on the Obersalzberg.

[258] Werner Foedisch (whose name the Himmlers spell inconsistently either Foedisch or Födisch) (b. 1910), the son of Marga's friend, was a member of the Waffen-SS and a *Gebietslandwirt* [district agriculturalist] in the Hegewald sector. He and his superior, Karl Sulkowski, head of the Rasse- und Siedlungsdienststelle [Office of Race and Resettlement Office] in Jytomyr, were charged in March 1943 with "profiteering from foodstuffs, black market trade, and illegal slaughtering of pigs and calves." Foedisch was threatened with a sentence for "undermining military morale by attempting suicide."

[259] The *SS-Leitheft* [*SS Leadership* magazine] was published from 1934 to 1945. [—Trans.]

[260] In 1934, when the Obersalzberg was expanded to create a second administrative center, the

This is meant as a little post-Easter greeting from your Pappi.[261]

Enclosed is a good picture of the three little Ribbentrop children, they really look nice! I shall take a package for Rudi with me to the front.[262]—I am again enclosing a copy of the *Leitheft* containing a number of very good articles. So tomorrow I shall be flying off, but I shall telephone you just beforehand. I shall be visiting all four SS divisions over there. I will be back in 8 days.

Many affectionate greetings and kisses to you and Püppi!—Get some good rest and get better.

Your Pappi

My best to Aunt Lydia and Frau Albers.—How is Püppi's English coming along?

———————

In January 1943 during a visit to Warsaw, Himmler ordered the complete destruction of the Jewish ghetto. Yet when SS troops entered the ghetto on April 19 to seize its remaining inhabitants, they unexpectedly encountered armed resistance. Despite the military superiority of the German troops, several hundred Jewish resistance fighters, men and women, defended themselves with desperate courage and inflicted appreciable losses on the SS. The SS had to resort to extreme brutality and employ heavy military equipment to crush the insurrection.

The courage and determination of the Jewish fighters shocked the NS leadership and intensified the resolution to implement the "Final Solution" as rapidly as possible without further thought of using this Jewish population as a source of labor. On June 19, 1943, Hitler gave Himmler the order that "despite the ensuing unrest that this measure will create over the next 3 or 4 months, the evacuation of Jews must be radically and thoroughly implemented and enforced."

◦⟨⟩◦

———————————————————

"Regierungsflughafen Reichenhall-Berchtesgaden" [Government Airport of Reichenhall-Berchtesgaden] was opened. This new facility could accommodate large aircraft.

[261] In 1943, Easter fell on April 25. Himmler, however, had visited Gmund a week before Easter (Gudrun's *Journal* of 7.6.43).

[262] Rudolf Ribbentrop (b. 1921), eldest son of the Ribbentrops, was at the time a führer in the Waffen-SS at the battle of Charkow (Kharkov) in the Ukraine, and also part of Operation Citadelle [the German offensive against the Kursk Salient, a major tank battle. [—Trans.]

15.5.43

My dear good Mami!

We have just spoken on the telephone.—Tomorrow is Mother's Day. Püppi and I are sending you the flowers and, along with them *many* affectionate, good wishes. When the flowers, the little package, and my letter arrive, then go get our Yule light from Berlin and light it. I will do the same outside here with my own, and Püppi will do it with ours in Gmund, and then we will all think of each other.

I will call you tomorrow morning and will be in Königsberg during the day, where I have meetings with Gauleiter Koch, and will also be visiting the widow and the children of one of my oldest SS people.[263]

With thanks in my heart I send you many affectionate greetings and kisses,

Your Pappi

We will both be telephoning our dear little daughter tomorrow morning. I am enclosing a little magazine by Colonel Scherff. You must read it, it is excellent, and there is a picture of me. Enjoy the sweet things!

21.5.43

My dear Mami!

I hope the little crabs taste good! These air raids are just too vile! I always feel so sorry for you when I have slept well and then I hear in the morning that the planes have been there.

Many many affectionate greetings and kisses,

Your Pappi

———

The Allies had been expanding their strategy of carpet bombing since the beginning of the year. Although the Ruhr area and other cities in the western part of Germany had at first been the primary target of the attacks, by 1943 the population in all of Germany was affected by American and British air raids. More

———

[263] Possibly the widow of SS-Oberführer [senior leader, Waffen-SS] Kurt Benson (1902–42).

and more often, people spent sleepless and fearful nights in air-raid shelters and the cellars of houses, and on the following day, were confronted with countless corpses, fires, and ruins. The aim of these attacks was not only to destroy German industry (specifically munitions plants) and infrastructure, but also to break the endurance of the populace. The consequences were devastating: by the end of the war only a handful of cities had been spared by the carpet bombing. In the firestorm that engulfed Hamburg from July 25 to August 3, 1943, thirty-four thousand people died. A total of four hundred thousand to six hundred thousand people fell victim to the Allied air raids upon German cities. Despite the growing doubts among the population about an "Endsieg" [final victory], the bombardments did not motivate the people to turn against the NS leadership as the Allies had hoped. Given the fact that political opposition had long since been destroyed and that terror had increased in the country since the declaration of "total war," this could hardly have been expected. Instead, the grueling bombardments led to increased resentment against the Allies and strengthened the population's determination to persevere stubbornly to the end.

On June 9, 1943, Marga writes in her *Journal*: "The calm within the German Red Cross is only superficial. We are finally going to be combined with the Wehrmacht. I cannot even write down all the other things that are happening outside the war. I do not know whether one can still even believe in a human being. Sometimes one thinks one cannot bear it anymore, but at least I have my child. How I despise people. Püppi asks me why I do not write in my journal more than I do. Only Elfriede has noticed the change in my nature. How well she knows me. I am in Gmund, we often have visitors."

————————

25.6.43

My good Mami!

I am enclosing a little package with sweets and candied fruits and brandy-filled [chocolate] beans, and a can of condensed milk. Also a few packets of glucose and marzipan, so that in those terrible nights, you have something to feast on and to help you fall asleep better.

You have to take the glucose if you are upset with the Red Cross—it will strengthen you.

Today I sent Püppi a package, something for our little gourmet, two books for Aunt Lydia (for Easter and her birthday) and books from me for the library. Then I sent a box of cookies to Gmund for you, which I am sure you can use.

I am including a couple of books for you, one of the *Constanze* (I would like to read this someday in Gmund), then the *König Geiserich* as a solstice present, and the Bismarck book. I would like to read this last one once you have read it.

There is so much work, one meeting after another.

From Saturday through Tuesday I will be on duty at parade grounds; I will be looking at very interesting new methods of shooting.—Tuesday afternoon I will be back and will call you.—I hope that the beasts do not chase you out too often. Do not stay in Berlin for too long.

Many affectionate greetings and kisses! And do be really careful.

Your Pappi

This letter, as well as other similar ones, make it clear that right until the end the relationship between these two spouses was much closer than had been formerly assumed, despite Heinrich's second wife. They telephoned each other regularly, and he looked after her well-being consistently. In offering her an endless stream of treats, he was surely trying not just to comfort his wife during the sleepless nights of the bombardment and about her constant "trouble" with the Red Cross, but also to calm her complaints about his frequent absence and her anger at his infidelity.

It becomes clear, furthermore, that they continued to find it important to give each other books for certain occasions, for example, at the solstice, and to exchange books that they had each been reading. Up until the end he continued to send her articles from magazines, his own speeches, and letters from shared acquaintances; and he wanted to know her opinion about these.

Constanze probably refers to the book by Robert Ries (1926) about the Empress Constance, the medieval queen of Sicily and wife of Heinrich VI. The book about King Geiserich was doubtless that of the same title by Hans

Friedrich Blunck (1937), *Eine Erzählung von Geiserich, und dem Zug der Wandalen* (A Story About Geiserich and the Migration of the Vandals). Geiserich, a king of the Vandals, had conquered North Africa and Carthage and was known as a wise, and also the mightiest, king, from the period of the great migrations.

After the invasion of the Soviet Union in 1941, issues concerning the Waffen-SS were at the core of Himmler's activity. The German armies desperately needed more and more soldiers, and the Wehrmacht could recruit only German men, whereas the Waffen-SS was able to create foreign units. An examination of Himmler's notes from his meetings with Hitler from 1941 to 1942 and thereafter, shows that establishing new Waffen-SS divisions was of paramount importance. Since the Waffen-SS units were under the control of the regular Army High Command, they were often split up, poorly equipped, and deployed in battle in order to spare the Wehrmacht. The result was high losses in Waffen-SS units. Himmler's inspection tours to the front often served to solve problems between SS and army units.

Norwegians, Finns, Swedes, and Danes were recruited for the SS, as were Flemings, Dutch, French, and even Bosnian Muslims. The SS made a special effort to create divisions composed of ethnic Germans in southeastern Europe. For this it was very important that the leaders of the German ethnic groups were placed directly under Himmler's authority in March 1941. Hungary alone provided almost twenty thousand men, who were partly recruited under false pretenses. In 1942 the Yugoslavian Germans were mobilized in the newly established SS Mountain Division Prinz Eugen. A tendency for enforced recruitment became increasingly evident, especially in Serbia and Croatia. In 1941–44, in this way, the number of Waffen-SS divisions was doubled from four to eight, and at the beginning of 1945, it even reached forty divisions—although most of these had long since lacked the requisite complement of soldiers.

30.6.43

My good Mami!

Enclosed are two eels and a couple of jars of fish. If you want, you can send an eel to our "little scamp," and give Frau Kränzlin[264] some of the jars.

Furthermore I am including the money for July as well as a shameless Russian caricature that is supposed to make you laugh and not get upset.—I wish you a good recovery from your poor back problem; if only I could help you with the work. An affectionate greeting and kiss your Pappi.

We will be speaking with each other tomorrow afternoon.

2.7.43

My good beloved Mami!

I wanted to write you a long letter, but now there are so terribly many people around, and time just does not permit it.

When you get this letter tomorrow, I will be thinking of you, full of love and gratitude, my dear little scamp, thinking of our 15th anniversary and our dear little daughter who soon will be turning 14.

All my good thoughts and wishes are of you and with you.

The roses are meant as a very affectionate greeting! In the little box there is a beautiful piece of amber; I got it at Christmas from Gauleiter Koch, and since then it has been standing here in East Prussia in my field command office, and I have enjoyed it every day and often held it in my hand. Precisely because I value this so highly, it should now become your present for our wedding anniversary, and in the future it should always stand in your room with you and then we will take joy in it together!

Stay healthy for my sake, and may God[265] preserve you always, when the airplanes come!

    I kiss your sweet mouth and your good hands! With love,

    Your Pappi

---

[264] Frau Krenzlin, or Kränzlin, lived with her eight-year-old son in Gmund during the war. Marga and Gudrun met them both on a vacation to the North Sea (Gudrun's *Journal* of 31.7.43).

[265] Himmler used the archaic Germanic spelling, *Got*, instead of the modern German *Gott* (God).

Hochwald, 16.7.43

My good Mami!

We just spoke together and now I only want to add a few more lines to you for his envelope.—I hope you like the peaches!—Have a look at this copy of the new magazine *Westland* and keep it; it is published by us. I think it is good. I am sending you two transcripts as well, one about my discussion with Mussert, who is unfortunately horribly petty and narrow-minded (feel free to keep this); I need to have the other one about the Bogomils returned.—In addition the book *Helden unter dem Sonnenbanner* [Heroes Under the Banner of the Sun] is enclosed, and then some stamps showing the face of our good man Heydrich for you. I have also sent Püppi some.

I thank you for your little letter of 10.7, it goes without saying that you should write me such things; but I really had not forgotten it.

Now many affectionate greetings and kisses,

Your Pappi

The journal *Westland* was published by Reichskommissar Arthur Seyss-Inquart for the occupied Netherlands. The book *Helden unter dem Sonnenbanner—von Hawai bis Singapur* (1943) [Heroes Under the Banner of the Sun—from Hawaii to Singapore], by Hans Steen, was a "factual report compiled from descriptions of Japanese soldiers." It was produced in cooperation with the military office of the imperial Japanese embassy in Berlin.

Anton Mussert (1894–1946) was the leader of the Nationaal-Socialistische Beweging in Nederland [National Socialist Movement in the Netherlands] (NSB). In 1941 he founded the SS-Freiwilligen Legion Niederlande [SS Volunteer Legion, Netherlands]; in 1942 he was named the "Leiter des Niederländischen Volkes" [Leader of the Dutch People]. On July 8, 1943, a meeting between Himmler and Mussert took place in the field command post, for which Rudolf Brandt recorded minutes. Previous to this there was disagreement about political influence on the NSB: whereas Hitler supported Mussert, Himmler was on the side of the more radical Rost van Tonningen, but he had to keep his ambitions in check. During the meeting, Mussert insisted upon partial independence for the Dutch and the Flemings and cited their seven hundred-year history as his authority. For his part, Himmler tried to persuade Mussert that, historically speaking, the German Reich had once lost the Netherlands, and that now the Dutch should really become part of a Germanic Reich. Mussert rejected that notion, and Brandt noted that "in the discussion one could not detect any trace of an acceptance or comprehension of the Germanic idea."

6.8.43

My good dear Mami!

On this day—when, 14 years ago, you gave me our sweet little daughter, with so much pain and in danger of your life—I think of you with special affection and send you many kisses.

Give our scamp a kiss from me.[266]

All my love,
Your Pappi

17.8.43

My dear good Mami!

Just quickly a greeting to accompany this package. Put the books in my room, but maybe have a look at them first. You can surely use the four cattle grooming combs.[267] Enclosed you will find a couple of films for your little camera. I ordered them for you.

Relax a little bit and do not do too much.

To you and to Püppi I send many affectionate greetings and kisses,
Your Pappi

On August 16, 1943, Marga wrote in her *Journal*: "Berlin is still standing, and people tell each other that it will be leveled on 15.8. I was in Berlin 2 weeks.

---

[266] On the evening of Gudrun's birthday, Heinrich Himmler paid a short surprise visit to Gmund (Gudrun's *Journal* of 3.9.43).

[267] *Kuhhandräppler*: unattested word, presumably a variant of *Striegel* (curry comb, grooming comb). [—Trans.]

My railroad stations were in perfect order. [. . .] As soon as Püppi has to go back to school I will return there. I miss the work."

———————

28.8.43

My good Mami!

I am enclosing the picture and press reactions to my speech at the Ministry of the Interior.

All my love to you and little daughter

Many greetings and kisses,

Your Pappi

———————

On August 20, 1943, Hitler named Himmler Reichsinnenminister [Reich minister of the interior]. Wilhelm Frick, the previous minister, had to content himself with the office of Reichsprotektor Böhmen und Mähren [Reich protector of Bohemia and Moravia]. Himmler's promotion shows how much power he had accumulated for himself during the war years. Now his task involved organizing and overseeing the security policies of the Third Reich. Himmler, however, was manifestly uninterested in any ministerial activity. He set foot in the ministry only a few times, directing it instead from his field command post, where his personal assistant, Rudolf Brandt, acted as liaison. He left the operational leadership of the Ministry of the Interior to Wilhelm Stuckart, who had been Staatsekretär [secretary of state] for years and a participant in the Wannsee Conference.

On August 26, 1943, Gudrun writes in her *Journal*, "Pappi Reichsinnenminister, that makes me incredibly happy." And on September 3, Marga writes, "What on earth will I live to see in this next new year of my life. I am not talking about the war. I believe in the Führer, and I believe that our people must not and cannot be destroyed. Even though things look very bad here.—H. has become minister of the interior. German people believe that he can save them. May God grant that. I want to go to Berlin, where the working people are, my place is there. I am so anxious about not being at my post." And on September

6: "I will soon be 50 years old and have endured so much strain. [. . .] There is nothing to look forward to. For my child's sake I must—and want to—bear everything."

———————

19.9.43

My dear good Mami!

The grapes, which sadly are no longer very beautiful, should not be sent without my note.—

In the large envelope I am sending you a number of letters that I received in response to my appointment to the office of Reich Minister of the Interior, letters that I wanted to show you in Gmund. You ought to give these back to me sometime. You should keep the article from the *Baseler Zeitung*[268] as well as the *Leitheft*. I am also sending you a book, *Spuk am Balkan*[269] [Balkan Ghost]; it is about King Carol. Why don't you read it and tell me what you think of it? I am again enclosing your birthday cards with the answers that I wrote. Do you not want to answer the letter from Fahrenkamp yourself; but we shall discuss this later by telephone.

I think that Mussolini is really very sick. A dying lion. A tragic fate.

I am well again. I slept for 11 hours. I wish that you could do that too, you good woman.

Many affectionate greetings and kisses,

Your Pappi

———————

After British and American trips had forced the surrender of the German Afrikakorps under General Erwin Rommel, they landed in Sicily on July 9, 1943. This led to the overthrow of Mussolini a few days later. On July 26, King Victor Emmanuel III had Il Duce arrested, and he named Marshal Pietro

———————

[268] Newspaper from Basel, Switzerland. [—Trans.]
[269] Alfred Gerigk, *Spuk am Balkan, Ein König, ein Oberst, ein General* [Balkan Ghost: A King, a Colonel, a General], (1943).

Badoglio prime minister of Italy. On September 8, 1943, Italy negotiated an armistice with the Allied forces. Germany reacted by occupying central and northern Italy, an area that included Rome. The Italian army was disarmed and more than six hundred thousand Italian soldiers were deported to Germany as forced laborers. After Mussolini was rescued in a spectacular operation by a German SS commando, a Fascist puppet government was established in northern Italy. In plain sight of the Vatican, Fascist militia in Rome actively helped in the deportation to Auschwitz of Italian Jews who had remained in Italy and previously been spared.

The German occupation forces moved with great brutality against the reinvigorated partisan movement in Italy. As retribution for attacks against German soldiers, Wehrmacht units as well as SS commandos massacred Italian civilians. But the terror inflicted on the populace could not forestall an Allied victory. During the course of 1944, Rome and Florence were liberated; at the end of April 1945 the German Wehrmacht units stationed in Italy surrendered to the Allies. Shortly beforehand, Mussolini had been recaptured and executed by Italian partisans.

On October 4, 1943, Himmler gave his infamous speech in Posen (Poznan) to the highest-ranking SS leaders. Here he bluntly described the hopeless situation with the war and, at the same time, appealed to the fighting spirit of the SS, telling them that they alone were in a position to turn the tide of the war because of their "virtues." Among these characteristics of the SS, he emphasized merciless cruelty. "What happens to the Russians, what happens to the Czechs, is absolutely unimportant to me. We shall take whatever good blood of our race is in these peoples; we shall do this when necessary by stealing their children and raising them in Germany. Whether the other peoples live in comfort or starve in misery interests me only to the extent that we need them as slaves for our culture. Otherwise, they do not interest me. Whether 10,000 Russian women die of exhaustion or not while building an anti-tank ditch interests me only to the extent that that it gets completed for Germany. We will never be brutal and heartless when it is unnecessary—that is clear. We Germans, the only people in the world who have a decent attitude toward animals, will also have a decent attitude toward these human animals."

Himmler expressed himself quite openly on the matter of Jewish genocide: "It is one of those things that is easily stated. 'The Jewish people shall be exterminated,' says every party member, 'it says so very clearly in our agenda, expulsion of the Jews, eradication, that is our task.' And then they start in, those 80 million virtuous Germans, and every one of them knows an honest Jew. Of course it is clear that the others are pigs, but this one is a fine Jew. All those people who talk that way—not one of them has seen, not one of them has endured, what you have. Most of you will know what it means to see 100 corpses laid out together, when 500, or when 1,000 lie there. To have endured this, and in doing so, nonetheless remained decent, that has made us tough—with the exception of a few human weaknesses. This is a glorious page in our history that has never been, and never will be, written."

In the airplane to Prague, 28.10.43

My dear good Mami!

Right now I am flying to Prague for the funeral of little Klaus.[270]

Again, many thanks for your sweet, good letters on my birthday and for your letter of 20.10.—I am enclosing a lot of things with today's letter. A nice note from Gulbranson [*sic*],[271] a pamphlet that we publish about protection from mosquitoes and flies, my letter to Grawitz about Frau Richter, my "Luftschutzanordnung und Briefe" [anti-aircraft directive and letters] for Gmund. Nice pictures from the SS [recreation] home in Sasbachwalden where we once were together. It has now been beautifully and tastefully renovated. Then there is a card from the local insurance office; a letter from Dr. Thönen in Switzerland with pictures of his nice family (you have the picture of Frau Thönen wearing folk costume).

I thank you so affectionately for the drinking glass that you chose so sweetly. I drink from it every day, it makes me so happy, full of love, and gratitude.

---

[270] Klaus Heydrich, the oldest son of Reinhard and Lina Heydrich, died at age ten. He was Himmler's godchild.

[271] Olaf Gulbransson (1873–1958), Norwegian painter and graphic artist, known for his covers of the satirical Weimar publication *Simplicissimus*. After 1929 he lived on the Tegernsee and never spoke out against the NS regime. [—Trans.]

I am so glad that you are taking a trip to the Daxenberg with our sweet little daughter, have a lovely, relaxing time there, both of you.[272] (I am enclosing the money for you), have a good, elegant time there! And on the 8th and 9th, I firmly hope to be with you in Gmund for 2 to 3 days.[273]

> Best wishes for the trip and many affectionate greetings and kisses,
> Your Pappi

On November 1, 1943, Gudrun wrote in her *Journal*, "My parents bought another large garden plot. Up behind the greenhouse as far as the back of the woods, next to the large meadow. The prisoners have moved the fence from inside our current garden. When peace comes we are sure to get an estate in the East. The estate would then bring us more money and make it possible to renovate the house in Gmund. So that the hallways are lighter and we get bigger rooms. Later Haus Lindenfycht will belong to me. When peace comes again we are going to move into the Reich Ministry of the Interior. Maybe we will even get a house on the Obersalzberg. Yes, once we have peace again, but that will take a long, long time (2, 3 years)."

29.12.43

My good beloved Mami!

Once again in this old year, which was so difficult for all our people and not very easy for you, you good woman, I am writing you a letter and thanking you *from my heart* for your love and generosity.

For the year 1944, which will confront our people, and all of us, not least of all me, with the burdens of courage, belief, determination to stay the course, and not least of all, our endurance—I wish all the best. Stay well and healthy for my sake, especially in horrible Berlin.—and this is what I wish,

---

[272] Gudrun noted in her *Journal* on October 31, 1943, that they were staying in the Gasthof Daxenberg [inn] because there had been an outbreak of diphtheria in Gmund.

[273] On November 8–9 Himmler came to Gmund and spent the night, as he did every year after the ceremonies in Munich (Gudrun's *Journal* of 1.1.44).

travel *often* and *in time*[274] to our beautiful Gmund so you can rest! (and to our little daughter=scamp),

> For now, *many affectionate greetings and kisses,*
> Your Pappi

I have already told you on the telephone about the things I am enclosing. I hope the floral greeting on New Year's morning brings you joy!

––––––––

On January 15, 1944, Marga wrote in her *Journal*, "Christmas and New Year's are over. H. was here for 8 days before Christmas and will come again on 8.1. Püppi was very excited and pleased with Christmas. Again it was a peaceful, quiet, beautiful holiday. [. . .] H. is healthy and cheery with his daughter and in general when we played bridge. Frau Albers is here now, nice and sweet as ever. Frau Krenzlin and Edith Boden often visit,

On July 15, 1944, looking back at the beginning of the year, Gudrun wrote, "On 8.1 the women's ice skating championship took place in Munich. It was great. Pappi was there too."

––––––––

21.1.1944

> This package is supposed to be an additional Christmas packet for you and Püppi. I hope it makes you both very happy. The fur (coat)—coat is an exaggeration, it looks more like a kaftan—should keep you warm, my good little scamp; the bridge cards are for your little box.

The book of animal illustrations is for our dear little daughter.

I cannot write much today because the courier is leaving soon.

I will write Püppi an extra letter soon. Enclosed find a few letters that are interesting to read.

> To you and Püppi many, many affectionate greetings and kisses,
> Your Pappi

––––––––

[274] "In time" (German: *rechtzeitig*) appears to sound a warning to Marga and Gudrun to escape to the countryside for their own safety. [—Trans.]

28.1.1944

My good Mami!

　　Many thanks for your sweet letter!—I also received the other letters, bills, and papers—enclosed are three larger photographs of my portrait (by Hommel),[275] as well as a beautiful magazine about the warriors from the time of the Parthenon.

　　I am not flying until the day after tomorrow, because tomorrow I have to see the Führer.

　　　　Many affectionate greetings and kisses,
　　　　Your P

Do not get too upset about incompetent people!

On March 25, 1944, Marga wrote in her *Journal*, "I went to Berlin on 22.1, there were many air raids and little one could do. [. . .] On 15.2 our house was badly burnt out. The first thing to do will be to put a roof on it."[276]

　　Berlin was bombed more heavily than any other German city. Today the number of dead can only be estimated. Probably around twenty thousand people in total died in the air raids in Berlin; whole districts, in particular Berlin-Mitte, with its government buildings, and the industrial areas, were especially hard hit. The actual air battle for Berlin took place from the fall of 1943 to the spring of 1944, and included countless bombing raids by day. Nearly ten thousand people lost their lives and one sixth of the housing stock was destroyed. Because very few air-raid bunkers were available, the population often had to seek shelter in the cellars of houses or subway tunnels. Even when the NSDAP tried to provide numerous helpers after every attack to support those who suffered in the bombings, it became harder and harder to procure adequate supplies. A majority of the schoolchildren had been evacuated from the city in the summer of 1943. Over two million Berliners, among them one hundred

---

[275] Conrad Hommel (1883–1971) began his painting career as a member of the Munich Secession. After 1938 he was commissioned to paint portraits of the most important National Socialists.

[276] According to Marga's *Journal*, "Haus Dohnenstieg" had already sustained bad bomb damage in early December 1943.

thousand children, were evacuated to surrounding areas. Those who stayed behind were mostly old people and women with small children.

———

28.3.1944

My dear good Mami!

Although we have been telephoning each other almost every day, it has been so long since I have written. First off, my affectionate thanks for your sweet little letter of 27.3!

Next, I am sending you 2 photographs, one of my barracks in East Prussia, and one of the two of us in Munich; then the copy of an order from the Führer. What a long, arduous path, full of struggle and difficulty lies before us.

The millet is for you and there is a small bag for Elfriede (I promised it to her).

Inside this package you will find an album that will be nice to look at (then please put it in my room), a few pamphlets, a nice book of theatrical sets, 2 little books on folk art [published] by the Ahnenerbe, a good pamphlet by us about Japan. A little book of *Feldpost* stamps [military postage] for you to give away, an interesting book, *People of Mont Blanc*. Püppi should have a look at this. The Passaquais[277] were in this region. In addition a nice coin from Lübeck for our collection, and also a handsome porcelain figurine of Götz von Berlichingen for you, and a cigarette lighter (to give away).

Do not worry yourself about Püppi, I really think that it has to do with a growth spurt. I will soon be with you both and then we can talk about it.—

I am so looking forward to our Easter!

Many affectionate greetings and kisses,

Your Pappi

———

Lydia Boden provides a glimpse of how the Himmlers celebrated Easter: "At Easter people ate a traditional breakfast. The cooked Easter ham lay in a basket, the Easter loaf—bread baked especially for this holiday, a stalk of horseradish,

———

[277] The Passaquais were French ancestors of the Himmlers, whom he first discovered through genealogical research.

some salt, and many hard-boiled eggs. Everything was decorated with spring flowers. This was accompanied by red wine. Even the children got wine, but mixed with a healthy dose of water. [. . .] One Easter there was a great surprise. The weather was lovely, and things were hidden in the garden. The adults said it was something big, and the children searched ever more eagerly. Finally, under the branches of a very old fir tree, there stood a child's car. The children's joy was indescribable. [. . .] Whenever the weather was bad, the Easter eggs were hidden in the hall."

Pictures of the car survive. Gerhard recalls it as custom-built especially for them and even equipped with a motor.

———

1.5.44

My good Mami!

Many thanks for your sweet letter! Today we spent a long time on the telephone together. Mami, *so many dear good thoughts* accompany you that nothing can happen to you.[278]

I wrote to Elfriede Reifschneider today; the transfer is impossible, it is absolutely forbidden.—I applied to Kalkreuth via telegram.

I am sending you (in addition to the money) a number of photos from my trip to France, among them a couple of very nice ones from Gmund with our scamp. When you have had a look at them please send the pictures to Püppi! As soon as I am with you in Gmund again, I will explain them to you and label them.

I hope you find the chocolate really delicious!

Many affectionate greetings and kisses,

Your Pappi

And get well, you good woman!

———

[278] This remark presumably applies to the heavy air raids on Berlin, upon which Marga looked back (May 25, 1944), and noted, "I was in Berlin 14 days. I experienced 4–5 five attacks. Terrifying. But other people even have to live there "

4.5.44

I hope you enjoy it! Many thanks for your letter and many affectionate greetings and kisses.

>Your Pappi

16.5.44

My good dear Mami!

For Mothers' Day I am sending you many many dear, good, grateful thoughts! Give our little daughter, the sweet scamp, a kiss!

The folder with the nice pictures that we are going to have framed once peacetime comes, and a "new" little deer [figurine?—Trans.], I hope you like them.

>Many kisses and greetings!
>With love, your Pappi

———————

At this time Hedwig Potthast was heavily pregnant with their second child. Himmler, nonetheless, was not only making plans with Marga for their peacetime life together, but was also still sending her "kisses" and signing his letters "with love."

———————

24.5.44

>A very affectionate greeting and kiss.
>from your Pappi

———————

On May 25, 1944, Marga writes in her *Journal*, "Yesterday I planted the last bushes and plants for the year in my garden [. . .]." On July 15, 1944, her daughter writes, "Mutti really loves her garden, and works in it alone and does not think there is anything wrong with that. I think that one simply cannot do that if one is the wife of the R.I.M. [Reich minister of the interior]."

31.5.44

My dear good Mami!

First let me thank you affectionately for both your sweet letters from 24. and 27.5. We looked into the matter of the dying SS man.[279] Waldeck has received two cables from me. I am enclosing the letter from SS-OGRUF Pohl for you again. To spare you the work, I have answered it, and I am enclosing the carbon copy for you.

I am sending you one of my recent speeches; when the others have been written, I shall send you those too because they are different in many ways. I am also enclosing *Mitteilungsblatt des SS-Oberabschnitt Main* [Bulletin of the Senior SS District of Main], which contains a very nice essay about the SS in Lower Bavaria and the early years [of the movement—Trans.], as well as a very pretty poem "Ablösung" [Renewal].[280] Püppi should read both things too.

For our good little daughter, Gudrun, I have enclosed a thank-you note from the SS Headquarters; both our names, however, are not included. You should take a look at the photographs, they are from Bosnia; I'll pick them up next time.

Allach has been instructed to allow you to purchase all their [porcelain] pieces, in perpetuity, with the exception of those that are meant for official SS and state presents, and what is more, you are to be allowed to get these at the same discount of 30–40% that I get.

I am still looking into the business in Apfeldorf, although it had already gone too far because the policeman had taken the matter to trial before Friedl told us about it. Nonetheless, I have intervened.

Put the books in my room!

950 M are in the envelope.

Dr. Stumpfegger[281] is bringing the letter. I really hope the physical therapist helps you both.

---

[279] Reference obscure. [—Trans.]

[280] Himmler refers to a poem by the Romantic poet Joseph von Eichendorff (1788–1857). The text explores some of Himmler's favorite subjects: the eternal cycle of nature, romantic love, mutability.

[281] Dr. Ludwig Stumpfegger (1910–45), SS-Obersturmbannführer, was the doctor who periodically treated Himmler and his family (Gudrun's *Journal* entry from 15.7.44). He carried out medical experiments on prisoners from Ravensbrück in the SS clinic at Hohenlychen.

To you, my dear Mami, and to our dear little daughter, I send many affectionate kisses and greetings. With love,

Your Pappi

———————

During these weeks, Himmler gave several speeches to Wehrmacht generals in which he openly referred to the Jewish genocide. On May 5, 1944, for example, he said, "The Jewish question is solved in Germany. It was solved without compromise, in accordance with the life struggle of our people, which is a matter of the existence of our blood." On May 24,: "The Jewish question was solved without compromise [. . .] according to orders and rational insight. I think, gentlemen, that you know me well enough, that I am not a bloodthirsty person, and not a man who feels any joy or amusement when he is obliged to do something ruthless. On the other hand, I have such strong nerves, and such a great devotion to duty—these things I can claim—that, when I recognize that something is necessary, I then pursue it to its conclusion without compromise. I did not consider myself authorized—I refer here namely to the Jewish women and children—to let the children grow up to be avengers who would then kill our fathers and grandchildren. I would have considered that cowardly. Consequently, the question was solved without compromise."

———————

8.6.44

My good Mami!

I want to quickly write a note to accompany the marmot salve and two speeches by me (1:00 at night). I really hope that I can come and visit you soon. The newspaper clipping is for Püppi.—I hope the marmot salve helps you!

Many affectionate greetings and kisses to you and Püppi!

Your Pappi

———————

On June 3, 1944, Nanette Dorothea, the second child of Hedwig Potthast and Heinrich Himmler, was born in Hohenlychen. Since the birth of her son, Helge, Hedwig Potthast had been living in Brückenthin, not far from

Hohenlychen, in an isolated forest house that Himmler had expanded. The only neighbors within two kilometers were the family of Oswald Pohl, with whom Himmler was friendly. At first, Heinrich Himmler was not named as father on the birth certificates of his illegitimate children. It was not until June 25, 1944, that he had his paternity recognized by an SS judge and the documents changed correspondingly, on July 20, at the Registry Office in Lychen.[282] Sepp Dietrich, for whose two younger sons Himmler was godfather, was the godfather of Himmler's daughter. Ursula Dietrich had stated the wish to the "dear Reichsführer" that "your dear little girl might always spread light and sun in the lives of her parents . . ." Oswald and Eleonora Pohl also paid their respects as "good neighbors" and promised to accompany "both children of fate with all good wishes into a strong future." On the day of the birth, Eleonora Pohl, who was herself the mother of three daughters, sent a little card to the "Liebe Frau Häschen" [Dear Mrs. Bunny Rabbit, i.e., Hedwig Potthast—Trans.] that included the comforting words "Nature takes its own paths and, with these many daughters, perhaps wants to predict a time that will not be shaped so much by men."

Heinrich Himmler was not present at the birth of his daughter because, on the same day, he had to be on the Obersalzberg as a witness at the wedding of SS-Gruppenführer Hermann Fegelein and Gretl Braun, the sister of Eva Braun. Hermann Fegelein was Himmler's liaison officer to Hitler. At the end of 1944, Frau Fegelein visited Hedwig Potthast in her new residence, Haus Schneewinkellehen (in Schönau, near Berchtesgaden), which Himmler had bought for his mistress from Martin Bormann in the summer of 1944 and had renovated using prisoners from Dachau.

After she stopped working, Hedwig Potthast stayed in touch with her old friends and colleagues primarily by letter. Nonetheless, she carried on an active correspondence with various wives of high-ranking National Socialists, such as Gerda Bormann, Lina Heydrich, Eleonara Pohl, and others. After the war, Lina Heydrich said of Hedwig Potthast, "This woman was neither *petit bourgeois* nor eccentric, not *SS*-chic, but rather intelligent and characterized by an innate warmth. Reinhard once said that you could warm your hands and feet [at her personality]."

---

[282] According to Peter-Ferdinand Koch (*Himmlers graue Eminenz*), Nanette Dorothea was not born in Hohenlychen, but rather on the Achensee (a lake) in Tyrol; her birthdate is consistently cited incorrectly in the literature as July 20.

By the same token, her primary contact with Heinrich Himmler was by letter and telephone as well. Short visits to her and the children were the exception. A letter from Martin Bormann to his wife in the beginning of October 1944 documents a visit that Himmler made to Haus Schneewinkellehen at the time: "Heinrich told me yesterday that he had hung pictures and worked in the house and played with the children all day. He did not accept any telephone calls either, but devoted himself completely and happily to his family." Hedwig Potthast apparently accepted her role as clandestine mistress without complaint. At the end of 1944 she wrote to Himmler, "My dear! [. . .] Above all I wish you the strength to carry out the task that Führer and Fatherland have assigned you. Compared to this everything is—we are—small—I am poor. Stay healthy and do not forget Your H." Hedwig Potthast never signed her letters to Himmler by name, but rather always with the Hagal rune, which stands for the sound of *H*. The following letters from the beginning of 1945 indicate that this letter was addressed to Himmler, for the date of receipt is noted on all of them in his handwriting.

In her only interview, which she gave to the journalist Peter-Ferdinand Koch in the 1980s, she not only said that Himmler had revealed doubts to her that the war could still be won, but also maintained that she had been a driving force behind Himmler's secret negotiations with the Western Allies and the liberation of concentration camp prisoners. She claimed, furthermore, that from the fall of 1944 onward, she had begun to alienate Himmler from the Führer because she wanted to survive, for the sake of the children.[283]

16.6.44

My good Mami!

Enclosed two more speeches by me; I am sorry for you, just skim them. I am enclosing two very decent letters from SS widows; please send them back to me again later!

I am also sending along 2 books and chocolate for Lydia, a couple of pamphlets and soap for you, and a book for the library.

---

[283] This at least is how Koch describes it. Nonetheless, his publication is so full of errors that one should be wary of this statement.

Many affectionate greetings and kisses for you, you good Mami, and
our little daughter (little goose).

From your Pappi

On June 6, 1944, Allied troops landed in Normandy and opened the long-
awaited second front. Within a few days the Allies were able to expand their
bridgehead and begin the liberation of France. In the east, Heeresgruppe Mitte
[Army Group Center] had long since collapsed, making the advance of the Red
Army unstoppable. The end of the war and the defeat of Nazi Germany were
only a matter of time.

On July 15, 1944, Gudrun wrote in her *Journal* about the course the war
was taking: "something is definitely happening, the invasion began in Normandy on the night of the 5–6 [June], we have already surrendered Cher-
bourg, [. . .] Rome surrendered long ago and in Russia the Russians are
almost at the border, just horrible, but we all believe so firmly in victory
(Pappi) that I, as the daughter of the man who is now especially respected and
beloved, have to think so too—and I do. It would be unthinkable if we were
to lose."

Given the desperate military situation, the resistance group in the circle of
Colonel Claus Count Schenk von Stauffenberg dared to attempt the assassination. On July 20, 1944, at a meeting in the Führer HQ, he planted a bomb
that was meant to kill Hitler and with that launch a coup d'état that had long
been prepared in conservative circles and certain segments of the military. Although slightly injured, Hitler survived the attack, and the conspirators were
not able to consolidate their power in Berlin. Units that were faithful to Hitler
imprisoned the resisters in the "Bendler Block"[284] and shot many of them immediately. Many more who were part of the plot were arrested and sentenced
to death in judge Roland Freisler's courtroom; their families were taken
prisoner as well, according to the practice of *Sippenhaft* [liability of kin]. In
total, roughly two hundred people were executed following the attempt on
Hitler's life.

---

[284] The Bendler Block was a building complex in Berlin that was also the headquarters of the
Wehrmacht (OKW). [—Trans.]

On July 22, 1944, Gudrun wrote, "On 20.7.44 German officers made an attempt on the Führer's life, almost all of them aristocrats. Almost nothing happened to the Führer, but his things around him were damaged. When I heard it, just when we were coming home from swimming, I almost burst out crying, thank God Pappi was not there, but he basically has final responsibility."

On July 26, 1944, hardly a week after the abortive assassination, Himmler gave a speech to the officers' corps of a division of grenadiers on the parade ground at Bitsch in which he spoke about soldiers' virtues: "And now we have all witnessed something that we all find unbelievable and incomprehensible: a German officer, a German colonel, has broken not only his sworn oath, but in violating all customs of Germanic and German military practice of many centuries and millennia, has raised his hand against his commander in chief. [. . .] It is the most terrible blow that has ever been dealt to the German army, and we shall [. . .] have to try to eradicate this deed from the memory of the German people with holy fire and a holy sense of duty for many years to come.—To eradicate from the spotless shield this blot that has tarnished it."

Marga noted on August 11, 1944, "This disgrace, German officers wanted to kill the Führer. A miracle he is alive."

Himmler's police apparatus had not been able to prevent the assassination attempt. On the one hand, they suspected something about the plans for the coup d'état at this time and had already made some individual arrests. On the other hand, the Gestapo was completely surprised by the extent of the resistance. This, however, did not make a dent in Himmler's prestige; on the contrary, he was able to consolidate his power base even more after the failed assassination.

18.8.44

My good dear Mami!

If you have been able to get out of bed and—as I hope—stay a few more days in Gmund, then this note and package should bring you a little joy! The book on Japan is very interesting. I hope that you can put the other things to good use!

Affectionate thanks for your note of 12.8! I have read all the enclosures. [. . .] As was predicted, the war has now entered its most difficult stage, putting all our strength and our nerves to the test.—But do not worry, all will be well, and I am working more than ever.

My good Mami, I wish you a speedy recovery with all my heart!

To you and our dear "clever" little daughter, many affectionate greetings and kisses from your Pappi.

Because Himmler feared a targeted attack, prisoners from the Dachau Aussen-kommando Gmund [Gmund satellite camp] began building an air-raid bunker in the garden of Haus Lindenfycht in July 1944. On July 15, 1944, Gudrun wrote about this in her *Journal*: "They are now building a bunker on the playground, I think it is awful, the constant noise, and the prisoners there all the time, so that you can't go near there, but Pappi really wanted to have it, and Mutti too."

The Gmund satellite camp, with its twenty prisoners, who were stationed at Bad Tölz, existed from May 1944 to the end of 1945. Marga Himmler oversaw the construction work and was soon complaining to the camp leadership in Dachau about the unsatisfactory progress of the prisoners' work. In September 1944 a new group of prisoners was put to work building an air-raid tunnel between Lindenfycht and the nearby villa of General Walter Warlimont. Despite the hard labor they had to perform, they were fed only in the mornings and evenings at the camp in Bad Tölz.

Himmler had previously used prisoners to work for him on his Berlin residence, Villa Dohnenstieg, and on the renovation of his hunting lodge in the Valepp. In 1944–45 another work detail of prisoners was sent to the Valepp. In the spring and summer of 1944 a detail had also been sent to renovate Haus Schneewinkellehen near Berchtesgaden, into which Hedwig Potthast and her two children moved that summer.

Immediately following the attempted assassination of July 20, Hitler appointed Himmler commander of the Army Reserve, which was a crucial military posi-

tion for the recruitment of new soldiers. The intention of Hitler's "decree regarding the formation of the German 'Volkssturm' [Home Guard, Civil
Defense]" of September 26, was to draft the last remnant of able-bodied men
between sixteen and sixty years of age. While the Gauleiters were responsible
for the formation of the Volkssturm, it was Himmler's responsibility, as commander of the Army Reserve, to take charge of its military organization, training, and equipment, as well as its combat missions. In one of Himmler's
speeches, broadcast on the radio on October 18 (not coincidentally, the anniversary of the Battle of the Nations at Leipzig), he proclaimed, "Let our enemies understand that every kilometer that they wish to advance into our country
will cost them rivers of their blood. Every city block, every village, every farm,
every forest, will be defended by men, boys, and the aged, and—if need be—by
women and girls."

He justified the drafting of those born in 1928—which meant sixteen-year-
olds—as follows: "it is better that a young generation die and a people be saved
than if I were to spare the young generation and let a people of 80 to 90 million
die out."

The military training as well as the equipment of the Volkssturm was sorely
insufficient, thus the young men and boys were, for the most part, deployed to
dig ditches and clear villages in the path of the advancing enemy. The fact that
the Volkssturm included all able-bodied men and boys, who immediately came
under SS jurisdiction, shows that the NS leadership feared a revolt on the home
front among an increasingly war-weary populace.

Himmler was even made commander of additional army groups: from early
December 1944 to mid-January 1945, he commanded the army group Oberrhein
[Upper Rhine]; from the end of January to March 1945, he commanded the
army group Weichsel [Vistula]. His military ability, however, was so cata-
strophically poor that in both cases he had to be relieved of his duties.

———————

22.12.44

My dear beloved Mami!

This is the first time we have not celebrated Christmas together; but
just yesterday I was thinking so much of you and Püppi. Did you both light
our Yule lights—I hope that my presents bring you joy. I have had terribly

little time and opportunity to look for something really nice. Perhaps, however, you will like the silver tray and the dish and the silk material (black and blue with white), and the blue handbag, and some underwear and stockings. 10 pounds of "1a" [?] are either included here or will follow later.

Our good little daughter should get the gold bracelet and the little sport dress. Goral fur [sheepskin] and a compass set and blue woolen material will follow. I have also included an old book on botany for her.

And the day after tomorrow, the 24th, I will be with the soldiers of *my* army group.—27 years ago, I enlisted as a young 17-year-old cadet, and today, in the 6th year of the war, in the midst of the most difficult situation, their leadership has now been transferred to me.—But it is a lot, besides all the other responsibilities, and this responsibility weighs heavily upon me. If one only knew anything about what I am in charge of here—the lives of so many Germans depend on it, whose wives and mothers will then have to mourn— and, in general, whatever I command or do not command affects the 90 million lives of our people.

It is now 3:00 a.m. I wish you, my good Mami, all my love at this Christmas festival and hope you get a little pleasure from my presents.

      Many affectionate greetings and kisses,
      Your Pappi

I am sending along the key. Lydia's fur coat to follow.

————

It is unclear how and where Himmler acquired these presents, especially because he had so little time, and because in 1944 these things were largely unavailable. One might surmise that their source was the stock of property stolen from the murdered victims of the National Socialists. This material was collected in the exterminations camps by the Wirstschaftsverwaltungshauptamt der SS [Head Office of the SS Business Administration], directed by Oswald Pohl. Members of the SS in particular enriched themselves from this material. Himmler placed great value on "honesty" and "decency" in the way stolen property was handled, which suggests that he bought the items from the Head

13.2.45

very difficult time, which we must, and *shall*, get through as ossible, to you, my good Mami, and my lovely little daughter, special loving greetings, thoughts, and kisses.

Your Pappi.

———

e end of 1944 Himmler had decided that Gerhard should interrupt his ultural training and join the SS. At age sixteen he began his training as a zergrenadier [armored infantryman] as *SS-Freiwilliger* [SS volunteer]. On bruary 21, 1945, Marga writes in her *Journal*, "It is questionable whether Gerhard will come visit before he is sent to the front. He is very brave and likes being in the SS in Brünn [Brno]."

Marga's last *Journal* entry from the same day reads: "The situation with the war is unchanged and very serious."

———

Gudrun wrote in her *Journal* on March 5:

[. . .] We no longer have any allies in Europe, and can only rely on ourselves. And among our own people there is *so much* betrayal. The officers are just deserting. Nobody wants war anymore. There is an indescribable terror from the air. They keep on bombing the civilian populations and the railroads. They bombed Dresden when it was full of refugees from the East. Even we are admitting that 10,000 people died, terrible. And yet there are still so many people who could join the battle, but just sit around and keep their heads down, and on the other hand, there is sooo much heroism. 16-year-olds are manning the front and the Hitler Youths have proven themselves, at least they still have their belief.—On 18.10 Pappi announced the formation of the Volkssturm in a magnificent speech. [. . .] Since 20 July Pappi has been the commander of this homeland army [. . .]. The general mood is at zero. The Luftwaffe is still so bad. Göring does not seem to care about anything, that windbag. Goebbels is doing a lot, but he always shows off. They all get medals and awards, except Pappi, and he should be the first to get one. If he did not exist, things would be very different. The people all look up to him. He always stays in the background and never shows off. [. . .]

Office. A list of presents for the personal staff at Christmas 1944 supports this. The list contains prices, and the entry for the fur coat for Lydia Boden is the most expensive, at 1700 RM. The only origin for these presents is given as "Items from Italy and Budapest."

For the normal population during the war years, the black market was the only source of presents and sweets such as those Himmler was always sending his family. Black marketeering was punished severely as an economic crime during wartime, but it nonetheless thrived while the resentment of the populace toward the party bosses increased because of the luxuries they enjoyed.

———

9.1.1945

My beloved good Mami!

A courier is just leaving by car for Munich, and I want him to take along something from me.

The Führer's packet of coffee (letter enclosed), gingerbread cookies, cookies from Nuremberg, and liver paté [. . .]—Among the books, you and Püppi have to have a look at the album of the Hitler-Jugend Division and the book *Die Vollendeten*.[285] Please keep the reviews. The missing ration cards (from last time) are enclosed. [. . .]

We have just spoken together on the telephone. This often works so poorly because the lines in Munich are so damaged.

And now let me thank you most warmly for your good, sweet letters of 21, 28, and 29.12. I also thank you for the sweet picture of both of you. Later, if you have a new one, where you do not look quite so serious, you have to send it to me, and then I will frame it, but this makes me very happy, and I look at it often. I am reading your book *Preussische Soldaten* [Prussian Soldiers][286]

———

[285] Book of photographs (the title translates roughly as "People of Accomplishment"), edited by Rosemarie Clausen (Stuttgart, 1941), showing the death masks of famous Germans, including Beethoven, Frederick the Great, Queen Louise, Richard and Cosima Wagner, but also the National Socialist Dietrich Eckart.

[286] Rudolf Thiel (Berlin, 1941).

with great pleasure, it is excellent, I have wrapped it with the book cover that Püppi sent me.—On Christmas eve I was in Metzeral near Münster in Alsace, and also in Gebweiler. I thought of you both so much and of the little room with Christmas decorations in your own little room.

[. . .] It is *very* difficult with the Air Force, how our poor people are forced to suffer! Our beautiful Munich and Nuremberg! And despite everything, I believe that the war in general will end victoriously this year!

I thank you for your good, good wishes.—You know how much I send you my very best, heartfelt good wishes, my good Mami. Stay wonderfully healthy for our sake!

I am glad that Frau Dr. Richter is treating you.

Many affectionate greetings and kisses,
Your Pappi

———

In January 1945 the Red Army had reached the border of the German Reich and mounted an attack with six million soldiers. The Wehrmacht, composed of two million soldiers with inadequate training, insufficient supplies, and no reserves at all, had almost nothing with which to defend against this onslaught. On January 31 the units under Marshal Georgy Zhukov reached Küstrin on the Oder, while, simultaneously, Soviet troops occupied Upper Silesia. A few days before, on January 27, the surviving inmates of Auschwitz were liberated by the Red Army. On April 25 the ring around the capital, Berlin, was closed; on the same day American and Soviet troops met at Torgau on the Elbe.

Millions of people from East Prussia, Pomerania, and Silesia fled before the approaching Soviet troops. National Socialist propaganda was not the only factor that created a terrifying scenario of the atrocities of the Bolshevik enemy and spread helpless panic among the civilian population. The unrestrained *soldateska* themselves, with their shootings, mass rapes, plundering, and deportation to forced-labor camps also caused people to flee in terror. The brutality of the war of extinction that the Germans had waged was now turned back against Germany itself.

The advance of the Red Army also meant that the SS dismantled the concentration camps in the East and drove the prisoners westward on horrific foot

marches and into the camps located on the roads through a German marches" took place through ice often without rest, as they marched thousands who could not keep up were tion on the way.

Marga writes in her *Journal* on January 16, 1945, in the West in addition to all his other work. It is to and in a good mood when he telephones." On February is in the East. If the situation turns serious, he will have to ful that he is called to such great tasks and can master the looks up to him."

———

On the train, 20.1.19

My good dear Mami!
My dear Püppi!

I am just on my way from the west to the east. This is bound to be the most difficult assignment that I have gotten up to now. I believe, however, that *I shall complete it* and, despite all the heavy burdens that oppress me, I am unswervingly *convinced of our final victory*.

Thank you so very much for your sweet letter of 16.1.—I am sending you a lot of books, among them two old ones for you and Püppi as well as a beautiful calendar. I am also sending along a number of letters, which will perhaps interest you.

I also received Püppi's sweet little letter from Reichersbeuern from 7.1. Many thanks, my dear little daughter!

Send me lots of good thoughts!

Many affectionate kisses and greetings!
Your Pappi

Hanns Johst is sending you a little description of our trip, along with a nice letter.

In March 1945, when Himmler realized that he had failed as an army commander, he retreated with angina for several weeks to the field hospital at Hohenlychen. On March 21, at the urging of the Wehrmacht generals, he was relieved of his command.

Even in the last weeks of the war, Himmler believed that the concentration camp prisoners represented veritable hostages with whom he could negotiate concessions from the western powers, possibly even a separate peace. Felix Kersten's mediation set up contacts in neutral Sweden. The vice president of the Swedish Red Cross, Count Folke Bernadotte, traveled to Germany in person in the beginning of 1945 in order to confirm this rescue mission with the SS leadership. When Bernadotte arrived in Berlin on February 16, Himmler at first avoided him and did not meet him for another two days, when he gave assurances that were once again postponed. It was not until April 1945 that the surviving Scandinavian prisoners were taken to the concentration camp Neuengamme in white buses belonging to the Swedish Red Cross, and taken from there via Denmark to Sweden.

On April 10 (16), 1945, Gudrun wrote, "Herr Schnitzler telephoned, Pappi is still near Berlin, has called all the Obergruppenführer to a meeting with him, so it cannot be all that bad, even though the Russian offensive has begun."And on April 17: "Yesterday we were in a very bad mood, they are not very far from Nuremberg. [. . .] and at 4:00 the alarm, attack on Munich, the house shook. Mutti was terribly upset. It made the whole house shudder. I did not mind it."

17.4.45

My good, beloved Mami!

My good dear little daughter!

Herr Baumert is driving down, which gives me the opportunity to include this note. He will tell Mami a lot in person.

But he should at least bring along a note together with a little package. For us all these times are unbelievably hard for all of us, and yet, things will—this is my firm belief—take a turn for the best. But it is hard.

You dear ones, just stay healthy for my sake.

The Ancient One will protect us, and especially the good German people and will not let us perish.

I send you both, you my beloved Mami, and you my Püppi, my dear one, many many affectionate kisses and greetings.

      Heil Hitler! With love,

      Your Pappi

This letter bears obvious characteristics of a farewell. It is one of the few that Himmler directed expressly to his wife and daughter, and it is the first and only time that he closes with "Heil Hitler"—ironically at a moment when he was trying to conduct secret negotiations with the western allies without Hitler's knowledge.

For quite a while Heinrich Himmler had no longer believed that everything would take a "turn for the best." Instead, he would retreat ever more frequently and for longer periods to Hohenlychen, where he had himself admitted for treatment and refused to speak to anyone. The fact that this letter refers to the possible downfall of the German people—which could be prevented by divine intervention—shows how hopeless his view of the situation was and how cynically the NS leadership equated the defeat of their regime with the end of Germany.

"The Ancient One" was the mythical Germanic divinity Waralda. Himmler mentioned him on July 26, 1944, in the speech cited earlier: "I have nothing to do with religious denominations, I leave that to each individual. In the ranks of the SS, however, I have never tolerated an atheist. Every man believes profoundly in fate, in the Lord God, whom my ancestors, in their own language called Waralda—theAncient One—who is more powerful than we are."

He probably wrote this farewell letter from Hohenlychen. While he was doing so, Paul Baumert, chief of the personal staff of the Reichsführer-SS, was driving to Bavaria in order to organize the escape of Marga and Gudrun, as well as that of Hedwig, Helge, and Nanette Dorothea.[287]

---

[287] After 1945, Hedwig Potthast first lived in Bavaria with her children and maintained contact with Eleonora Pohl , Karl Wolff, and Gebhard Himmler, among others. In 1953 she severed all contacts in Bavaria and moved to Sinzheim, near Baden-Baden, where she began to work as a secretary again, and lived with her (female) friend Sigurd Peiper, former secretary on the personal staff of the Reichsführer-SS. The families went their separate ways when her friend's husband, Jochen Peiper (an SS general and former adjutant of Himmler's, responsible for the 1944 massacre of American prisoners of war at Malmedy), was released from prison in 1957. Hedwig Potthast married, and died in Baden-Baden in 1994.

On April 18, 1945, Gudrun wrote, "Yesterday a *Tagesbefehl* [order of the day] was broadcast by the Führer. Now things must surely get better again. Now I firmly believe in victory again. Yesterday the battle began in the East. The military report in the West was not very good. There is nothing but war talk, even though people try not to."

———————

And on 19 April:

When I came home [yesterday] Schnitzler and Baumert were here and talking with Mutti. [. . .] Baumert was trying to convince Mutti that we should go to the Vallepp [*sic*] with Frau Heydrich using false passports. Mutti does not want to, people would know us there. [. . .] Baumert came from Pappi and is driving back again. Now they have reached an agreement. We are going south, Mutti and I to one place, Ulla and Aunt Martha to another. Where we are going (under a false name) must remain *very* secret. [. . .] A lot of things are being taken to the Valepp, we might still have to go there, when everything is over and our house is gone, which we hope will not happen. Pappi sent along a sweet letter and chocolate.

On April 20, 1945, Hitler's birthday, Himmler visited the Führer for the last time in the Reich Chancellery in Berlin. Eight days later an intercepted British communiqué reached the Führer's bunker containing the intelligence that Himmler was negotiating with the western Allies. In response, Hitler ordered that Himmler be removed from all offices in the state and in the party. At this point Himmler had fled to North Germany and was living in Flensburg.

Admiral Karl Dönitz, whom Hitler had proclaimed as his successor before his suicide on April 30, was also staying in Flensburg. When he learned of Himmler's demotion, he chose not to include him in his new transitional cabinet.

Himmler moved around in Flensburg unrecognized for two more weeks. He received devoted SS leaders, kept a staff of 150 people, together with a radio communications office and a motor pool. He wrote letters to the British field marshal Bernard Montgomery but never received an answer. On May 20, three days before the arrest of the Dönitz government, Himmler left the city with several members of his staff. He had shaved off his moustache and wore an eye patch, as well as the uniform of the Geheime Feldpolizei [Secret Military

Police], and he held identification papers issued under the name of Heinrich Hitzinger. The plan to escape to the south through the English cordon did not succeed. He and his entourage were suspected of being Gestapo agents, and on May 22, 1945, were taken to Lüneburg, headquarters of the British Second Army. There Himmler identified himself and shortly afterward committed suicide with a cyanide capsule.

Aftermath

On the night of the nineteenth to the twentieth of April 1945, Erich Schnitzler drove Marga and Gudrun Himmler, Lydia Boden, and an aunt of the two sisters to South Tyrol. American troops reached the region around Gmund on May 2 and confiscated the private documents in Haus Lindenfycht. On May 13, Marga and Gudrun were arrested by American soldiers in Wolkenstein, near the villa belonging to Karl Wolff. They were taken to an internment camp in Rome, where Marga was interrogated by British officers.

On July 13, 1945, the journalist Anne Stringer visited Marga in a luxurious villa outside Rome for an interview for the *Giornale del Mattino*. There she informed Marga for the first time of her husband's death: "Frau Himmler showed not the slightest hint of emotion. It was the coldest demonstration of absolute control of human feelings that I have ever experienced." Stringer reported that Marga Himmler, a "corpulent woman with her hair in a severe bun, and numerous gold teeth," spoke relatively good English. She confirmed that she had known about her husband's assignments in his role as the head of the Gestapo. She was not surprised that some people hated him: "He was a policeman, and no one likes policemen." To the question of whether or not she had ever been in Dachau, Marga responded that she had been in the vicinity of this sad place almost every day to buy the vegetables and fruits that the SS grew there. She placed the guilt for the war on the English, but in response to more pointed questions, she said evasively, "I am just a woman; I do not understand much about politics."

Marga and Gudrun were later interned in different camps in Italy and France.

During the Nuremberg trials of the major war criminals they were moved into the witness building in Nuremberg for a few weeks; there Marga was interrogated by an American officer on September 26. She asserted that her husband had always acted only upon orders from the Führer, and because of his countless tasks, was always overworked, and had had a delicate constitution. "He had so terribly much to do." She doubted that he had ever visited the concentration camps, although she admitted to having known that he was responsible for them and, for her own part, to having visited the women's concentration camp at Ravensbrück.

At the end of 1946, Marga and her daughter were released from the women's camp Ludwigsburg 77 and placed in the Bodelschwingh Bethel home,[288] near Bielefeld. Both worked in the weaving and spinning mills, and Gudrun completed an apprenticeship as a seamstress. Life with other residents was not without its tensions. As Pastor Bodelschwingh remembered in 1962, Marga Himmler's behavior became "more and more hostile and difficult." She continued to identify herself as "religious" but kept herself apart from the Christian community in Bethel.

The denazification commission in Bielefeld at first classified Marga as only a *Minderbelastete* [someone only "minimally incriminated]." In 1951 her classification was revised to *Mitläuferin* [collaborator]. In Bavaria, in the fall of 1952, further denazification proceedings were brought against her having to do with the question of ownership of Haus Lindenfycht. In the verdict of January 1953 she was now classified as *belastet* [incriminated], which entailed loss of property and the right to vote. In the fall of 1955, Marga moved into her own apartment in Bielefeld-Heepen with her sister Lydia. The parting from Bethel was not exactly friendly because, according to Pastor Bodelschwingh, "Frau Himmler persisted in absolute delusion until she left us without thanks and moved back in among her 'brown' [i.e., National Socialist—Trans.] accomplices, who in the meantime, had gotten back on their feet." Marga Himmler lived the last years of her life with her daughter, Gudrun, and Gudrun's husband in Munich. She died in August 1967. It is not known when and where her sister Lydia died.

---

[288] Friedrich von Bodelschwingh (1877–1946) was a Protestant pastor and public health advocate who founded the charitable institutions known as Bethel. These offered health care and shelter to the poor. [—Trans.]

Gudrun, who had moved to Munich in 1952, had a difficult time finding work as a seamstress in Munich because of her last name. Because she kept her name in the years before her marriage, apparently with stubborn defiance, she often had to change jobs, as she told the journalist Norbert Lebert in 1960 in her only interview. She worked as a cutter, pieceworker, office worker, and, finally, as a secretary. At that time, she was planning to write a book rehabilitating her father, but the project was never realized. At the end of the 1960s she expressed to Josef Ackermann, the Himmler biographer, the point of view that Hitler could only have delegated the "garbage disposal of the Reich" to "the most loyal"—in other words, to her father.

Gudrun Burwitz, as she was called after her marriage, gave birth to two children after her mother died and for decades was active in the organization Silent Help for Prisoners of War and Internees, an aid group that supports imprisoned war criminals and their families. Furthermore, she was a regular guest at veterans' meetings of the Waffen-SS and a member of the Wiking-Jugend [Viking Youth], a successor to the Hitler Youth that was not banned until 1994. She lives in Munich to this day.

Gerhard von der Ahé—who in the fall of 1944 at age sixteen had gone to Brünn [Brno] as an SS candidate for his training as an armored infantryman—was captured by the Russians at the end of the war after seeing only two days of active duty. In December 1949 he was sentenced to twenty-five years of hard labor. He spent the next years in various camps, where he worked as a miner and also a plasterer on construction sites.

He returned to Germany in October 1955. At age twenty-seven he was the youngest repatriated prisoner of war. On his repatriation registration form, dated October 10, 1955, he still identified himself as "religious." Marga, with whom he had carried on a correspondence during the last three years of his imprisonment, picked him up at the Friedland camp. At first he lived with her and Lydia in Bielefeld for a short while. During this time his aunt wrote the *Memoirs* about their time together in Gmund. In those pages one reads the following about the end of the war: "And our *fate* was fulfilled. We lost the war. We became prisoners. We lost our rights, and all our property was taken."

In the spring of 1956, Gerhard moved to Lübeck, soon married, and had a son. All his life he worked as a truck driver. He kept contact with Marga and Gudrun up until Marga's death. In 2001 he gave the newspaper *Lübecker Nachrichten* a three-page interview in which he recounted his childhood and the mostly "peaceful idyll" with his foster mother and aunt in Gmund—an idyll that was disturbed now and then by his feared, authoritarian foster father. When Gerhard died in a hospital in Lübeck in December 2010, his son found two portrait photographs in a folder in his nightstand. The first showed Gerhard as a young man, the other, his foster father, Heinrich Himmler—each wearing an SS uniform.

Acknowledgments

Our greatest thanks go to Vanessa Lapa, who granted us the opportunity to work with these unique documents. In particular, the many conversations we had with her about the material were very productive for us all. Without her tireless dedication in recent years, our joint book and film project would never have come about.

Special thanks as well to all the colleagues who worked on the film production, especially to Hermann Pölking-Eiken, whose thorough research for the film frequently helped us. Sharon Brook, Dorothea Otto, and Sarah Strebelow we thank for the good cooperation and exchange of information; thanks especially to Sharon for watching the children.

We thank Horst von der Ahé, who spoke to us about his father and gave us access to his father's extensive posthumous papers.

Anne Pütz and Alexandra Wiersch thankfully relieved us of typing the letter transcripts.

The countless colleagues in the various archives, the Munich State Archive, the Bundesarchiv Berlin-Lichterfelde, Koblenz, including the photo archives, always answered our countless questions and fulfilled our requests. Michael Hollmann of the Bundesarchiv Koblenz deserves special mention here.

Thanks also to those colleagues at various libraries, especially the Library of the Foundation Topographie des Terrors, Berlin, and the main library of Humboldt University in Berlin.

Linde Appel subjected the introduction to a critical reading and helped us with her suggestions.

Christina Wittler provided us with many important references to Marga Himmler. Similarly, Jens Westemeier gave us many references to Hedwig Potthast.

Thanks also to Mair Glain, whose support made possible many days of research in archives and libraries.

Finally, our thanks go to our editors: Kristin Rotter of the Piper Verlag and Cécile Majorel of Plon-Perrin in Paris, whose countless valuable suggestions transformed our manuscript into an actual book.

Short Biographies of Persons Mentioned in the Text

Ahé, Anna von der, née Knaack
Born February 15, 1899, Neukalen (Mecklenburg); died 1945/46, Sachsenhausen.
In 1921 married Kurt von der Ahé (1897–1933), a laborer; mother of Horst (b. 1924)
   and Gerhard (b. 1928). Husband (1931, NSDAP and SS) died February 19, 1933,
   Berlin, after street fight with Communists. 1940, NSDAP; 1945, imprisoned in spe-
   cial camp at Sachsenhausen, reasons unknown. Declared dead 1956.

Ahé, Horst Kurt von der
Born April, 28, 1924, Berlin, died (killed in action) January 24, 1943, Illowaisk
   (Ukraine); precision mechanic, SS-Sturmmann, older brother of Gerhard.

Albers, Frau [Mrs.]
Native Englishwoman, tutored Marga and Gudrun in English; occasionally lived in
   Gmund with them after 1942.

Attolico, Bernardo
Born January 17, 1880, Canneto di Bari; died February 9, 1942, Rome.
In 1935–39, Italian ambassor to Berlin; he and his wife friends of the Himmlers; re-
   called 1940 because lacked clearly pro-German attitude.

Aumeier, Georg
Born November 14, 1895, Amberg (Palatinate)
Merchant; Himmler's adjutant before 1933. 1922–26, NSDAP; 1928, SS; 1922–26, SA
   leader; 1930, adjutant of the Reichsführer-SS; SS business manager; 1934, SS colonel. In World War II, cared for patients in SS field hospital, Hohenlychen.

Bach-Zelewski, Erich von dem

Born March 1, 1899, Lauenburg; died March 8, 1972, Munich.

SS-Obergruppenführer and general in the police force. World War I veteran; lieutenant, Freikorps; day laborer; 1930, NSDAP; 1931 SS; 1932, Reichstag delegate; 1941; head of Einsatzgruppe B; 1943, in charge of the elimination of partisans and Jews. August 1944, put down the resistenace in the Warsaw ghetto. During the Nuremberg war trials, witness for the prosecution, imprisoned until 1950; 1961, sentenced to four years and ten months' imprisonment for role in murders of SA men in 1934; 1962, sentenced to life in prison for murder of three Communists in 1933.

Bach-Zelewski, Ruth von dem, née Apfeld

Born August 22, 1901, Neisse.

Wife of Erich von dem Bach-Zelewski; six children; youngest (b. 1940) was Himmler's godchild.

Bastians, Hans

Born November 2, 1894; died (accidental death) June 14, 1940, Brûly-de-Pesche.

Himmler's first driver until death at Führer HQ Wolfsschlucht; shot himself while cleaning a pistol.

Baumert, Paul

Born May 20, 1904, Breslau; died March 5, 1961, Munich.

Merchant; 1934, assistant on personal staff of the Reichsführer-SS; 1938, Himmler's adjutant; 1942, chief of staff of the personal staff.

Berkelmann, Gabriele, née von Wolffersdorf

Wife of Theodor Berkelmann; with Marga and Gudrun in Unterwössen and Marquartstein (Chiemgau) in summer of 1942.

Berkelmann, Theodor

Born April 17, 1894, Le Ban-St.-Martin (Lorraine); died (brain tumor) December 27, 1943, Posen.

World War I veteran; Freikorps; 1920–31, gym teacher, miner, merchant, farmer in Canada; 1929, NSDAP; 1931, SS. Highest echelons of SA leadership; Himmler's adjutant until 1936; 1936 Reichstag delegate; 1942 SS-Obergruppenführer; 1940 head of the civilian administration of Lorraine, and later same function in 1943 in the Wartheland district.

Blösl, Hans

Owner of the Daxenberg guest house in the Chiemgau region; Himmlers stayed here in August 1932 and later again in October 1943, due to diphtheria epidemic in Gmund.

Bocchini, Arturo

Born February 12, 1880, San Giorgio, died November 20, 1940, Rome.

Chief of Police and Secret Police in Italy, 1926–40. Himmler and Heydrich attended his funeral.

Boden, Berta

Marga Himmler's married sister.

Boden, Edith (Edit)

Wife of Franz Boden; during the war lived with her two children in Gmund in the Himmlers' guest house, Haus Erika.

Boden, Elfriede, née Popp

Marga's mother, first wife of Hans Boden.

Boden, Franz

Husband of Edith; relationship to Marga unclear.

Boden, Grete

Second wife of Hans Boden.

Boden, Hans

Born December 12, 1863, Pyritz, died August 15. 1939, Blandikow (Brandenburg).

Marga's father; pensioner; formerly landowner in Goncerzewo, near Bromberg; first marriage with Elfriede, née Popp; six children; oldesest son killed in action in World War I; second marriage with Grete Boden; witness at the wedding of Marga and Heinrich; 1930, NSDAP.

Boden, Helmut

Marga's younger brother; witness at the wedding of Marga and Heinrich.

Boden, Lydia

Born June 18, 1899, Goncerzewo.

Marga's youngest sister; dressmaker; unmarried; 1932, NSDAP; lived in Berlin and Röntgental, 1932 in Munich; 1934–45, Gmund (Haus Lindenfycht); 1945, interned; 1955, with Marga in Bielefeld.

Boden, Martha

Sister of Marga.

Bouhler, Helene, née Mayer

Born April 20, 1912, Lauingen.

In 1934 married Philipp Bouhler; 1933, NSDAP; acquaintance of Marga's in Munich and Berlin.

Bouhler, Philipp

Born September 11, 1899, Munich; died (suicide) May 19, 1945, near Dachau.

Politician; World War I veteran; publicist at J. F. Lehmanns publishers; after 1921, with the *Völkischer Beobachter*; 1925–34, business manager of the NSDAP; 1933, Reich leader of the NSDAP and SS-Gruppenführer. Chief of the Aktion T4 program, which carried out euthanasia on thousands of people.

Brandt, Dr. Rudolf Hermann

Born June 2, 1909, Frankfurt an der Oder, died (executed) June 2, 1948, Landsberg.

Stenographer and jurist; 1932, NSDAP; 1933, SS; 1934, Ph.D.; 1933, personal staff of the Reichsführer-SS; 1935 married Annemarie Willeck (b. 1914); 1933, stenographer at Gestapo HQ; 1936–45, Himmler's personal aide and liaison officer to the Ministry of the Interior; organized murders of eighty-six Jews for skeleton collection of SS anatomist August Hirt in Strasburg; August 20, 1947, sentenced to death at Nuremberg.

Brekenfeld, Dr. Friedrich Wilhelm

Born September 13, 1887, Neubarmen.

Medical specialist and instructor in hygiene; World War I veteran; high-ranking staff physician (ret.) DRK; 1937, NSDAP; c. 1941, director of the DRK.

Bruger, Ferdinand

Born July 19, 1889, Frankfurt am Main.

Writer; World War I veteran; 1923, founded local NSDAP chapter near Landshut; from 1926, acting Gauleiter, Lower Bavaria; engaged as speaker by Himmler; 1927, editorial staff *Völkischer Beobachter;* 1932, editor NS publication *Illustrierter Beobachter;* financial support from Reichführer-SS; 1937, editor at *Münchner Illustrierten Presse,* on Himmler's recommendation; 1943, cared for wounded, SS field hospital, Tutzing.

Bruns

Born 12, 5. 1931.

SS-Standartenführer, Oldenburg.

Burgstaller, Alois

Born September 22, 1871, Holzkirchen; died April 19, 1945, Gmund am Tegernsee.

Opera singer at Bayreuth Festivals; protégé of Cosima Wagner; 1934, sold Haus Lindenfycht to Himmler for 65,000 gold Marks.

Darré, Richard Walther

Born 14. 7. 1895 Buenos Aires; died 5. 9. 1953 Munich

Leader of Reichsbauern. World War I veteran; 1927, met Himmler in the Bund Artam; 1930, NSDA; 1931, SS adviser to Hitler on agrarian matters; author of several "Blood and Soil" tracts; 1931–38, head of SS Central Office for Race and Resettlement; 1938, removed from office after conflicts with Himmler; 1932, Reichstag; 1933, Reich minister of nutrition and agriculture, leader of Reich farmers, Prussian state counselor, November 1933, Reich leader, SS-Gruppenführer; 1942, removed as minister; 1949, sentenced to seven years' internment; 1950 released from prison.

Deininger, Johann

Born April 9, 1896, Burtenbach (Günzburg-Schwaben); died July 2, 1973.

Farmer; World War I veteran; 1921, mayor of Burtenbach; late 1920s, NSDAP and SS; 1932, Reichstag delegate; 1943, SS-Brigadenführer.

Dietl, Eduard

Born July 21, 1890, Bad Aibling; died June 23, 1944, Waldbach (Styria, Austria).

July 28, 1942, colonel-general; Dietl was comber in chief of the twentieth Army Mountain Corps in Norway and the Alps. Veteran of World War I; member of Freikorps Epp (like Himmler); 1920, Reichswehr and NSDAP; helped establish Munich SA; participant in Hitler Putsch; 1944, died in airplane crash.

Dietrich, Josef (Sepp)

Born May 28, 1892, Hawangen (Unterallgäu); died April 21, 1966, Ludwigsburg.

Butcher, SS-Führer; World War I veteran; Hitler Putsch; 1928, NSDAP and first SS-Standarte Munich; 1930, Reichstag delegate; 1933, "personal attendant of the Führer"; leader of "SS Guard Battalion Berlin" (1934 Leibstandarte Adolf Hitler); 1934, organized Röhm Putsch; in World War II as commander of Sixth Tank Army, responsible for war crimes in Kharkov; 1944, godfather of Nanette Dorothea Potthast; 1942, SS general; 1944–45, responsible for massacre at Malmedy; 1946, sentenced to twenty-five years' imprisonment; 1955, released; 1957, sentenced for SA murders; 1958, released; seven thousand people attend his funeral.

Dollmann, Dr. Eugen

Born August 21, 1900, Regensburg; May 17, 1985, Munich.

World War I volunteer; 1926, Ph.D., Munich; 1927–30, studied in Italy; apparently met Himmler in Rome; 1934, NSDAP; 1935, translator and foreign correspondent in Rome; Himmler's liaison officer to Mussolini; 1937, staff of National Youth leadership movement in Italy; special envoy of SS in Italy.

Dwinger, Edwin-Erich

Born April 23, 1898, Kiel; died December 17, 1981, Gmund am Tegernsee.

World War I volunteer; 1915, Russian prisoner of war; from 1920, fought in White Army (possibly Bolsheviks); 1921, return to Germany, farmer and writer in Bavaria; numerous books; 1941, war correspondent USSR with authority from Himmler; after 1942, increasing criticism of Germany's politics in the East; house arrest and under surveillance by Secret Police.

Eberstein, Karl Friedrich von

Born January 14, 1894, Halle; died 1979, Tegernsee.

World War I veteran, Stahlhelm; Kapp Putsch. Bank trainee; 1924, private secretary of SA-Führer Wolf von Heldorf; 1925, NSDAP; 1930, SS-Führer in Thüringen. Introduced Heydrich to Himmler (mother was Heydrich's godmother); 1933, Reichstag delegate; 1936–42, police president of Munich; 1942, leader, police department, Bavaria; Ministry of Interior; after 1945, categorized as collaborator.

Ebner, Dr. Gregor

Born June 24, 1892, Ichenhausen (Bavaria); died March 22, 1974, Wolfratshausen.

World War I field medic; Freikorps Epp; 1920, Ph.D., practicing doctor in Kirchseeon; 1930, NSDAP; 1931, SS; 1930, district group leader Ichenhausen; before 1933, party speaker on topics such as declining birthrate; occasionally Himmler's family doctor; 1936, Central Office for Race and Resettlement; head doctor SS Mothers' Home, Steinhöring; personal staff of Reichsführer-SS; head of SS "Lebensborn Initiative;" head of all Lebensborn homes until 1945; 1948, Nuremberg, sentenced to brief incarceration; subsequently practiced medicine.

Ettel, Erwin

Born 1895, Cologne; died 1971, Bad Bevensen.

World War I veteran; 1930, merchant in Colombia; 1936, Foreign Office, legation counselor in Rome; 1937, SS; 1939, German ambassador, Teheran; 1943, resignation from diplomatic service, Waffen-SS; 1944, Haupsturmführer, reserves; 1950–56, under pseudonym "Ernst Krüger," editor at *Die Zeit* [newspaper].

Fahrenkamp, Dr. Karl

Born April 20, 1889, Aachen; died (Suicide) September 21, 1945, Pabenschwandt Estate.

Internist; 1913, received degree; World War I veteran, as senior physician; 1920, specialist, internal medicine, private practice Munich, head of Institute for Biochemical Therapies; 1933–44, staff physician of the Waffen-SS in Dachau; leader of "Department F" in the personal staff of the Reichsführer-SS; head of his own research garden in Dachau; experimented with glycocides, also using prisoners; experiments involving nutrition and hormones with prisoners in Dachau; advised Siegmund Rascher on deadly vacuum chamber experiments on prisoners. Had own SS cosmetic factory in Dachau. Personal physician and friend of Himmler family; informed Himmler on the results of all physical examinations of his personal staff.

Fahrenkamp, Frau [Mrs.]

Wife of Karl Fahrenkamp, friend of Marga Himmler; lived with husband and family in Munich; after 1943 lived in Pabenschwandt, SS experimental agricultural estate near Salzburg.

Foedisch, Frau [Mrs.]

Girlhood friend of Marga Himmler's from the region near Bromberg; estate owner in Rogalin.

Foedisch, Werner Gustav Wilhelm

Born December 13, 1910, Rogalin.

Farmer, ethnic German, son of Frau Foedisch; 1939, civil defense, Danzig; 1940, SS training; 1940, SS-Scharführer in the Central Office for Race and Resettlement;

1942–44 Waffen-SS. Februay 1943, farmer in Hegewald; March 1943, sentenced, along with his superior officer, SS-Untersturmführer Karl Sulkowski by SS Judiciary; accused of black marketeering and economic crimes against the Reich; attempted suicide; 1944, charges dropped.

Frank, Hans ("Frank II")
Born May, 23, 1900, Karlsruhe; died (executed) October 16, 1946, Nuremberg.

Jurist and Generalgouverneur in Poland: 1919, studied law and economics; Freikorps Epp; 1923, NSDAP and SA; Hitler Putsch; 1926, state examinations, assistant professor, Technical University, Munich; 1930, Reichstag delegate; 1929–42, head of legal branch of the NSDAP; 1934, minister without portfolio; president, Academy of German Law; 1939–45, Generalgouverneur for occupied Poland, 1946, condemned to death in Nuremberg.

Frentz, Walter
Born August 21, 1907, Heilbronn; died July 6, 2004, Überlingen.

Cameraman and photographer; 1933–36 cameraman for Leni Riefenstahl; afterwards in Hitler's entourage; filmed in all Führer HQs; war correspondent for weekly German newsreels; August 1941, trip to Minsk with Himmler; witnessed mass shootings; afterward, accepted into SS.

Friedrich, Dr. Traude
Pharmacist; head of laboratory opened in 1940 in Dachau dedicated to curative and nutritional properties of plants. Experiments in plant breeding, nutrition, and naturopathy.

Gebhardt, Prof. Karl
Born November 23, 1897, Haag (Oberbayern); died (executed) June 2, 1948, Landsberg.

Surgeon, "chief clinician" in Reichsarzt-SS [Medical Branch, SS]; 1919, medical studies in Munich; Hitler Putsch; 1932, instructor in Munich; 1933, NSDAP; 1935, SS; 1933, chief physician in the Sanatoriums at Hohenlychen, near Ravensbrück concentration camp. Remodeled as surgical clinic in World War II; also field hospital of the Waffen-SS; 1940, consulting surgeon of the Waffen-S; experiments on gas burns and transplants using female Polish prisoners from Ravensbrück; 1943, Himmler's doctor; in final days of war, president of the DRK; godfather of Helge Potthast; 1947, death sentence in Nuremberg.

Globocnik, Odilo
Born April 21, 1904, Triest; died (suicide) May 31, 1945.

Contractor; 1931, NSDAP Austria; 1934, SS; 1933, acting Gauleiter, Vienna; 1938, secretary of state, Reichstag delegate, and Gauleiter Vienna; 1938, removed from office to the personal staff, Führer-SS; 1939, SS and Police führer, Lublin. Assigned to "Final Solution" in Poland by Himmler (Aktion Reinhard"); responsible for extermination camps Bełżec, Sobibór, and Treblinka; 1943, business manager of the *Ostindustrie* [industry, East]; responsible for confiscation of Jewish property and exploitation of Jewish workers marked for extermination. In 1943, Höherer SS und Polizeiführer [senior SS and police chief] Adriatic coast.

Göring, Ilse, née Borchardt

Born April 28, 1898, Kiel.

Cousin of Hermann Göring; in World War II DRK nurse, colleague of Marga Himmler; 1933, NSDAP; 1940, DRK trip to France and Belgium with Marga Himmler.

Görlitzer, Frl. [Miss]

Tutor; visited Gmund several times, reviewing and tutoring for Gudrun.

Grawitz, Prof. Dr. Ernst-Robert

Born June 8, 1899, Berlin; died (suicide) April 24, 1945, Potsdam-Babelsberg.

Reichsarzt-SS [Reich doctor, SS] and general in the Waffen-SS. World War I veteran; Freikorps, Kapp Putsch; medical studies; 1925, licensed; 1929, specialist internal medicine; 1931, NSDAP; 1932, SS; 1935, head of the Sanitation Bureau and Reichsarzt-SS; 1937, managing director, DRK; 1941, honorary degree, University of Graz; SS Gruppenführer and lieutenant general, Waffen-SS. Performed medical experiments on prisoners; 1945, suicide with family.

Grawitz, Ilse, née Taubert

Born February 8, 1905, Wesel; died (suicide) April 24, 1945, Potsdam-Babelsberg.

Daughter of the captain in charge of Wewelsburg Castle, SS-Führer Siegfried Taubert and his wife, Arnoldine; 1926, married Dr. Grawitz, five children, 1932, NSDAP; suicide, with husband and children, in villa in Potsdam-Babelsberg (hand grenade).

Grynszpan, Herschel

Born March 28, 1921, Hannover; death unconfirmed.

In 1935, dismissed from elementary school, Hannover, without finishing; Polish passport (parents emigrated from Russia to Poland); 1936, traveled illegally to Paris; July 1938, expelled for lack of residence permit; hidden by uncle. In October 28, 1938, fifteen thousand Jews forcibly deported from Germany to Poland, Grynszpan's parents among them. In desperation, he shoots Ernst vom Rath, secretary at German embassy, Paris. This assassination used as propaganda for Reichskristallnacht on November 9, 1938. Arrested July 1940, in Vichy, France, and handed over to Germany; imprisoned in Berlin and Sachsenhausen. Unclear whether he survived the war.

Gulbransson, Olaf

Born May 26, 1873, Christiania (Oslo); September 18, 1958, Schererhof (Tegernsee).

Painter, graphic artist and caricaturist for the satirical journal *Simplicissimus*. 1929, professor at Munich Academy of Art; after 1929, lived on the Tegernsee. Uncritical of NS regime. 1943, seventieth birthday, receives Goethe Medal for Art and Science.

Günther, Hans Friedrich Karl ("Rassengünther")

Born February 16, 1891, Freiburg im Breisgau; died September 25, 1968.

Political author and eugenicist. World War I veteran. 1920, author of *Ritter, Tod und Teufel* [Knight, Death, and the Devil]; 1922, *Rassenkunde des deutschen Volkes* [Race Primer for the German People]. One of the most widely read publicists between the wars and one of the most controversial. 1930, chair of Racial Studies, University of Jena; 1932, NSDAP; 1935, professor for Racial Studies, Humboldt University, Berlin; 1940–45, professor, University of Freiburg; 1951, denazified as a collaborator.

Gutensohn, Dr. Wilhelm

Born January 21, 1905, Munich.

Dentist; 1921, Gymnasics and Sport Sector (later SA); Hitler Putsch; 1924–28, studies; 1926, NSDAP; 1931–32, SS Press Office; 1934, SS. Himmler godfather to his son.

Hahne, Prof. Hans

Born March 18, 1875, Piesdorf; died February 2, 1935, Halle.

Medical doctor, special interest in prehistory; 1921, professor in Halle, researched local bog bodies; director of the Museum of Prehistory in Halle; 1933, president of the University of Halle; in the 1920s, joined NSDAP; speaker at leadership training courses for the Artam League.

Hallermann, Dr. August

Born October 10, 1896, Hamm (Westphalia).

Agricultural counselor; World War I veteran; licensed agronomist; animal breeding inspector in Halle; 1928, NSDAP, agricultural district expert adviser for the NSDAP; 1934, SS; 1942, SS-Oberführer.

Hallermann, Prof. Wilhelm

Born March 14, 1901, Arnsberg, died March 28, 1975, Kiel.

Forensic pathologist, brother of August Hallermann; 1935, instructor and senior officer at the Institute of Legal and Social Medicine, University, Berlin; NS-Dozentenbund [NS German Lecturers League]; 1937, NSDAP; 1941–71, director of Legal and Social Medicine, University of Kiel.

Hammerl, Sebastian

Born January, 20, 1894, Todtenweis.

Detective, Reich Secret Service; farmer; World War I veteran; police training; 1921–35, police administration, Munich, afterward "Braunes Haus" [Brown House,

NSDAP HQ]; 1933, NSDA; June 1934, in charge of SS HQ, Gmund; 1944, SS-Obersturmführer; daughter was a friend of Gudrun Himmler.

Hauschild, Dr. Bernhard

Surgeon and gynecologist-obstetrician; co-owner of the private clinic in Berlin-Schöneberg, colleague of Marga Siegroth, 1928 purchased her share of the clinic; after 1935, no further Berlin address, presumably emigrated.

Hermann, Nora

Colleague and close friend of Marga Himmler's at the DRK.

Heydrich, Klaus

Born June 17, 1933; died October 24, 1943, Jungfern-Breschan.

Elder son of Reinhard and Lina Heydrich; Himmler's godson.

Heydrich, Lina, née von Osten

Born June 14, 1911, Avendorf (Fehmarn); died August 14, 1985, Burg auf Fehmarn.

December 1931 marries Reinhard Heydrich (1904–1942), four children, 1931, NSDAP; after husband's assassination and death on June 4, 1942, continued to live in Jungfern-Breschan, near Prague; used Jewish prisoners as forced labor. April 1945 fled to Gmund with her children; 1948, sentenced to life in prison by Czech court; 1949, classified as collaborator in denazification proceedings; 1951, cleared of charges; 1956, receives husband's full public pension ("war victim"); 1976, publishes exculpatory memoir, *Leben mit einem Kriegsverbrecher* [Life with a War Criminal].

Himmler, Anna Maria, née Heyder

Born 19, January 19, 1866, Munich; died September 10, 1941, Munich.

Mother of Heinrich Himmler and his brothers, Gebhard and Ernst; 1897, married Gebhard Himmler; 1927, visits Hitler rally in Munich; 1933, NSDAP.

Himmler, Ernst Hermann

Born December 23, 1905, Munich; died (missing) early May 1945, Berlin.

Younger brother of Heinrich Himmler; 1924, secondary school diploma; 1924–28, studies engineering in Munich, becomes electrical engineer in Berlin; 1931, NSDAP; 1933, SS; senior engineer at the Reich Radio Service, Berlin; 1933, marries Paula Melters, Heinrich Himmler as witness; four children, son (b. 1939) godchild of Heinrich Himmler; 1934, acting technical director and acting chief engineer of Reich Radio; 1939, SS-Sturmbahnführer; 1942–45, senior engineer and technical head of Reich Radio Service; went missing in Berlin in 1945; declared dead 1955.

Himmler, Gebhard Ludwig, Jr.

Born July 29, 1899, Munich; died June 22, 1982, Munich.

Older brother of Heinrich Himmler, engineer; 1917, secondary school degree, officer candidate school; veteran of World War I; Freikorps Epp; studied in Munich; Hitler Putsch, 1924; teaches in vocational school; 1926 marries Mathilde Wendler, three children; 1933, NSDAP and SS; 1933, Deputy Gauleiter in the NS Teachers' League; division head, Central Administration for Technology, Munich; 1935–39, director of the Oskar-von-Miller-Polytechnic, Munich; 1939, officer in campaign against Poland; December 1939, head of the Division for Engineering Problems in the Reichserziehungsministerium [REM, Reich Ministry of Education]; 1944, SS-Standartenführer; 1944, *Ministerialdirektor* [Director of the Ministry, REM] 1945–48, interned; in denazification proceedings, designated "incriminated"; mid-1950s, at the Afghan Cultural Institute, Munich.

Himmler, Gebhard, Sr.

Born May 17, 1865, Lindau; died October 29, 1936, Munich.

Father of Heinrich Himmler, Gymnasium teacher of Latin and ancient Greek; 1893–97, private tutor of Prince Heinrich von Wittelsbach (godfather of Heinrich Himmler) in Munich; 1897, marries Anna Heyder; from 1897, secondary school teacher in Munich and Passau; 1913–19, co-director in Landshut; 1919–22, director of the secondary school in Ingolstadt; 1922–30, director of the Wittelsbacher-Gymnasium in Munich until retirement; 1933, NSDAP; 1936, state funeral, with an obituary in the *Völkischer Beobachter.*

Himmler, Johanna, née Mildner

Born September 20, 1894, Chemnitz; died October 13, 1972, Nordhausen.

KPD (Communist Party) politician, no relation to Heinrich Himmler. Sales clerk; 1917, Spartakusbund; 1919, KPD; 1927–31, city councellor in Chemnitz; 1930–33, Reichstag delegate from Chemnitz-Zwickau. After the Reichstag file in February 1933, arrested several times and released; after July 20, 1944, interned in Ravensbrück until liberation.

Himmler, Mathilde (Hilde), née Wendler

Born May 25, 1899, Neuburg am Inn; died September 2, 1986, Munich.

Wife of Gebhard Jr., sister of Richard Wendler; 1926, marriage; three children; youngest daughter (b. 1940) was Himmler's godchild; 1932, NSDAP; 1935, gave her party membership to husband because of the favorably low membership number. After 1943, lived with children in Gmund, in Guesthouse Erika of Haus Lindenfycht.

Himmler, Paula (Gertrud), née Melters

Born March 27, 1905, Dinslaken; died November 24, 1985, Dinslaken.

Wife of Ernst; milliner; in Berlin after 1930; meets Ernst Himmler; marries 1933; four children; son was Himmler's godchild. After 1943, lived in the Warthegau district; 1945, escapes with help of brother-in-law Heinrich via Horn, near Detmold,

Hohenlychen to Timmendorf. After 1947 lived again in Dinslaken; 1948, denazification, became milliner again.

Hofer, Franz

*Born November 27, 1902, Hofgastein (Österreich); died February 18, 1975, Mülheim
an der Ruhr.*

Merchant; 1931, member of the banned NSDAP Austria; 1932, Gauleiter of Tyrol;
1933, imprisoned, freed by SA men; 1935, German citizenship; 1938, after the
Anschluss, again Gauleiter of Tyrol-Vor-Vorarlberg; from 1940, also Reichsstatthalter; 1944, suggests the building of the Alpine fortress to Hitler; 1945–48, interned, flees to Germany; 1949, in Austria, sentenced to death in absentia; from
1949, merchant in Mülheim, lived under a false name until 1954.

Höfl, Frieda, née Nässl ("Friedl")

Born September 5, 1886, Steingaden.

Cousin of Anna Himmler; 1913, marriage to Hugo Höfl in Apfeldorf am Lech; one
daughter (b. 1919, see Klingshirn); 1930, NSDAP; the Höfls later lived in Weilheim,
Freising, and Schongau.

Höfl, Dr. Hugo

Born July 17, 1886, Munich.

Husband of Frieda; general practitioner in Apfeldorf, later in Weilheim, Freising,
and Issing. Veteran of World War I, staff doctor in the Reserves; 1930, NSDAP;
1933, SS; 1935, SD; 1937, honorary SD field office director; April 1941, SS-
Obersturmbahführer. Close contact with Heinrich Himmler and his family.

Hofmann, Frieda (Frida)

Marga's relative, presumably a cousin. Often visited Gmund during summer holidays
with her family (Marga's *Journal*).

Hofmeister, Frau [Mrs.]

Colleague and friend of Marga's in the field hospital.

Hofmeister, Georg

Born April 15, 1892, Pilberskofen (Dingolfing).

Colonel, major general; World War I veteran; officer training; 1941, lieutenant colonel
of the Wehrmacht, led the Mountaineer Regiment 136 of the second Mountaineer Division; 1942, badly wounded; 1944, city commander of greater Berlin, successor to Paul von Hase (executed after July 20).

Holfelder, Hans

Born September 17, 1900, Wien; January 1, 1929, Halle.

Estate manager; knew Himmler from their student days in Munich; 1924, Artam
League; 1925, NSDAP; 1927, business manager of the Artam League; his goal, to
make the league financially independent from the NSDAP; manager of various es-

tates in Saxony; edited a supplement in the journal *Die Kommenden*, "Die Artamanenbewegung" [The Artaman Movement]; 1928, motorcycle accident, succumbs to injuries shortly thereafter.

Hommel, Conrad

Born February 16, 1883, Mainz; died November 11, 1971, Sielbeck.

NS painter; uncle of Albert Speer; trained at Munich Academy of Arts; member of Munich Secession and late Impressionist; portraits of Albert Einstein and Friedrich Ebert; later Goebbels, Göring, Hitler, Himmler, and others.

Hühnlein, Adolf

Born September 12, 1881, bei Kulmbach; died June 18, 1942, Munich.

Reich leader and corps leader, NS automotive corps; military academy; World War I veteran; General Staff officer; company leader in Freikorps Epp; Hitler Putsch; six months' imprisonment; 1925, quartermaster NSDAP and SA-Obergruppenführer; 1927, chief SA-Automotive Corps; 1931, founding of the NS Automotive Corps; 1933, Reichstag delegate; 1934, after murder of Röhm, corps leader in NSKK; 1936, major general; 1940, serves under Göring; in World War II, assigned to Motorized Transport for the War Economy. Under him the NSKK becomes a paramilitary unit subordinate to the Wehrmacht also deployed for deportations to extermination camps.

Johst, Hanns

Born July 8, 1890, Seerhausen (Saxony); died November 23, 1978, Ruhpolding (Bayern).

Author, literary functionary, "Bard of the SS"; c. 1923, first meeting with Hitler; 1932, NSDAP; 1933, artistic director of the State Theater, Berlin; 1933, head German "Akademie der Dichtung" [Academy of Literature]; 1935, president of the Reichsschrifttumskammer [Reich Literary Association]; Prussian state counsellor; 1942, SS-Gruppenführer; 1939–40, travels with Himmler through occupied Poland; 1949, identified as "major offender"; 1951, denazified to category of "offender."

Johst, Johanna, née Feder (Hanne)

Born 1892, Nürnberg.

Wife of Hanns Johst, marries 1915; one daughter (b. 1920). Family lived in Allmannshausen (Starnberger See) and were close friends of the Himmler family.

Kalkreuth, Herr and Frau [Mr. and Mrs.]

Employees in Gmund; 1939, gardener (Marga's *Geschenkebuch* [*Gift Book*]).

Karl, Josef (Sepp)

Born March 1, 1910, Salzburg.

Lived Munich from 1913; 1930–35, brewer; 1933, NSDAP and SS; January 1935, assistant in SS HQ; 1937, Führer on the staff of SS HQ; 1940, Waffen-SS.

Kersten, Felix

Born September 30, 1898, Dorpat (Estonia); died April 16, 1960, Hamm.

Estate manager; Finnish citizenship after Russian Revolution; trained as masseur; 1928, health consultant to Dutch royal ramily; 1934, return to Germany; Heinrich Himmler a godfather to his son; (b. 1943); 1939, begins regular treatment of Himmler's chronic stomach pains (other patients include Hess, Ribbentrop); 1943, Sweden; 1944–45, mediated release of concentration camp prisoners among Swedish Red Cross, World Jewish Congress, and Himmler; 1953, Swedish citizenship.

Killinger, Manfred Freiherr von

Born July 14, 1886, Lindigt (Meissen); died (suicide) September 2, 1944, Bucharest.

World War I navy; captain lieutenant in Freikorps "Marinebrigade Ehrhardt"; head of "Sturmkompanie Killinger"; participated in overthrow of Soviet republic in Bavaria and in murder plot against Matthias Erzberger; 1927, NSDA; until 1933, SA leadership, Dresden; 1932, Reichstag delegate; 1933, governor of Saxony, pensioned off after the "Röhm Affair"; 1935, dismissed by Hitler; Foreign Service; 1936, general consul, San Francisco; 1939, ambassador, Bratislava; 1941–44, responsible for "matters relating to Jews" in Bucharest.

Kiss, Edmund

Born 1886, Kassel; died 1960.

Architect and author; World War I veteran; 1920s, expedition to Tiwa na ku (Brazil); author, several books, admirer of Hanns Hörbiger's Welteislehre; ("Glacial Cosmogony"); 1938, SS-Ahnenerbe; SS-Haupsturmführer; 1939, together with Kiss, the Ahnenerbe planned expedition to South America to research ruins of extraterrestrial harbors on Lake Titicaca, which Kiss thought he had discovered; did not take place because of the war.

Klingshirn, Irmgard, née Höfl

Born May 21, 1919, Apfeldorf am Lech.

Daughter of von Hugo and Frieda Höfl, marries Dr. Richard Klingshirn (b. 1910; 1937, NSDAP); son (b. 1941) was Himmler's godson.

Koch, Erich

Born June 19, 1896, Elberfeld (Wuppertal); died November 12. 1986, Prison Barczewo (Poland).

Gauleiter and Oberpräsident East Prussia; railroad official; World War I veteran; Freikorps; 1922, NSDAP in Ruhr region, member of circle around Leo Schlageter; early supporter of Gregor Strasser; friend of Himmler from 1925; 1928, Gauleiter East Prussia; January 1929, invited Himmler as one of first NS speakers there; 1933, Reichstag delegate; Oberpräsident East Prussia; 1938, SA-Obergruppenführer;

November 1941, Reichskommissar for the Ukraine; known as one of most successful and brutal of all Gauleiters; 1959, death sentence, Warsaw, commuted to life in
prison.

Kolbe, Martchen

Friend of Marga's in Berlin.

Krenzlin (Kränzlin), Frau [Mrs.]

Acquaintance of Marga and Gudrun's from their Baltic vacation; lived in Gmund with
her son during the war.

Laur, Herr [Mr.]

SS member of the Gmund HQ.

Litzmann, Karl

Born January 22, 1850, Neuglobsow (Mecklenburg); died May 28, 1936.

General; March 1, 1930, NSDAP; 1932, Reichstag delegate; after invasion of Poland,
city of Łódź renamed Litzmannstadt in his honor.

Litzmann, Karl-Siegmund

Born August 1, 1893, Minden; died August 1945, Kappeln (Holstein).

Career officer and farmer; son of the general; military school, Potsdam; World War I
veteran; Freikorps; 1919, studies agriculture in Halle; 1921, administers the state
Althof-Didlaken, near Insterburg (East Prussia); 1926–29, Stahlhelm; 1929,
NSDAP and SA; establishes the SA in East Prussia; 1930, establishes the Reiter-
SA [mounted SA]; 1931, SA-Führer in East Prussia and Danzig; 1933, SA-
Obergruppenführer and Reichstag delegate; 1939, leader of the SA-Hauptamt for
Rider and Driver Training; summer 1941, sent to the front, White Russia; 1941,
Generalkommissar of Estonia.

Loeper, Wilhelm ("Hauptmann [captain] Loeper")

Born October 13, 1883, Schwerin; died October 23, 1935, Dessau.

Gauleiter; career officer; World War I veteran; leader of a Freikorps unit in the Ruhr
and Baltic regions; 1920, officer in the Reichswehr; 1923, teacher at School for
Pioneers, in Munich, where he met Hitler; Hitler Putsch; dismissed from Reichswehr; 1925, NSDAP; 1928, Gauleiter Magdeburg-Anhalt; 1930, head of the Personnel Department of the NSDAP and Reichstag delegate; 1933, governor of
Braunschweig and Anhalt; 1934, SS-Gruppenführer.

Lorenz, Werner

Born October 2, 1891, Grünberg (Pommerania); died March 13, 1974, Hamburg.

Farmer, officer; World War I veteran; Freikorps "Grenzschutz Ost," 1919; 1929,
NSDAP; 1931, SS; 1933, Reichstag delegate; 1937–45, Head of the Main Welfare
Office for Ethnic Germans (VoMi); 1936, SS-Obergruppenführer; general in the
Waffen-SS and the Police; Organizes the resettlement of c. nine hundred thousand

ethnic Germans, including expulsion and murder of local population; 1948, sentenced at Nuremberg to twenty years' imprisonment; released 1955.

Lucas, Franz (Lukas)

Born December 12, 1901, Stahnsdorf.

Head of the automotive division of the personal staff of Reichsführer-SS; Himmler's driver; occasionally photographed in role as SS war reporter; 1944, SS-Sturmbahnführer.

Melters, Walter

Born September 1, 1913, Dinslaken; died (killed in action) September 14, 1941, Dnjepropetrowsk.

Younger brother of Paula Himmler; painter; 1935, SS training Munich; 1937, NSDAP; 1940, SS-Verfügungstruppe (SS-VT) [SS Dispositional Troops] (later SS Division "Das Reich"); deployed in the Netherlands and France; 1940, SS war reporter; 1941, accompanied war correspondents on the Russian campaign; September 4, 1941, mortally wounded near Dnjepropetrowsk.

Menke, Miens and Frida (Mieze)

Nurses in Obersiegersdorf (Silesia); Miens was a friend of Marga's.

Mielsch, Max Hermann

After 1927, leader of the Artam League, responsible for the regional offices; 1929, successor to Hans Holfelders as business manager.

Moulin Eckart, Karl Leon du

Born January 11, 1900, Munich; died 31, March 1991, Oberviechtach.

Student of law, politician, and SA-Führer; World War I veteran; Freikorps Epp; Hitler Putsch; friend of Himmler's at least as early as 1924 (*Journal* entry of February 15, 1924); 1927, law degree; estate manager; 1930–32, head of the SA Press Office in the Brown House; 1933, SA-Brigadenführer; adjutant of Röhm's; 1934, narrowly escapes being murdered; 1934–36, in Lichtenburg concentration camp; later retreats from public life.

Oeynhausen, Carl Freiherr von

Born October 24, 1880, Grevenburg.

Brother of Adolf, SS-Standartenführer; lived at Schloss Grevenburg with wife and three sons.

Oeynhausen, (Friedrich) Adolf Freiherr von

Born August 27, 1877, Holthausen bei Büren; died June 7, 1953, Grevenburg (Westphalia).

Tax official; 1919–23, head of the tax office Hildesheim; Stahlhelm; 1931, NSDAP; in January 1933, shelters Adolf Hitler and his entourage at his castle, Schloss Grevenburg, during the so-called *Lipper Durchbruchswahlkampf* [Breakthrough Election in Lippe, 1933]. Also, suggested the nearby castle of Wewelsburg to Himmler as a Reichsführerschule [training institute] for the SS. Daughter (b. 1935) was god-child of Hitler and Himmler.

Oldenburg, Grossherzogin [grand duchess] Elisabeth von, née zu Mecklenburg-Schwerin

Born August 10, 1869, Ludwigslust; died September 3, 1955, Schaumburg-Lippe.

Wife of Grand Duke Friedrich August von Oldenburg; published travel journals.

Ossietzky, Carl von

Born October 3, 1889, Hamburg; died May 4, 1938, Berlin.

One of the most significant journalists of the Weimar Republic; 1913, marries Maud Lichfield-Woods in Hamburg; one daughter; World War I veteran, general secretary of German Society for Peace; from 1920, worked on Social Democratic newspapers; 1927, editor-in-chief of the *Weltbühne* [World Stage]; his editorials criticized party politics, clandestine rearmament; 1931, sentenced to eighteen months in prison for betraying state secrets; 1932, released early; February 1933, imprisoned and tortured by Gestapo; through 1936, various concentration camps; sent to hospital in Berlin with severe tuberculosis; died of his maltreatment. Received Nobel Peace Prize posthumously for the year 1935.

Oswald, Herr and Frau (Mr. and Mrs.)

Friends of the Himmlers' in Berlin. Probably Herr von Oswald, embassy attaché; wife née Princess zu Lippe.

Pfeffer von Salomon, Franz

Born February 19, 1888, Düsseldorf; died April 12, 1968, Munich.

Jurist, officer, politician; World War I veteran; participated with Freikorps Westphalia in the Kapp Putsch; 1924, founded NSDAP–Gau Westphalia with Joseph Goebbels and Karl Kaufmann; 1926–30, Oberster-SA-Führer. Himmler was his secretary in Munich; 1930, Hitler took over SA leadership personally; 1932–41, Reichstag delegate; Hitler's liaison staff in the Reich Chancellory; 1941, fell from favor with Hitler, relieved of duties.

Pohl, Oswald

Born June 30, 1892, Duisburg; died (executed) June 8, 1951, Landsberg.

Career soldier; 1918, navy bursar, Freikorps; 1921, NSDAP; 1922, SA; 1929 Ortsgruppenleiter and SA-Führer, Swinemünde; 1935, administrative head of the SS (concentration camps); 1939, head of SS main divisions, budget and buildings, administration, and business, and SS administrative headquarters; 1942, SS-Obergruppenführer and general of the Waffen-SS; head of the board of directors of the DRK; family lived on estate Comthurey, near Hohenlychen; there, neighbors and friends of Hedwig Potthast; sentenced to death in Nuremberg on November 3, 1947.

Potthast, Hedwig
Born February 5, 1912, Cologne; died September 22, 1994, Baden-Baden.
Secretary; 1933, studied at vocational high school for business, Mannheim; employment in Coblenz; 1935, Gestapo, Berlin; 1935, moved to Personal Staff Reichsführer-SS; from 1936, Himmler's private secretary; from end 1938 on, Himmler's mistress; end 1940 to beginning 1941, end of employment on Personal Staff; February 15, 1942, birth of (Himmler's) son, Helge; June 3, 1944, birth of their daughter, Nanette Dorothea, both births in SS clinic, Hohenlychen; 1942–44, lived in Brückenthin with her children, near Hohenlychen; 1944–45, in Schönaunear Berchtesgaden; after 1945, first in Teisendorf (Bavaria); 1953, to Sinzheim (Baden); worked as secretary; 1957, marries Hans Adolf Staeck (Baden-Baden).

Pracher, Auguste von, (formerly Zipperer, widowed)
Mother of Falk Zipperer; second marriage to Ferdinand von Pracher, one daughter; friendly with the Himmler family in Landshut.

Pracher, Ferdinand von
Stepfather of Falk Zipperer; father of his half-sister; 1914–23, government president of Lower Bavaria.

Prützmann, Christa, née von Boddien
Born March 13, 1916, Leissienen (Wehlau, East Prussia).
Wife of Hans-Adolf Prützmann; 1935, the Himmlers were guests at her wedding.

Prützmann, Hans-Adolf
Born August 31, 1901, Tolkemit (East Prussia); died (suicide) May 21, 1945, Lüneburg.
Farmer, Höherer SS- und Polizeiführer and general of the Waffen-SS; 1935, marries Christa von Boddien; 1937, Höherer SS- und Polizeiführer, Nordwest (Hamburg); 1941, SS-Obergruppenführer, Höherer SS- und Polizeiführer Nordost (Königsberg), Russland-Nord [Russia, North], *Russland-Süd* [Russia, South], and Ukraine; 1944, general, Croatia (empowered to govern); Himmler assigned him to Operation Werewolf [mission: to operate as resistance force behind advancing enemy lines—Trans.]; 1945, interned in Lüneburg by the British.

Rainer, Friedrich ("Dr. Reiner")
Born July 28, 1903, St. Veit (Carinthia); died (executed) July 19, 1947, Ljubljana.
Jurist, Gauleiter; 1923, SS; 1930, NSDAP; friend of Globocnik and Kaltenbrunner as one of the *Kärntner Erneuerer* [Carinithian Modernizers]; 1938, Gauleiter of Salzburg; Reichstag delegate; 1940, Reichsstatthalter [Reich governor], Salzburg; expanded police apparatus there. 1941, Reichsstatthalter Kärnten [Carinthia]; chief of the civilian government of Carniola [Kranjska] (Slovenia); 1943, SS-Obergruppenführer; married; youngest daughter (b. 1939) godchild of Himmler; May 31, 1945, interned; July 19, 1947, sentenced to death, military court Ljubljana.

Aires, where she worked to organize German women expatriates; active in the Red Cross; 1943, after return, SS-Führerin [SS woman leader] of the SS-Helferinnenkorps. After 1945, active in the Stille Hilfe organization.

Schaumburg-Lippe, Stephan Prinz zu

Born June 21, 1891, Stadthagen; died February 10, 1965, Kempfenhausen.

Husband of Ingeborg Alix; 1922, secretary to the legation of the embassy in Sofia, Rome, Rio de Janeiro; 1940, Buenos Aires; 1936, SS; 1937, SS-Hauptsturmführer; 1939, SS-Obersturmbahnführer; 1943, retires from Foreign Service; returns to Germany.

Scheubner-Richter, Mathilde von, née von Scheubner

Born 1855, Riga.

In 1911, marries the twenty-nine-year-younger Baltic German diplomat Max Erwin Richter (1884–1923; 1920, NSDAP) one of the most important early supporters of Hitler in Munich, who, dies in 1923 in the failed Putsch attempt; Hitler dedicated the first part of *Mein Kampf* to him); 1926, Hitler appointed her to work with Himmler to establish a collection documenting the NS press and the press of its opponents (later the Central Archive of the Reich Press); today in the Bundesarchiv (Department Berlin-Lichterfelde), main archive of the NSDAP.

Schick

Servant of Marga Himmler.

Schirach, Baldur Benedikt von

Born May 9, 1907, Berlin; died August 8, 1974, Kröv (Mosel).

Gauleiter and Reichsjugendführer; 1925, married daughter of Hitler's favorite photographer; four children; 1932, leader of the Hitler Youth, Reichstag delegate; 1940, Reichsstatthalter and Gauleiter of Vienna; leader of the *Kinderlandverschickung* (evacuation of five million children); from 1941, responsible for deportation of Jewish population of Vienna; 1945, sentenced in Nuremberg to twenty years' imprisonment; released 1966.

Schirach, Carl Baily von

November 10, 1873, Kiel; died July 11, 1948, Weimar.

Father of Baldur; Prussian officer, cavalry captain and chamberlain at court of Saxony; 1908–18, director of National Theater of Weimar; married Emma Middleton Baily (1872–1944).

Schnitzler, Erich

Born April 12, 1902, Eschweiler (Aachen).

SS-Führer on the personal staff of the Reichsführer-SS; 1932, SS; 1935, NSDAP; 1939, with SS adjutant office in Munich; 1942, SS-Hauptsturmführer; did personal favors and ran errands for the Himmler and Wolff families; 1945, merchant in Starnberg.

Raubal, Angelika ("Geli")

Born June 4, 1908, Linz; died (suicide or accident) September 18, 1931, Munich.

Daughter of Hitler's sister, Angela Raubal; 1923, Hitler becomes her guardian; 1927, medical studies, Munich; 1927, studies medicine in Munich, musical training (singing); friend of Henriette Hoffmann (married Schirach), daughter of Hitler's personal photographer; 1928, engagement to Hitler's close friend and driver, Emil Maurice (broken off); 1929, lived in Hitler's apartment on Prinzregentenplatz; 1931, shot herself there with a pistol; suicide or accident, unclear.

Rehrl, Alois ("Rehrls")

Born September 6, 1890, Spoeck.

Agrarian entrepreneur in Fridolfing; 1921, Himmler did apprenticeship; friendship continued; 1936, SS; 1942, Obersturmführer [SS lieutenant]; 1942, travels to Crimea with Himmler; 1944, forced laborer on the farm through Himmler's intervention.

Reifschneider, Carl

Husband of Elfriede Reifschneider; merchant; from 1928, Berlin.

Reifschneider, Elfriede

Born January 23, 1883, Lobendau (Bohemia).

Nurse, best friend of Marga Himmler; godmother of Gudrun; 1929–31, head of her own private clinic; 1931, NSDAP; 1932, lived with the Himmlers in Waldtrudering; 1933, in Munich; 1935, back in Berlin; 1941, opened a private clinic.

Reiner, Rolf

Born January 2, 1899, Gmunden am Traunsee; died August 27, 1944, Brăila (Romania).

Consul; World War I veteran; Freikorps; 1920, university studies in Munich; 1921, member of Röhm's Reichsflagge; Hitler Putsch, one-year prison sentence; 1930, NSDA; 1931, Röhm's personal adjutant and chief of staff; 1934, expelled from NSDAP and SS for homosexuality and proximity to Röhm; March 1935, released from prison; World War II, thanks to close friendship with Himmler, probationary post as Luftwaffe officer; 1943, sent into action; 1944, missing in action; presumed dead.

Reinhardt, Fritz

Born April 3, 1895, Ilmenau (Thuringia); died June 17, 1969, Regensburg.

Gauleiter and head of the Speakers' School; 1923, NSDAP; 1926, district group leader in Herrsching am Ammersee; 1928–30, Gauleiter of Upper Bavaria; 1928–33, head of NSDAP Speakers' School; trained circa six thousand party members as political speakers in nine-month course; 1930, Reich propaganda leader and Reichstag delegate; 1935, "representative of the Führer" and adviser on financial policy; 1941–42, board of overseers of the AG Reichswerke [business] "Hermann Göring"; 1950, denazified as "major offender."

Reitzenstein, Elizabeth von, née Heimburg ("Baroness")

Born January 10, 1889.

1925, NSDAP; 1927, married Friedemann von Reitzenstein.

Reitzenstein, Friedemann Freiherr von ("Baron")

Born November 29, 1888, Dillingen.

Hauptmann a. D. 1927; married Elizabeth Heimburg; 1928, NSDAP.

Ribbentrop, Annelies von, née Henkell

Born January 12, 1896, Mainz; died October 5, 1973, Wuppertal-Elberfeld.

Art historian; daughter of sparkling wine producer Otto Henkell; 1920, married Joachim Ribbentrop; five children; 1922, family lived in Berlin, villa in Dahlem, with valuable painting collection; 1920s, mainly Jewish circle of friends; 1932, NSDAP; generally seen as the power behind her otherwise insignificant husband; advised him and made decisions that he implemented; close friend of Marga Himmler's; after 1945, published several books meant to justify her husband's politics.

Ribbentrop, Joachim von

Born April 30, 1893, Wesel; died (executed) October 16, 1946, Nuremberg.

Reich foreign minister; no high school diploma; four years laborer in Canada; World War I veteran; 1919, wine merchant; 1920, married Annelies Henkell; 1920s, generated a fortune in wine trade; 1932, NSDAP; 1933, SS; 1930s, close friend of Himmler's. Foreign policy adviser to Hitler; 1935, naval treaty with Great Britian; 1936–37, ambassador in London; 1938, Reich foreign minister; 1940, SS-Obergruppenführer; appropriated the Castle of Fuschl, near Salzburg, interned owner in Dacha; October 1, 1946, sentenced to death in Nuremberg for war crimes.

Ribbentrop, Rudolf ("Rudi") von

Born May 10, 1921, Wiesbaden.

Elder son of Ribbentrops; SS-Führer; boarding school in England; Napola; Reichsarbeitsdienst; 1933, SS; 1939, NSDAP, Waffen-SS; campaign in France; 1941, Russian campaign; saw action in Finland; 1942, tank division of the "Leibstandarte Adolf Hitler"; 1943, participated in battle of Kharkof and "Citadel" campaign; later, chief of SS division "Hitlerjugend"; 1943, Knight's Cross; 1945, SS-Hauptsurmführer; after 1945, managing director of the Henkell firm in Wiesbaden; published a book that tried to justify his father's politics.

Röhm, Ernst

Born November 28, 1887, Munich; died (shot) July 1, 1934, Stadelheim prison.

Captain; leader of the "Reichsflagge" and "Reichskriegsflagge;" Himmler's mentor

until 1924; Himmler participated in the Hitler Putsch under Röhm; [...] from prison; Reichstag delegate (party: Völkischer Block); 1925, retr[...] itics after power struggle with Hitler; various civilian careers; 1928, [...] livian army; fought in Chaco war until 1930; 1931, took over SA (Hit[...] Supreme SA Führer); expanded power of the SA; July 1, 1934, unti[...] by Himmler's SS, in power struggle between SA and SS.

Rosenberg, Alfred

Born January 12, 1893, Reval (Estonia); died (executed) October 16, 1946, [...]

Architect, Reich minister for the occupied territories in the east; 1919, [...] Deutsche Arbeiterpartei (DAP; later NSDAP); 1921, publisher and, [...] editor of the *Völkischer* Beobachter; Hitler Putsch; 1929, adviser to Arta [...] 1930, Reichstag delegate; author of *Der Mythus des 20. Jahrhanderts* (19[...] of the Twentieth Century]; 1933, head of foreign policy office NSDAP; R[...] 1934, assigned by Führer to supervise intellectual and ideological train[...] NSDAP; 1941, Reich minister for the eastern territories; October 1, 1[...] tenced to death in Nuremberg.

Rühmer, Dr. Karl

Born December 18, 1883 Bayreuth.

Agricultural engineer and expert on fisheries; captain in World War I; 1930, Sta[...] founder of publishing house Germanenverlag in Ebenhausen, near Munic[...] NSDAP; 1942, SS; 1944, Obersturmbahnführer; 1941, SS business admini[...] thanks to Marga's influence; expanded a department of fishery in Unterfa[...] May 1942, uses prisoners from Dachau in fishery; Marga Himmler ordered fi[...] Rühmer.

Schade, Erna von, née Wagener ("Tante Schadi")

Born July 17, 1891, Küstrin.

Good friend of Marga's; married Hermann, Baron von Schade; NSDAP membe[...]

Schade, Hermann Freiherr von

Born October 3, 1888, Münster (Westphalia).

Officer and SS-Oberführer, World War I captain; 1932, NSDAP and SS; 1935, [...] uty head of SS law court; 1936, SS-Oberführer; 1940–42, on the personal sta[...] the Reichsführer-SS 1939–41, manager of factory in Altenburg (Thüringia); 1[...] 44, head of SS-Oberabschnitt Elbe.

Schaumburg-Lippe, Ingeborg Alix zu, née von Oldenburg

Born July 20, 1901, Oldenburg; died January 10, 1996, Bienebek (Schleswig-Holste[...]

Wife of Stephan Prince of Schaumburg-Lippe, two children; from 1928, attend[...] NSDAP meetings in Munich with husband and brother-in-law, Waldeck; 19[...] NSDAP; accompanied husband to Sofia, Rome, Rio de Janeiro, and Buen[...]

Schönbohm, Heinrich

Born June 19, 1869, Berlin; died July 25, 1941, Aalen (Württemberg).

Retired book dealer; 1925, NSDAP, family lived in Stolp, Lindau (Bodensee), Waldtrudering; became friendly with the Himmlers; January 20, 1934, received commendation from the party.

Schönbohm, Margarete

Married Heinrich; friendly with the Himmlers.

Schreiner, Dr.

Died February 10, 1931.

Married Gerda Schreiner; 1926, Ortsgruppenführer of the SS, Plattling, Lower Bavaria; c. 1927, SS-Führer there; 1929, district leader; knew Himmler from time together in Landshut; appeared together as party speakers.

Schultze-Naumburg, Paul

Born June 10, 1869, Naumburg; died May 19, 1949, Jena.

Architect; 1895, Munich Secession 1934; 1904, founded Saaleck workshop; 1928, author *Kunst and Rasse* [Art and Race]; 1930, NSDAP; 1932, Reichstag delegate; 1929–33, meetings of the "Saaleck Circle" (including Hans F. K. Günther, Richard Walther Darré, and Wilhelm Frick) at his house; Hitler, Himmler, and Goebbels were frequent visitors; 1934, Schultze-Naumburg's ex-wife married Wilhelm Frick; 1930–40, director of State Academy for Architecture in Weimar, from which so-called "degenerate" works of art were removed.

Schwarz, Berta, née Breher

Wife of Franz Xaver Schwarz.

Schwarz, Franz Xaver

Born November 27, 1875, Günzburg; died December 2, 1947, Regensburg Internment Camp.

Reich treasurer of the NSDAP; 1896–1925, Oberamtmann, city of Munich; World War I veteran, citizens' defense, Munich; 1922, NSDAP, (Nr. 6); Hitler Putsch; 1925–45, Reich treasurer, NSDAP; 1931, SS; 1933, Reichstag delegate; 1935, Reich leader; 1942, SS Oberstgruppenführer, responsible for all assets of the NSDAP and financing the T4-Aktion [euthanasia program]. Interned after 1945, died in internment camp. Posthumously designated as a "major offender."

Seidl, Siegfried

Born August 24, 1911, Tulln (Lower Austria); died (executed) February 4, 1947, Vienna.

Historian and scholar of German studies; 1930, NSDAP Austria; 1931, SA; 1932, SS; 1941, Ph.D. In World War II in Security Police, Vienna; 1940, *Mitarbeiter des Reichssicherheitshauptamt* [Main Office of Reich Security], Section IV B4, under Adolf Eichmann in Posen; 1941, established Theresienstadt ghetto; commander of same until 1943; transferred to Bergen-Belsen, Mauthausen; 1944, with Eichmann's commandos to Budapest; 1945, arrest in Vienna; 1946, sentenced to death by People's Court, Vienna.

Stang, Frau

Born 13.8.1941. Possible wife of Walter Stang (b 1895), Reichshauptamtsleiter of NSDAP.

Stegmann, Wilhelm Ferdinand

June 13, 1899, Munich; died (killed in action) December 15, 1944, Šahy (Slovakia).

Farmer; World War I veteran; Freikorps Epp; leader in the Bund Oberland; 1920–23, study of agriculture in Munich; marries Emmy Holz (b. 1900); estate inspector; 1924, NSDAP; before 1933, Gauleiter of Franconia; party speaker; 1930–33, Reichstag delegate; early 1933, loyalty oath; leaves the party; founds Freikorps Franken; 1944, probationary transfer to punishment detail Oskar Dirlewanger.

Strasser, Gregor

Born May 31, 1892, Geisenfeld; died (murdered) June 30, 1934, Berlin.

Pharmacist; World War I veteran; Freikorps Epp; 1920, pharmacy in Landshut; there, led the Sturmbataillon Niederbayern [Lower Bavaria]; Himmler occsasionally his adjutant; Hitler Putsch; 1924, delegate to Bavarian parliament, party: Völkischer Block; December 1924, Reichstag delegate, party: Deutschvölkische Freiheitspartei (substitute party for NSDAP); 1925, NSDAP (Nr. 9); Gauleiter of Lower Bavaria/Upper Palatinate. With his brother, Otto, they represented their own "social revolutionary" party platform; 1926–28, Reich propaganda leader of the NSDAP; 1928–32, Reich organization leader of the NSDAP; June 1924, Himmler his secretary in Landshut; 1932, escalation of rivalry between Strasser and Hitler; June 30, 1934, arrest and murder by Berlin Gestapo (during the SA murders, part of the Röhm Putsch).

Strasser, Otto

Born September 10, 1897, Windsheim; died August 27, 1974, Munich.

Political scientist and NS politician; brother of Gregor Strasser; World War I veteran; Freikorps Epp; 1917–20, member of SPD; minister of nutrition; 1925, NSDAP, where, with his brother and Joseph Goebbels, he established the "left," social-revolutionary wing of the party, 1930, left the party; 1933, emigrated via Prague to Portugal and Canada; 1955, returned to Germany.

Stumpfegger, Dr. Ludwig

Born July 11, 1910, Munich; died (suicide) May 2 1945, Berlin.

Doctor; marries Gertrud, née Spengler. Occasionally family doctor to the Himmlers; 1944, also for Hitler. In Hohenlychen, directed medical experiments on female prisoners from Ravensbrück; 1943, SS-Osturmbahnführer; in last days of the war, committed suicide together with Martin Bormann.

Tannberger, Herr

Employee in Gmund.

Terboven, Josef

Born May 23, 1898, Essen; died (suicide) May 11, 1945, Skaugum (Oslo).

NSDAP Gauleiter and SA Ogruppenführer; bank official; 1923, NSDAP, Hitler Putsch; 1925 founder local NSDAP group in Essen; 1928, Gauleiter Essen; 1930, Reichstag delegate; 1928–45, Oberpräsident of the Rhine province; 1940, Reich commissioner in Norway.

Thermann, Edmund von

Born March 6, 1883, Cologne; died February 27, 1951, Bonn.

Diplomat; 1913, diplomatic service; World War I veteran; 1919–21, German embassy Budapest; 1923, legation counselor; 1925–32, general consul, Danzig; 1933, NSDAP and SS; 1933, German emissary in Buenos Aires; 1941, persona non grata with Argentine government; 1943, sent into retirement.

Thermann, Vilma von

Wife of Edmund von Thermann; two children.

Wagner, Adolf

Born October 1, 1890, Algringen (Lorraine); died April 12, 1944, Bad Reichenhall.

Gauleiter; World War I veteran, officer; 1922, NSDAP; Hitler Putsch; 1924, delegate to local parliament; 1930, Gauleiter of Munich–Upper Bavaria; 1933, deputy Ministerpräsident and Innenminister of Bavaria; 1933, Reichstag delegate; 1939, Reich commissionar of defense; most powerful of all the Gauleiters; his access to Hitler won him the nickname "Despot of Munich"; 1942, retired from all official duties after suffering stroke.

Waldeck and Pyrmont, Josias Erbprinz [hereditary prince] zu

Born May 13, 1896, Arolsen; died November 30, 1967, Schloss Schaumburg (Diez).

Farmer and officer; World War I veteran; Freikorps; 1927, university studies in Munich; 1929, NSDAP and SS; 1930, Himmler's adjutant and member of first SS-Standarte Munich (Sepp Dietrich); 1933, Reichstag delegate and legation Counselor with the Foreign Service; 1934, returns to SS; married to Altburg von Oldenburg (1903–2001; 1929, NSDAP), five children, one son (b. 1936), a godchild of Hitler and Himmler; June 30, 1934, organized the executions of SA leaders in Munich-Stadelheim; 1936, SS-Obergruppenführer; 1941, general in the police force; 1944, general in the Waffen-SS; close friend of Himmler; 1947, sentenced to life imprisonment in the Buchenwald trial; 1950, released.

Wedel, Ida Gräfin [countess] von, née von Schubert

Born July 2, 1895, Berlin; died October 15, 1971.

Daughter of a general; wife, later widow of Count Graf Wilhelm von Wedel; three
    children; 1931, NSDAP; 1932, NS-Frauenschaft; very close friend of Marga
    Himmler's.

Wedel, Wilhelm Alfred Graf [Count] von

Born November 18, 1891, Berlin; died October 19, 1939, Potsdam.

Officer and president of the police; World War I veteran, cavalry captain; 1919,
    marries Ida von Schubert; estate owner and Hitler's host prior to the "Seizure
    of Power" in 1933; 1930–32, Stahlhelm; 1932, NSDAP and SA; 1933, district
    administrator Ostprignitz; 1935, SS; 1938, SS-Brigadenführer; 1935–39, police
    president Potsdam.

Wedel, Wilhelm Graf [Count] von

*Born August 30, 1922, Berlin; died (killed in action) August (July) 30, 1941,
    Tarnopol.*

Youngest son of the Wedels; SS-Untersturmführer.

Weiss, Ferdl (Ferdinand Weisheitinger)

Born June 28, 1883, Altötting; died June 19, 1949, Munich.

Comedian, actor, Munich's most beloved folk singer; 1907, first theatrical appearance;
    1921, director of Münchner Platzl Theater; sympathized early with NS; 1930, made
    countless "Heimat films" ["homeland films," rural, sentimental portrayals of simple
    values—Trans.]; 1940, NSDAP.

Wendler, Maria, née Haggenmüller

Born February 22, 1908, Auerbach.

Wife of Richard Wendler; medical studies; married 1934 NS-Frauenschaft; during the
    war, lived in the Generalgouvernement with husband; after 1945, doctor in Rosen-
    heim.

Wendler, Richard

Born January 22, 1898, Oberdorf; died August 24, 1972, Prien am Chiemsee.

Law studies; brother of Hilde Himmler; Freikorps Epp; 1927, founded local NSDAP
    in Deggendorf; 1928, SA- Führer and speaker for the NSDAP; 1933, SS and mayor
    of Hof; 1934, third marriage to Maria Haggenmüller; 1939, civilian governor in
    various Polish cities, including Krakow and Lublin; 1943, SS-Gruppenführer;
    close contact with Himmler; 1945, disappeared under false name; 1948, interned,
    sentenced, as a "major offender," to a work camp; 1949, released; 1955, categorized
    as "fellow traveler" [*Mitlaüfer*], allowed to work as lawyer in Munich, 1971, charged
    with "suspicion of participating in deportation of the Jews from Cracow—
    termination of proceedings for reasons of health.

Wiligut, Karl Maria ("Karl Maria Weisthor")

Born December 10, 1866, Wien; died January 3, 1946, Arolsen.

Colonel, occultist; 1924–27, in sanatorium in Salzburg; 1933, SS; Himmler's closest adviser in ideological matters; dabbled in "rune lore," heraldry, astrology; asserted that he was direct descendant of the "Ase," a race of Norse gods; because of his influence upon Himmler, sometimes called his Rasputin; 1934, RuSHA [*Rasse-und Siedlungshauptamt*]; 1936, SS-Brigadenführer; 1939, left SS because of fraud and alcoholism. Himmler continued to seek his advice.

Wolff, Karl

Born May 13, 1900, Darmstadt; died July 15, 1984, Rosenheim.

Chief of personal staff Reichsführer-SS and general of the Waffen-SS; World War I veteran, officer; merchant; 1923, married Frieda von Römheld (b. 1901; 1932, NSDAP); four children, two sons (b. 1936 and 1938) godchildren of Himmler; 1931, NSDAP and SS; 1933, staff of Reichsführer-SS; 1935, Himmler's chief adjutant; 1936, chief of Personal Staff Reichsführer-SS; 1939, liaison officer of SS to the Führer; 1942, SS-Obergruppenführer and general of the Waffen-SS; 1943, Höhrer SS und Polizeiführer Italy and leader of Army Group B; family lived in Munich, Berlin-Dahlem, and Rottach-Egern (Tegernsee); eldest daughter (b. 1930) schoolmate of Gudrun in Berlin and Reichersbeuern; 1943, divorce against wishes of his wife and Himmler's will; married his mistress, Countess Inge von Bernstorff; Himmler godfather to their son (b. 1937); 1964, sentenced to fifteen years' imprisonment; 1969, released for health reasons.

Zipperer, Falk Wolfgang

Born December 24, 1899, Darmstadt.

Legal expert; Himmler's best friend from schooldays in Landshut; World War I veteran; Freikorps Landshut and Freikorps Epp; studies in Munich; 1937, NSDAP; 1938, SS Führer, personal staff Reichsführer-SS; 1943, Hauptsturmführer; 1937, adviser at the "German Legal Institute of the Reichsführer-SS" in Bonn (SS-Ahnenerbe); Ph.D.; married. 1937, Lieselotte Lubowski (b. 1908); their daughter (b. 1944) was Himmler's godchild; 1944, professor in Innsbruck through Himmler's influence; 1945, prisoner of war.

Glossary of German Terms and Abbreviations

ANSCHLUSS   Literally, "annexation," specifically the German annexation of Austria in 1938

AUSSENMINISTER   Foreign minister

BAYERN   Bavaria

BRAUNES HAUS   "Brown House," NS party headquarters in Munich

BUND ARTAM   Artam Alliance, an early right-wing folkish organization. See commentary accompanying letter of 18.11.1929.

BUND OBERLAND   Paramilitary organization that supported Hitler and marched in the Putsch of 1923

BUND REICHSFLAGGE   Also Wehrverband Reichsflagge. Paramilitary organization founded 1919, later amalgamated into the Stahlhelm

BUND REICHSKRIEGSFLAGGE   Paramilitary organization founded in 1923 by Ernst Röhm. See commentary on letter from Himmler to Marga, 2.1.28.

BUNDSCHUH   Journal of the Artam League. See commentary following Himmler's letter of 18.11.29.

CHEF DES ERSATZHEERES   Chief of the Army Reserve

DEUTSCHES REICH   Literally, "German realm," a designation without monarchical connotations. Official name for the German state from 1871 to 1943

DEUTSCHES ROTES KREUZ (DRK)   German Red Cross

DEUTSCHE VERSUCHSANSTALT FÜR ERNÄHRUNG UND VERPFLEGUNG (DVA)
German Experimental Institute for Nutrition and Provisions

DEUTSCHNATIONALE PARTEI   DNP; right-wing German national party

DICKKOPF, DICKKOPP, DICKSCHÄDEL   Colloquialism, also teasing endearment meaning roughly "pig-headed man" or "thick head," to connote
stubbornness. Marga first teases Heinrich with this word in her letter of
21.12.27. They sometimes use the North German form *Dickkopp*.
The variant, *Dickschädel*, or "thick skull," appears in the letter of
31.12.1927.

DIENSTKALENDAR   Official appointment book

DNP DEUTSCHNATIONALE PARTEI   Right-wing German national party

DNVP, DEUTSCHNATIONALE VOLKSPARTEI   Conservative party in the Weimar Republic before the rise of the NSDAP

DRK, DEUTSCHES ROTES KREUZ   German Red Cross

DUMMERLE   Primarily South German expression meaning "silly little thing,"
"silly goose," or even "nitwit"

EINSATZGRUPPE   Special unit or detachment; euphemism for "death squad"

ERRINERUNGEN   Memoirs

ERSATZHEER   Army Reserve

FHQ, FÜHRER-HAUPTQUARTIER   Führer headquarters

FRATZ   Little rascal, scamp, little cutie

FREIKORPS   Voluntary paramilitary organizations that opposed the Weimar
Republic

FRIEDELEHE   State-sanctioned concubinage for SS men who met Aryanization guidelines. The goal was to promote a higher birth rate. See section
III of the introduction.

GAU   District

GAULEITER   Regional leader

GAULEITUNG   Regional administration

GENERALFÜHRERIN   Rank in the DRK, "general"

GENERALGOUVERNEMENT   Areas in western Poland (population c. ten million, the majority of whom were Poles) annexed by the German Reich and

slated for "Germanicization" under Hans Frank, the Generalgouverneur [governor-general].

GENERALHAUPTFÜHRER Director

GENERALMAJOR Major general

GENERALOBERST Colonel general, a four-star rank

HILFSPOLIZEI Auxiliary police of the SS

HÖHERER SS- UND POLIZEIFÜHRER Senior SS and police chief

INNENMINISTER Minister of the interior

INNENMINISTER DES DEUTSCHEN REICHES Minister of the interior for the German Reich

JUGENDTAGEBUCH Marga's childhood diary, from 1909 to 1916

JULLEUCHTER Yule light; see note to letter from Marga Himmler, 9.8.41

KAPITÄN LEUTNANT Lieutenant-commander

KAPP PUTSCH Failed attempt by Freikorps brigade Ehrhardt to install right-wing journalist Wolfgang Kapp as chancellor in 1920

KINDERLANDVERSCHICKUNG Initiative to evacuate five million children to the countryside from German cities threatened by aerial bombardment during the war

KINDHEITSTAGEBUCH Childhood journal

KOMMENDEN, DIE ["They Who Are Coming"] A publication of the Bündische Jugend (an early phase of the German Youth Movement), which had close ties to the Bund Artam

KORPSFÜHRER Corps leader

LANDSKNECHT Originally associated with mercenary soldiers, a term connoting roughness and strength

LANDTAG Representative assembly at the state level; state or local parliament.

LEBENSBORN Literally "life source"; designation of the system of maternity homes and support provided to the women who bore illegitimate children fathered by SS members

LESELISTE reading list

M   Mark(s), also RM, Reichsmark(s)
MÄDCHENTAGEBUCH   Girlhood album
MINISTERPRÄSIDENT   Governor

NAPOLA, NATIONALPOLITISCHE ERZIEHUNGSANSTALT   National-political edu-
    cational establishment. Academies to train future military personnel; under
    the SS after 1936
NS, NATIONALSOZIALISMUS   National socialism
NSDAP, NATIONAL SOZIALISTISCHE DEUTSCHE ARBEITERPARTEI   National
    Socialist German Workers' Party
NS-FRAUENSCHAFT   NS Women's League
NSKK, NS-KRAFTFAHRERKORPS   Automotive Corps

OBERAMTMANN   Senior civil service administrator
OBERFÜHRER   Colonel
OBERFÜHRERIN   Female senior leader [colonel in the DRK]
OBERPRÄSIDENT   Title of top civil servant in Prussian provinces
OBERST   Colonel
OGRUF, OBERGRUPPENFÜHRER-SS   Lieutenant-general
ORDNUNGSPOLIZEI (ORPO)   Uniformed police who served under the SS and
    wore green uniforms and were sometimes referred to as "the green
    police"
OSAF, OBERSTER SA-FÜHRER   Supreme commander of the SA
OSTLAND   Baltic States

PG., PARTEIGENOSSE, PG   (NS) party member
POESIEALBUM   Friendship album
PREUSSEN   Prussia
PÜPPI   Pet name for Himmler's daughter, Gudrun, roughly "Little Doll"

REICHPRÄSIDENT   Reich president
REICHSARBEITSDIENST, RAD   Reich labor service
REICHSARTZT-SS   Medical branch of the SS
REICHSFÜHRER-SS   SS commander, highest rank in the SS (Reichsführer SS
    in this book); Himmler's title as highest-ranking officer and commander of
    the SS

REICHSHAUPTAMT   Reich head office

REICHSJUGENDFÜHRER   Reich Youth leader

REICHSKOMMISSAR   Reich commissioner

REICHSKOMMISSAR FÜR DIE FESTIGUNG DEUTSCHEN VOLKSTUMS   Reich commissioner for promoting German national character

REICHSLANDBUND (RLB)   Farmers' association

REICHSLEITER   Reich leader

REICHSORGANISATIONSLEITER   Organizational leader of the Reich

REICHSPARTEITAG   Annual party rally of the NSDAP

REICHSPARTEITAG   Party congress of the NSDAP

REICHSPROPAGANDALEITER   Propaganda chief

REICHSSCHRIFTTUMSKAMMER, RSK   Reich literary association

REICHSSICHERHEITSDIENST, SD   Reich security service, security police

REICHSTAG   The parliament building in Berlin; by extension, the representative assembly itself

REICHSSTATTHALTER   Reich governor

REICHSWEHR   German army of one hundred thousand soldiers permitted by the Treaty of Versailles

RF-SS, REICHSFÜHRER-SS   Special title and rank for the commander of the SS; Himmler is appointed RF-SS in 1929.

RLB, REICHSLANDBUND   Nationalistic right-wing organization representing farmers' interests during the Weimar Republic in opposition to labor unions

RM REICHSMARK(S)   German currency from 1924 to 1948

SA STURMABTEILUNG   Literally, "Assault Division"; also called Storm Troopers or Brownshirts; founded by Hitler in 1921

SD SICHERHEITSDIENST SS   intelligence agency, sister organization to the Gestapo

SS, SCHUTZSTAFFEL   Literally, "defense unit"; originally Hitler's personal bodyguard, expanded by Himmler into units of police, camp guards, and combat troops

SS-BRIGADEFÜHRER   Brigadier general

SS-FORSCHUNGSSTÄTTE AHNENERBE   Research and Teaching Group for Ancestral Heritage

SS-GRUPPENFÜHRER   Major general

SS-Hauptscharführer Master sergeant

SS-Hauptsturmführer Captain

SS-Helferinnenkorps SS women's volunteer corps

SS-Oberabschnitt Division, often translated as "district"; a division-strength command of the general SS

SS-Oberführer Senior leader

SS-Oberführer Senior leader of the Waffen SS (no equivalent military rank)

SS-Obergruppenführer (Ogruf) Lieutenant general

SS-Oberstgruppenführer General

SS-Obersturmbannführer Lieutenant colonel

SS-Obersturmführer First lieutenant

SS-Ogruf (Obergruppenführer) Lieutenant general

SS-Ortsgruppenführer Local group leader (also Ortsgruppenleiter)

SS-Ostuf, Obersturmführer Senior assault leader, or first lieutenant

SS–Rasse und Siedlungshauptamt SS Central Office for Race and Resettlement

SS-Reichsgeschäftsführer Business manager of the SS

SS-Scharführer Staff sergeant

SS-Standartenführer Colonel

SS-Sturmbannführer Major

SS-Untersturmführer Second lieutenant

SS-Wirtschaftsverwaltungshauptamt SS business administration headquarters

Stadtkommandant City commander

Stahlhelm Literally, "steel helmet"; paramilitary wing of the DNVP

Stille Hilfe, Die Stille Hilfe für Kriegsgefangene und Internierte "Silent Help for Prisoners of War and Those Who Are Interned," postwar relief organization for former SS members

Strasse, Str. Street, St.

Tagebuch, Tagebücher journal, diary; journals, diaries

Taschenkalender pocket calendar

T4-Programm Euthanasia program targeting the incurably ill and physically or mentally disabled

VALEPP A mountain valley as well as a stream and a village in the Bavarian Alps

VB Völkischer Beobachter Literally, Folkish Observer

VÖLKISCH "folkish"; see note to section II in introduction; national socialist term blending meanings of an idealized German people with an archaic notion of the people as a primitive tribe, suggesting the concept of "nation" as an ethnic unity based on blood ties

VÖLKISCHER BEOBACHTER Main ideological and propagandistic newspaper of the NSDAP, literally, "Folkish Observer"

VÖLKISCHER BLOCK Folkish right-wing splinter party in the 1920s

VOLKSDEUTSCHE Ethnic Germans from the east

VOLKSGESUNDHEIT Racial hygiene

VOLKSSTURM Home Guard, civil defense

VOLKSTUM NS term connoting racial essence, replacing "nationality"

WAFFEN-SS Armed SS; the military branch of the SS, an army that numbered forty combat divisions at its height

WINTERHILFSWERK Winter charity drive, annual appeal for funds and donations to provide food, clothing, coal, etc. during the winter months

WIRSTSCHAFTSVERWALTUNGSHAUPTAMT DER SS Head office of the SS business administration

Index